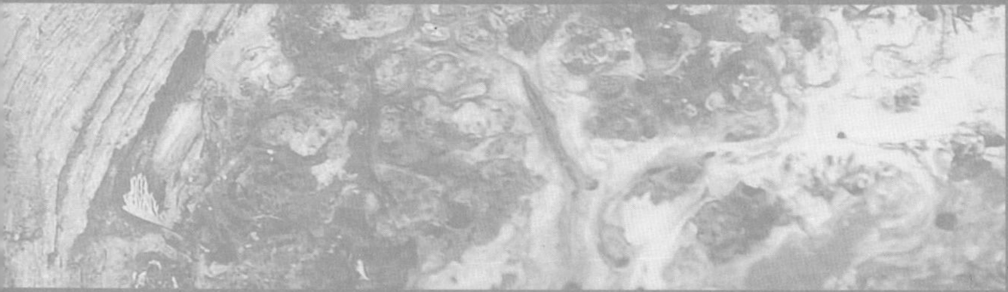

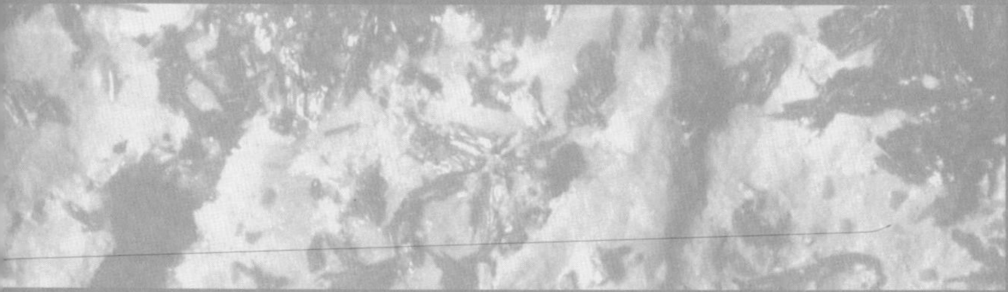

HANDBOOKS

ROCKS & MINERALS

DK HANDBOOKS

ROCKS & MINERALS

CHRIS PELLANT

HELEN PELLANT

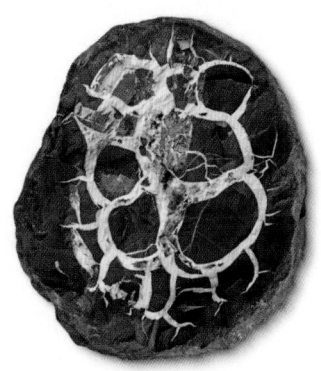

Photography by
HARRY TAYLOR
(Natural History Museum)

NEW EDITION

DK LONDON

Editor Kate Taylor
US Editor Kayla Dugger
Managing Editor Angeles Gavira
Managing Art Editor Michael Duffy
Jacket Design Development Manager Sophia MTT
Jacket Designer Surabhi Wadhwa-Gandhi
Senior Production Controller Meskerm Berhane
Senior Production Editor Andy Hillard

DK DELHI

Editors Devangana Ojha, Rishi Bryan
Senior Art Editor Ira Sharma
Art Editors Shipra Jain, Kavita Dutta
Assistant Art Editors Sampda Mago, Adhithi Priya
Managing Editor Soma B. Chowdhury
Senior Managing Art Editor Arunesh Talapatra
Jacket Designer Priyanka Bansal
Production Manager Pankaj Sharma
Pre-production Manager Balwant Singh
DTP Designers Syed Md Farhan, Jaypal Singh Chauhan, Mrinmoy Mazumdar

FIRST EDITION

Editors Stella Vayne, James Harrison
Art Editor Clive Hayball

Technical Consultant Dr. Robert Symes
(Natural History Museum, London)
Production Controller Caroline Weber

This American Edition, 2021
First American Edition, 1992
Published in the United States by DK Publishing
1450 Broadway, Suite 801, New York, NY 10018

A catalog record for this book
is available from the Library of Congress.
ISBN 978-1-4654-9774-1

Printed and bound in China

For the curious
www.dk.com

MIX
Paper from
responsible sources
FSC™ C018179

This book was made with Forest
Stewardship Council ™ certified
paper – one small step in DK's
commitment to a sustainable future.
For more information go to
www.dk.com/our-green-pledge

Contents

COLLECTING ROCKS AND MINERALS

ROCKS AND MINERALS are a fundamental part of the Earth's crust. Collecting and studying them can be both a rewarding and an absorbing hobby. This can involve traveling to exciting places, a lot of research, and some time spent cataloging and displaying finds. As your collection grows, you can exchange material with other collectors and purchase rare or exceptional specimens from mineral dealers.

A COLLECTING TRIP can take you to a site a mile away or to the other side of the world. Wherever your exact destination is, you may find rock faces and surfaces in sea or river cliffs or in man-made exposures such as quarries, road or rail cuttings, and artificial drainage channels. Seek permission to collect on private land, and remember to take specimens in moderation. Always treat natural exposures with care, and don't quarry away natural rock faces. Collectors can also be conservationists.

FIELD SPECIMENS

You may come to explore an area where, millions of years ago, hot fluids—possibly associated with molten magma beneath the Earth's surface—have deposited minerals in overlying strata. In such an area, you can find many different specimens: rocks like granite and limestone and minerals such as fluorite may all occur within a short distance of each other.

Seaside cliff exposure
Search the shore below the cliffs for rocks and minerals. The spoil heaps of abandoned mines, as on the cliff top here, are an excellent area to hunt for minerals.

crinoidal limestone can occur on limestone cliffs

granite is often found in disused quarries

Fluorite can be found on old mine spoil heaps

Crinoidal limestone

Granite

Crystalline fluorite

GEOLOGICAL MAPS

Geological maps show the surface distribution of rocks, their age relationships, and structural features. The colored patterns of a geological map represent individual rock types. Geological maps also give information about how the rocks behave below the ground. Dip arrows provide clues to predict the structure, indicating the angle that a rock bed makes with the horizontal. Interpreting a geological map is a matter of experience and common sense. For instance, note that the mineral veins shown below occur near a metamorphic contact zone. Geological maps are obtainable from specialty map and museum stores.

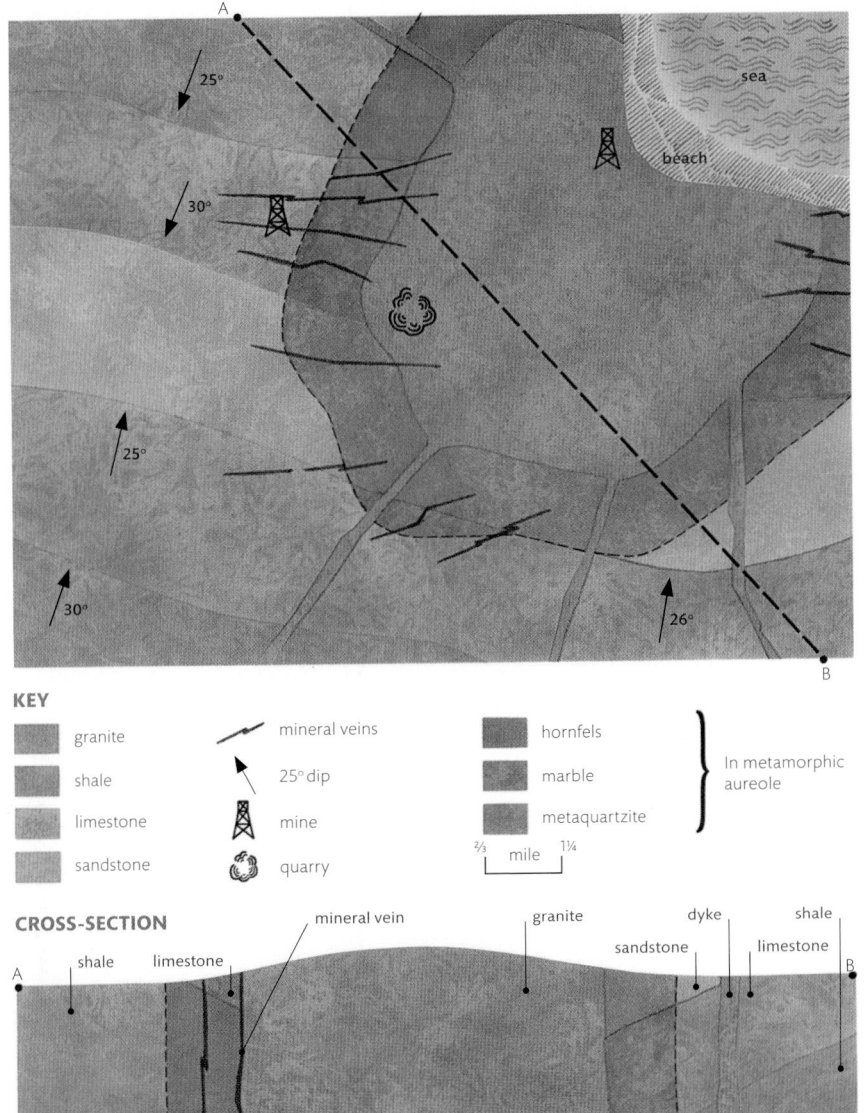

KEY

- granite
- shale
- limestone
- sandstone

- mineral veins
- 25° dip
- mine
- quarry

- hornfels
- marble
- metaquartzite

} In metamorphic aureole

⅔ mile 1¼

CROSS-SECTION

FIELD EQUIPMENT

IT IS BEST TO do some homework before a field trip, checking locality reference material, such as guide books and detailed maps. Geological maps are a great asset (see page 7), but, because overprinted colors may obscure features like roads and quarries, a large-scale map (either a physical copy or one downloaded to a smartphone) may be needed to pinpoint the actual site. A compass will be helpful for areas where there are few topographic features on the ground. Protective clothing is essential.

When working below a high cliff or quarry face, a hard hat is a must. Goggles will shield your eyes from chips of rock flying off during hammering to break up fallen blocks of material, and strong gloves will protect your hands. Several hardened steel chisels are handy for extracting minerals and for splitting rocks. Written notes, photographs, or videos showing the location of specimens should be taken. Without field notes, especially of a location, specimens are of little scientific value.

Locating the site
Satellite navigation can pinpoint locations. A compass will help find a site when there are few landmarks for reference.

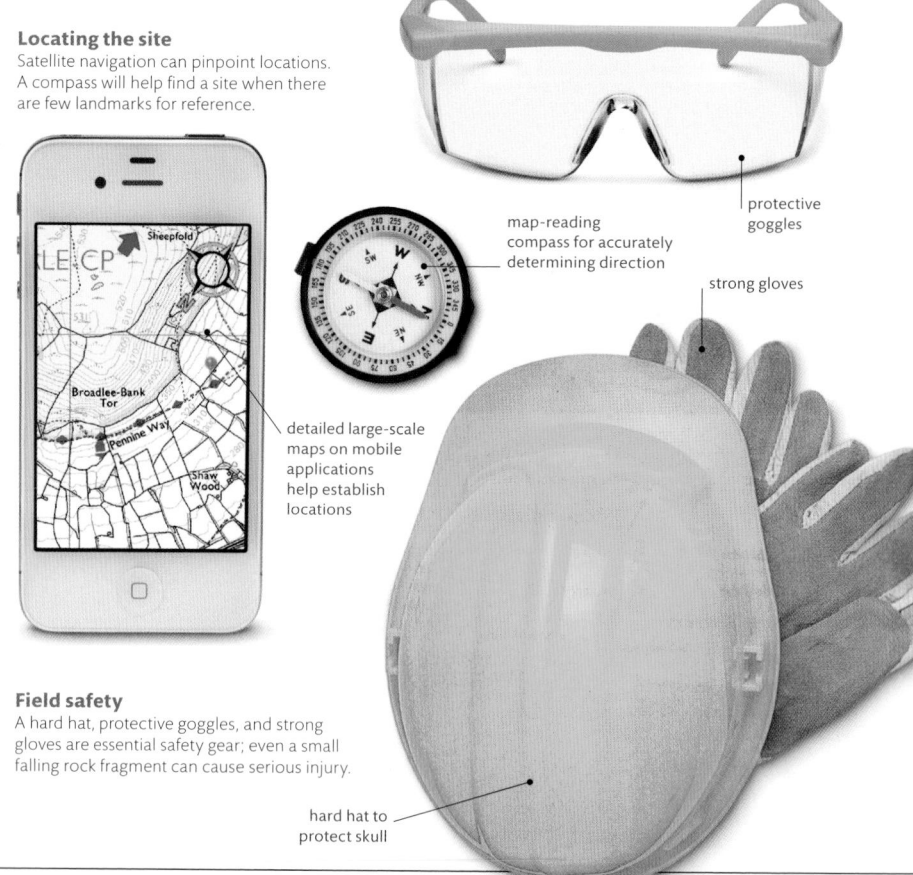

protective goggles

map-reading compass for accurately determining direction

strong gloves

detailed large-scale maps on mobile applications help establish locations

Field safety
A hard hat, protective goggles, and strong gloves are essential safety gear; even a small falling rock fragment can cause serious injury.

hard hat to protect skull

pencil

ballpoint pen

notepad

camera

Recording specimens

Mineral or rock specimens are of little scientific interest without a detailed record of the location. It is important to record details on site, not after returning home. Notes and sketches should be made in a small notebook and pictures taken of the strata, rock structures, and geological location. A camera or a smartphone can be used to make an audiovisual record.

Hand lens

A 10× hand lens provides much better detail of rock and mineral specimens, making on-the-spot identification easier.

Prying out and packing

A geological hammer should only be used to break up rocks that are already on the ground and not for quarrying exposures. Specimens must only be collected in moderation and safely wrapped in newspaper, cloth, or "bubble wrap," with each clearly labeled.

newspaper for wrapping

cloth bag to pack specimens

geological hammer for breaking up fallen rocks

multipurpose knife to test hardness (see p.11)

wide-ended chisel

"bubble wrap"

thin, sharp-pointed chisel

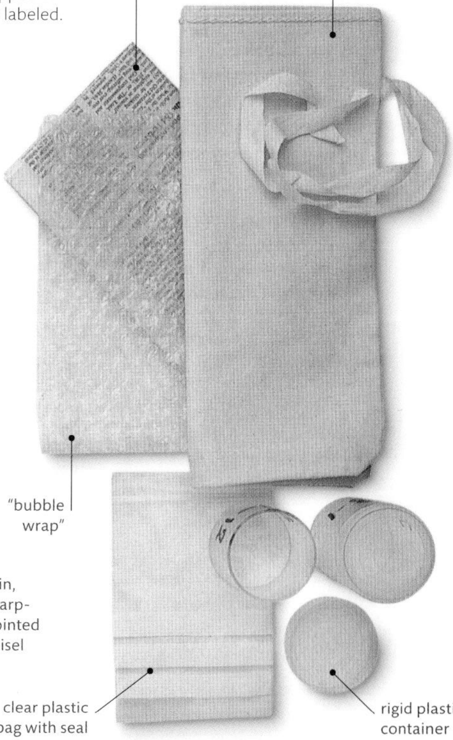

clear plastic bag with seal

rigid plastic container

HOME KIT

YOU HAVE COLLECTED your specimens and brought them home. Now you should prepare them carefully for identification, then for display or storage. Your home kit must have the essential identification equipment shown here. Many specimens will have soil and/or rock matrix stuck to them, which you will have to clean off. Use a soft brush to remove very loose soil and other rock debris. Avoid hammering at specimens with heavy or sharp tools unless you want to reveal fresh surfaces. Hold the specimens in your hand while you brush away the loose material—a vise or metal clamp may cause damage.

If you are preparing a hard rock specimen, such as granite or gneiss, you can do very little damage even with a fairly coarse brush and running water. For delicate minerals, such as calcite crystals, use distilled water (which doesn't contain reactive chemical additives) and a very fine brush. For minerals that dissolve in water, such as halite, use other liquids. Alcohol can be used to clean nitrates, sulfates, and borates, and weak hydrochloric acid is a good cleaner for silicates but will dissolve carbonates. Soaking silicates overnight in weak acid will remove coatings of carbonate debris.

Scraping and prying tools
Clean off loose debris from specimens with sharp metal implements. A pointed tool like a bradawl is useful for prying debris off, but take great care not to damage the underlying material. This is a preliminary stage of specimen preparation.

Cleaning brushes
You can clean rocks and minerals using brushes of various sizes—from a soft paintbrush to a nail brush—depending on the fragility of the specimen. A soft sable brush is best for removal of tiny sediment grains from minerals, while a nail brush is best restricted to hard rocks, such as gneiss or gabbro, which it can't damage.

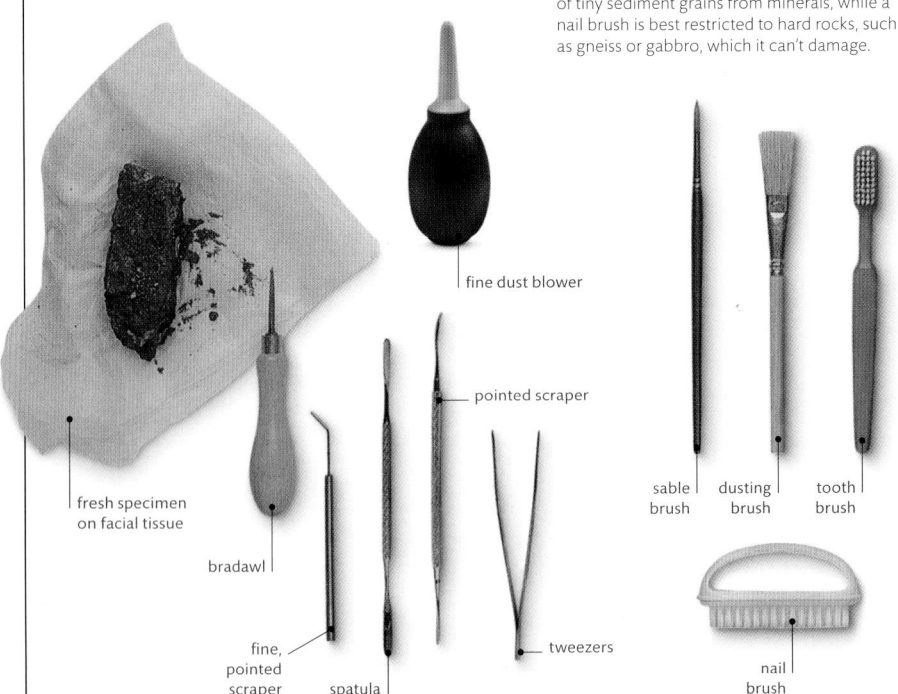

fine dust blower

pointed scraper

fresh specimen on facial tissue

bradawl

fine, pointed scraper

spatula

tweezers

sable brush

dusting brush

tooth brush

nail brush

Cleaning liquids

Use distilled water, if possible, for cleaning, because tap water contains various chemicals that may react with minerals. Dilute hydrochloric acid will dissolve carbonate material. This acid is safe to use.

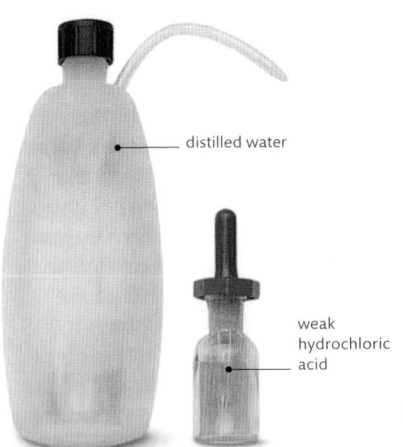

distilled water

weak hydrochloric acid

soft facial tissue for absorbing cleaning liquids

MINERAL TESTS

At home, basic chemistry tests are a good way of establishing a mineral's identity. Dilute acids will give consistent reactions on a given mineral—for example, carbonates effervesce in dilute hydrochloric acid. Always wear gloves when working with acids. A controlled flame is another test. Place a specimen on a charcoal block and concentrate a Bunsen flame onto it, using a blowpipe. The mineral may color the flame, indicating chemical composition, or it may fuse—forming a small, globular, beadlike mass—or give off odors.

Identification aids

A streak plate, hardness-testing tools, and hand lens are all indispensable identification aids. The properties of hardness and streak are explained on pages 25 and 26 respectively.

porcelain streak plate or tile

10× hand lens for identifying specimens

Hardness testing

If you scratch a mineral with everyday objects in sequence—say, a coin followed by a knife, followed by a piece of glass or quartz—you can determine the mineral's hardness.

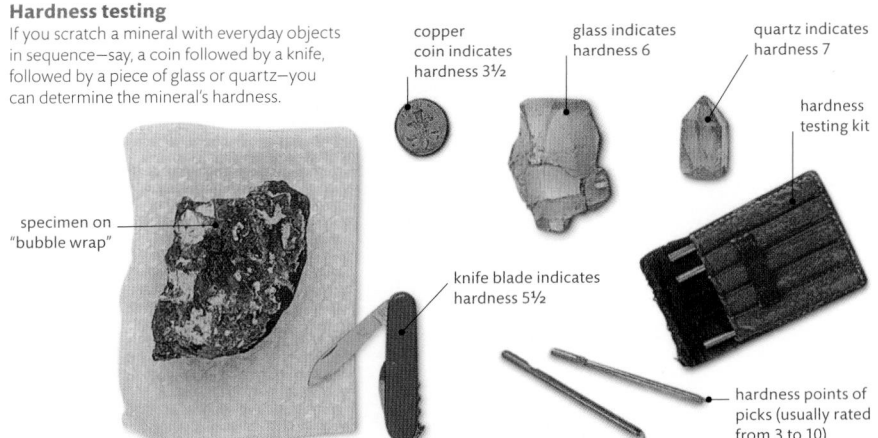

copper coin indicates hardness 3½

glass indicates hardness 6

quartz indicates hardness 7

hardness testing kit

specimen on "bubble wrap"

knife blade indicates hardness 5½

hardness points of picks (usually rated from 3 to 10)

ORGANIZING YOUR COLLECTION

A COLLECTION OF ROCKS and minerals is of no scientific value unless it is sensibly curated. Once you have collected and cleaned your specimens, they have to be organized for storage and display, as well as cataloged and labeled. You'll probably want to display the more attractive specimens and those which are fairly robust. These can be stored in a glass-fronted cabinet to prevent dust from collecting in the hollows and cavities. Keep delicate specimens in individual card trays or boxes, slightly larger than the specimens themselves, in the drawers of a cabinet. Put a data card in the base of each specimen tray, with the specimen's name, location, date of collection, and catalog number. Enter

each specimen in your catalog—this can be an index card or home computer-based system. Number the catalog entries to correspond with the numbers on the cards in the specimen trays. There will also be room for more detailed information in the catalog than on the specimen tray. Write or key in any map references and any local geology, such as other minerals or rocks at that location. Also include details of the rock structure and any large-scale formation and field features you saw there—perhaps a mineral vein and the rock in which the vein was running—along with important identifying features, which you can cross-reference with in the relevant rock or mineral entry in this book.

Notes and records
Transfer field notes to an index card or a computer. Put a small patch of correcting fluid or white paint on each specimen (in an unimportant area) and write a catalog number on this.

USB flash drive

notepad and ballpoint pen

correcting fluid

mark for numbering

Computer records
A computer-based system is a very convenient way to store, add, and amend data.

index card box

Index card
A catalog on an index card is inexpensive, reliable, and quick to use. Enter the specimens alphabetically. There is space to transcribe field notes and even copy location sketches.

cards for cataloging

well-sorted drawer

Storing your specimens

House your rocks and minerals in card trays within a drawer. You can easily make the trays at home, to fit the drawer and the specimens, or buy them from a specialty supplier. Pack the more delicate items with facial tissue to prevent them from moving or rubbing against each other. Small, plastic, transparent-topped boxes are also useful for storage.

tissue-lined cardboard trays

specimen labels

HOW THIS BOOK WORKS

THE BOOK IS ARRANGED in two parts: minerals, followed by rocks. The minerals, pages 46–179, are organized into eight main chemical groups (see pages 20–21 for an explanation). The mineral groups with the simplest chemistry come first and are followed by the more complex varieties. Each separate group has a short introduction describing its general characteristics. The entries that follow give detailed information about the minerals found in the groups. The annotated example below shows how a typical entry is organized. The rocks, pages 180–249, are set out in the three large recognized classes (see pages 30–31). Typical annotated entries are shown opposite.

MINERALS

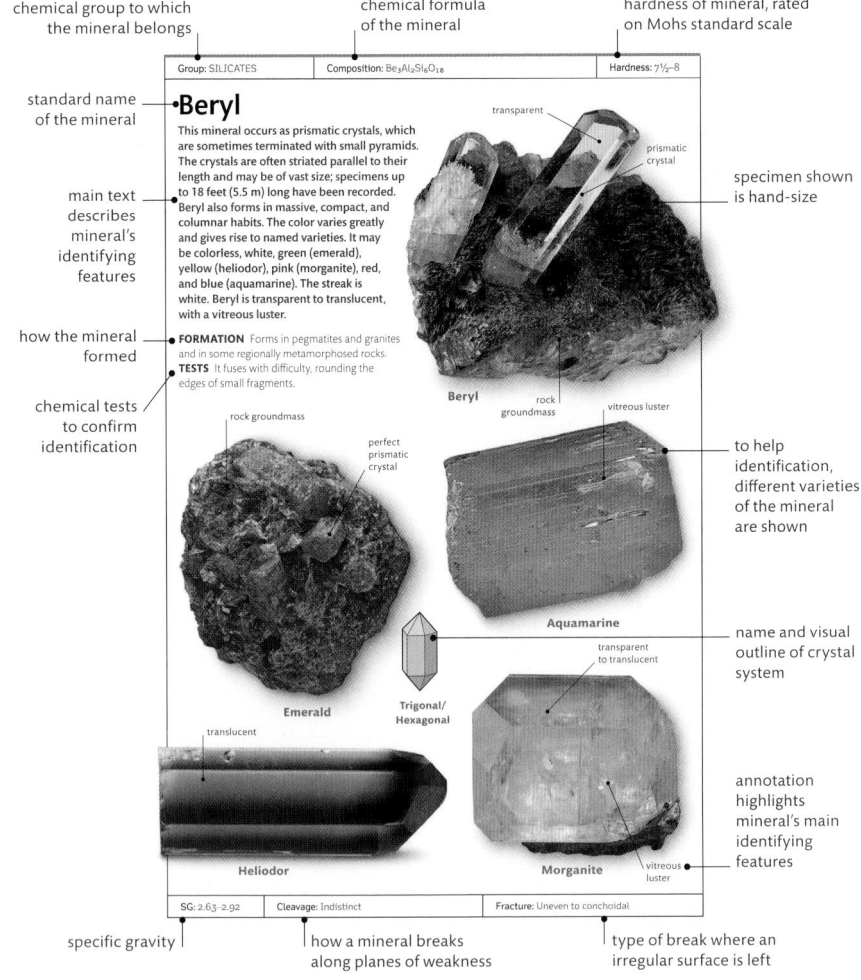

chemical group to which the mineral belongs

chemical formula of the mineral

hardness of mineral, rated on Mohs standard scale

| Group: SILICATES | Composition: Be₃Al₂Si₆O₁₈ | Hardness: 7½–8 |

standard name of the mineral

Beryl

This mineral occurs as prismatic crystals, which are sometimes terminated with small pyramids. The crystals are often striated parallel to their length and may be of vast size; specimens up to 18 feet (5.5 m) long have been recorded. Beryl also forms in massive, compact, and columnar habits. The color varies greatly and gives rise to named varieties. It may be colorless, white, green (emerald), yellow (heliodor), pink (morganite), red, and blue (aquamarine). The streak is white. Beryl is transparent to translucent, with a vitreous luster.

main text describes mineral's identifying features

how the mineral formed

FORMATION Forms in pegmatites and granites and in some regionally metamorphosed rocks.

TESTS It fuses with difficulty, rounding the edges of small fragments.

chemical tests to confirm identification

transparent

prismatic crystal

specimen shown is hand-size

Beryl

rock groundmass

vitreous luster

rock groundmass

perfect prismatic crystal

to help identification, different varieties of the mineral are shown

Aquamarine

transparent to translucent

name and visual outline of crystal system

Emerald

Trigonal/ Hexagonal

translucent

annotation highlights mineral's main identifying features

Heliodor

Morganite

vitreous luster

| SG: 2.63–2.92 | Cleavage: Indistinct | Fracture: Uneven to conchoidal |

specific gravity

how a mineral breaks along planes of weakness

type of break where an irregular surface is left

IGNEOUS ROCKS

classification of the rock

whether formed on the surface (extrusive) or below the surface (intrusive)

size of grains in the rock

crystal shape: euhedral is well formed, anhedral is poorly formed

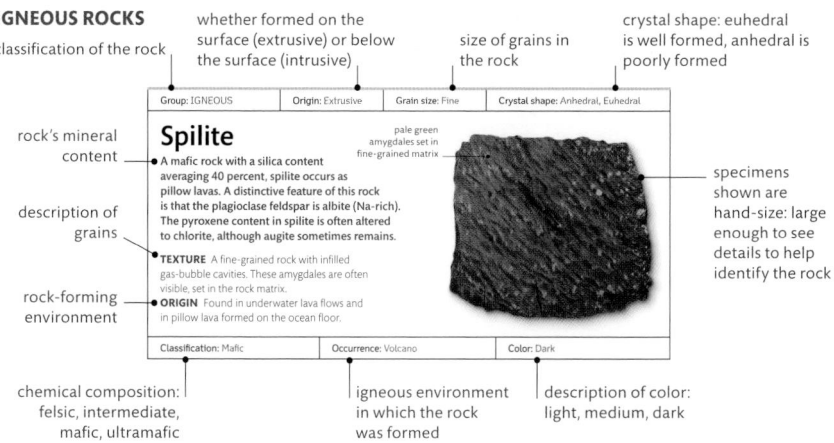

rock's mineral content

description of grains

rock-forming environment

| Group: IGNEOUS | Origin: Extrusive | Grain size: Fine | Crystal shape: Anhedral, Euhedral |

Spilite

pale green amygdales set in fine-grained matrix

A mafic rock with a silica content averaging 40 percent, spilite occurs as pillow lavas. A distinctive feature of this rock is that the plagioclase feldspar is albite (Na-rich). The pyroxene content in spilite is often altered to chlorite, although augite sometimes remains.

TEXTURE A fine-grained rock with infilled gas-bubble cavities. These amygdales are often visible, set in the rock matrix.

ORIGIN Found in underwater lava flows and in pillow lava formed on the ocean floor.

| Classification: Mafic | Occurrence: Volcano | Color: Dark |

specimens shown are hand-size: large enough to see details to help identify the rock

chemical composition: felsic, intermediate, mafic, ultramafic

igneous environment in which the rock was formed

description of color: light, medium, dark

METAMORPHIC ROCKS

| Group: METAMORPHIC | Origin: Contact aureoles | Grain size: Fine | Classification: Contact |

type of metamorphism

Chiastolite hornfels

chiastolite crystal

A gray or brownish rock, this hornfels contains minerals such as quartz and mica, with andalusite and cordierite. The thin-bladed crystals that are clearly seen in the matrix are of chiastolite, a variety of andalusite.

TEXTURE This rock consists of fine-grained crystals of even size. Porphyroblasts of andalusite occur as inclusions of chiastolite, which are cross-shaped in section.

ORIGIN Forms close to the igneous intrusion that provides the heat for metamorphism.

bladed chiastolite

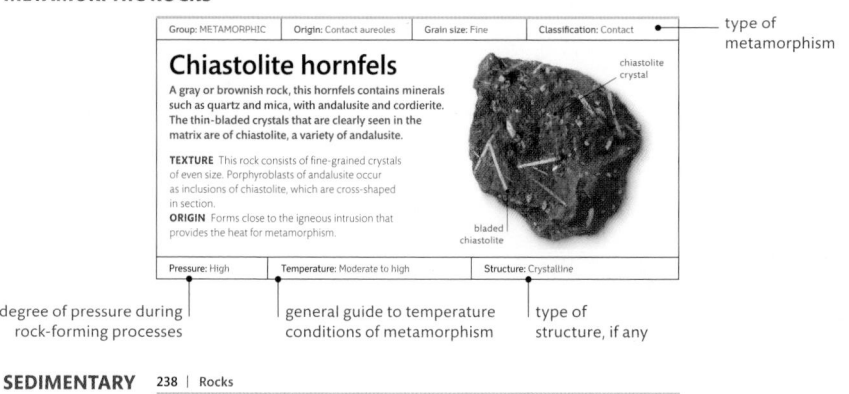

| Pressure: High | Temperature: Moderate to high | Structure: Crystalline |

degree of pressure during rock-forming processes

general guide to temperature conditions of metamorphism

type of structure, if any

SEDIMENTARY ROCKS

238 | Rocks

| Group: SEDIMENTARY | Origin: Marine | Grain size: Fine to coarse |

Crinoidal limestone

pale grayish-pink rock with a lot of fragmented calcite

This rock is essentially formed of calcite as fine or larger crystals. These may have been derived from animal skeletons such as crinoid plates. Ossicles of crinoid stems are conspicuous ingredients of this rock.

TEXTURE The large fragments in the rock are the broken stems of crinoids. These may be long, cylindrical pieces, as well as single, rounded ossicles. They are bound in a matrix of massive calcite, with a calcite cement.

ORIGIN This limestone is formed in marine conditions and takes its name from crinoids— a group of sea-dwelling creatures related to starfish and sea urchins. Crinoids' presence in coral limestone suggests that they inhabited shallow marine environments. Crinoids are not the only fossils that are commonly found in crinoidal limestone—it can be rich in brachiopods, mollusks, and corals.

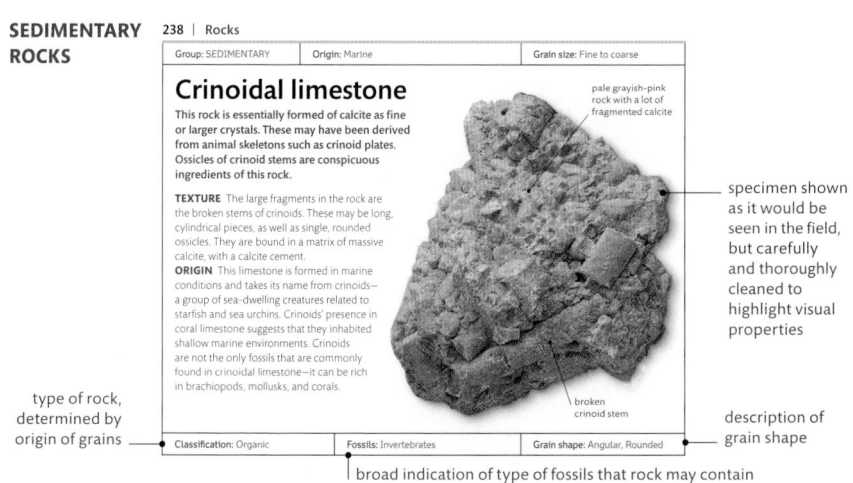

broken crinoid stem

specimen shown as it would be seen in the field, but carefully and thoroughly cleaned to highlight visual properties

type of rock, determined by origin of grains

description of grain shape

| Classification: Organic | Fossils: Invertebrates | Grain shape: Angular, Rounded |

broad indication of type of fossils that rock may contain

MINERAL OR ROCK?

ROCKS ARE aggregates of minerals— usually several, but sometimes only one or two. Similarly, minerals are either free, uncombined native elements, or elemental compounds. Gold, silver, and copper are metallic native elements. Feldspars, pyroxenes, amphiboles, and micas are rock-forming silicates— compounds in which metallic elements combine with linked silicon and oxygen.

WHAT IS A MINERAL?

With a few notable exceptions (mercury), minerals are solid, inorganic elements or elemental compounds. They have definite atomic structures and chemical compositions which vary within fixed limits. Each and every quartz crystal, whether crystallized in a sandstone vein, or in volcanic lava, possesses the same chemical and physical properties.

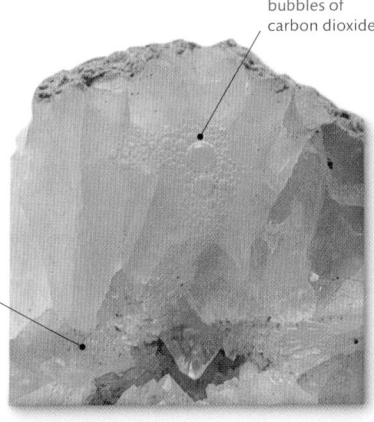

bubbles of carbon dioxide

calcite always effervesces with cold, dilute hydrochloric acid

crystal face

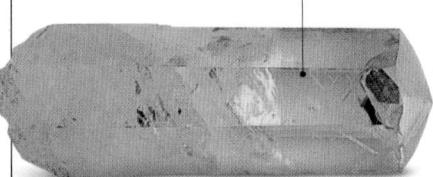

Physical property

All specimens of the same mineral will have a similar atomic structure.

Chemical property

Every mineral has a definite composition which varies within fixed limits.

Cleaved calcite rhombs

Natural occurrence

Minerals often crystallize from fluids associated with volcanic lava (left). Crusts of minerals may also form around the volcano's vent.

WHAT IS A ROCK?

Rocks are the essential components of our planet. They are classified into three major groups, determined by how the rocks were formed: igneous, metamorphic, and sedimentary (see pages 30–31). Rocks are aggregates of many different mineral grains, which are fused, cemented, or otherwise held together.

Rock: a mineral aggregate

Granite is a rock composed essentially of three minerals: quartz, alkali feldspar, and plagioclase feldspar. Their crystals interlock as a result of crystallization during the cooling of molten magma. The quartz is gray with a glassy luster, the alkali feldspar is sometimes a light pink-reddish color, and the plagioclase feldspar is often a light color. Both feldspars are often in prismatic crystals.

alkali feldspar

plagioclase feldspar

feldspar

quartz

mica

Granite

Quartz
A common mineral in granite, quartz is light-colored and hard.

Feldspar
Two types of feldspar occur in granite, often as very well-formed crystals.

Mica
Forming as small glittery crystals in granite, mica can be both dark biotite and light muscovite.

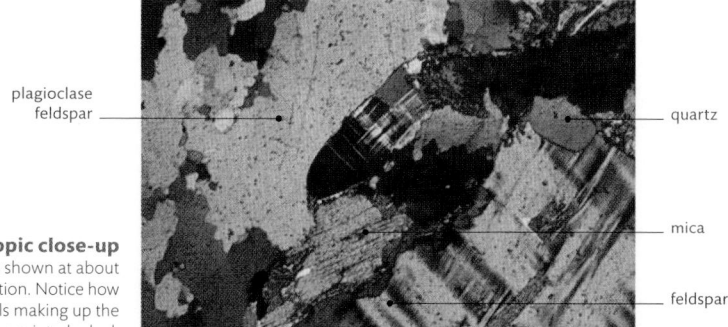

plagioclase feldspar

quartz

mica

feldspar

Microscopic close-up
This granite is shown at about ×30 magnification. Notice how the crystals making up the rock are interlocked.

MINERAL FORMATION

THE EARTH'S CRUST is made of rocks, which themselves are aggregates of minerals. Many fine mineral specimens occur in hydrothermal veins, fractures in the Earth's crust through which very hot fluids circulate. These fluids contain the elements from which many minerals form. Mineral specimens also occur in igneous rocks, crystallizing directly from cooling magma (molten rock beneath the Earth's surface) or lava (molten rock ejected at the Earth's surface). Various minerals form in metamorphic rocks when preexisting rocks are recrystallized. In some sedimentary rocks, such as limestones, evaporites, and ironstones, minerals crystallize from low-temperature solutions, often very near the surface of the Earth.

MINERAL VEINS

These are sheetlike areas of minerals that often cut through existing rock structures. Originally, they may have been faults, where rocks were broken and one rock mass moved in relation to another, or joints, where fractures occurred without movement. In the vein, there can be a complete mineral filling or crystallization around rock fragments.

typical mineral from a hydrothermal vein

Cassiterite

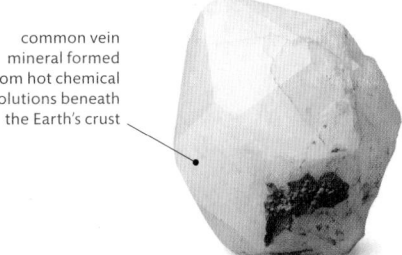

common vein mineral formed from hot chemical solutions beneath the Earth's crust

Milky quartz

Quartz vein
A vein of white milky quartz cutting through dark slates. Originally formed at great depth, this has been exposed by both weathering and erosion.

IGNEOUS ROCKS

Minerals develop in igneous rocks (see page 32) when molten magma solidifies. The densest minerals, ferromagnesian silicates like olivine and pyroxene, form at the highest temperatures, whereas less dense minerals, such as feldspar and quartz, occur later in the cooling sequence. Minerals forming in molten rock often grow unrestricted and can have a fine crystal form.

silicate mineral commonly found in many igneous rocks

Orthoclase feldspar

Granite exposure
An exposure of the igneous rock granite, showing large feldspar crystals set in the rock groundmass (above).

METAMORPHIC ROCKS

A range of minerals, including garnet, mica, and kyanite, develop in metamorphic rocks (see page 34). Temperature and pressure may rearrange chemicals in the existing rocks to create new minerals, or chemically potent fluids circulating through the rock may add extra elements.

almandine, a garnet commonly found in metamorphic rocks

Garnet

shiny mineral found in many metamorphic rocks, especially schist

Muscovite mica

Schist outcrop
Schist forms where rocks have been folded deep in the Earth's crust due to intense pressures (left).

MINERAL COMPOSITION

MINERALS ARE free, uncombined elements or elemental compounds. Their compositions are given as chemical formulae. The formula for fluorite is CaF_2. This indicates that calcium (Ca) atoms have combined with fluorine (F) atoms. The subscripted number ($_2$) shows there are twice as many fluorine atoms as there are of calcium. Minerals are arranged into groups according to their chemical composition and their crystal structure.

NATIVE ELEMENTS
These are free, uncombined elements. This relatively small group consists of around 50 members, some of which (such as gold, silver) are commercially valuable.

HALIDES
All minerals in this group contain one of the halogens: fluorine, chlorine, bromine, or iodine. Atoms of these elements combine with metallic atoms to form minerals such as halite (sodium and chlorine) or fluorite (calcium and fluorine). This is a small group of minerals, with around 100 members in all.

Silver

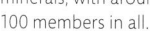

Halite

Sulfur

SULFIDES
A common group of over 300 minerals, sulfides are chemical compounds in which sulfur has combined with metallic and semimetallic elements. Pyrite and realgar are examples of this group.

Pyrite

Realgar

OXIDES AND HYDROXIDES
This group has over 250 minerals. Oxides are compounds in which one or two metallic elements combine with oxygen. A metallic element combining with water and hydroxyl forms a hydroxide.

Hematite

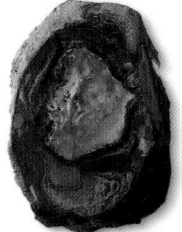

Opal

CARBONATES

A group of some 200 minerals, carbonates are compounds in which one or more metallic elements combine with the $(CO_3)^{-2}$ carbonate radical. Calcite, the most common carbonate, forms when calcium combines with the carbonate radical.

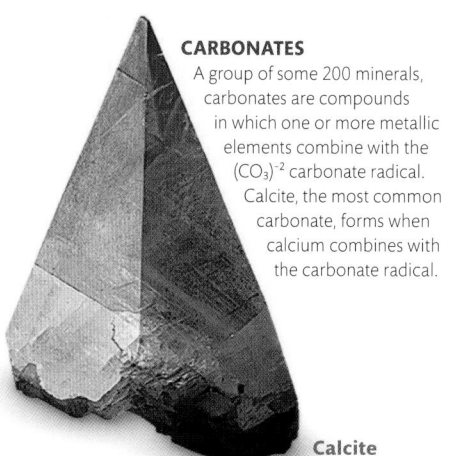

Calcite

SULFATES

These are compounds in which one or more metallic elements combine with the sulfate $(SO_4)^{-2}$ radical.

Gypsum

CHEMICAL ELEMENTS

SYMBOL	NAME	SYMBOL	NAME
Ac	Actinium	Mn	Manganese
Ag	Silver	Mo	Molybdenum
Al	Aluminum	N	Nitrogen
Am	Americium	Na	Sodium
Ar	Argon	Nb	Niobium
As	Arsenic	Nd	Neodymium
At	Astatine	Ne	Neon
Au	Gold	Ni	Nickel
B	Boron	No	Nobelium
Ba	Barium	Np	Neptinium
Be	Beryllium	O	Oxygen
Bi	Bismuth	Os	Osmium
Bk	Berkelium	P	Phosphorus
Br	Bromine	Pa	Protactinium
C	Carbon	Pb	Lead
Ca	Calcium	Pd	Palladium
Cd	Cadmium	Pm	Promathium
Ce	Cerium	Po	Polonium
Cf	Californium	Pr	Praseodymium
Cl	Chlorine	Pt	Platinum
Cm	Curium	Pu	Plutonium
Co	Cobalt	Ra	Radium
Cr	Chromium	Rb	Rubidium
Cs	Cesium	Re	Rhenium
Cu	Copper	Rh	Rhodium
Dy	Dysprosium	Rn	Radon
Er	Erbium	S	Sulfur
Es	Einsteinium	Sb	Antimony
F	Fluorine	Sc	Scandium
Fe	Iron	Se	Selenium
Fm	Fermium	Si	Silicon
Fr	Francium	Sm	Samarium
Ga	Gallium	Sn	Tin
Gd	Gadolinium	Sr	Strontium
Ge	Germanium	Ta	Tantalum
H	Hydrogen	Tb	Terbium
He	Helium	Tc	Technetium
Hf	Hafinium	Te	Tellurium
Hg	Mercury	Th	Thorium
Ho	Holmium	Ti	Titanium
I	Iodine	Tl	Thallium
In	Indium	Tu	Thulium
Ir	Iridium	U	Uranium
K	Potassium	V	Vanadium
Kr	Krypton	W	Tungsten
La	Lanthanum	Xe	Xenon
Li	Lithium	Y	Yttrium
Lu	Lutetium	Yb	Ytterbium
Lw	Lawrencium	Zn	Zinc
Md	Mendelevium	Zr	Zirconium
Mg	Magnesium		

PHOSPHATES

A group of minerals, many of which are brightly colored, phosphates are compounds in which one or more metallic elements combine with the phosphate $(PO_4)^{-3}$ radical. Arsenates and vanadates are associated with this group.

Pyromorphite

MINERAL CHARACTERISTICS

MINERALS EXHIBIT a number of properties that are used for identification. It is essential to take a scientific approach when testing a mineral. First, observe the color (see page 26), luster (page 27), and habit (page 23). Then test for hardness (page 25), specific gravity (page 25), and streak (page 26). Fracture and cleavage (page 24) may be obvious, or you may have to break the mineral.

CRYSTAL SYSTEMS

The geometrical shapes in which minerals crystallize are organized, according to their symmetry, into six main groups called crystal systems. Within each of these systems, many different forms are possible, but all the forms in a crystal system can be related to the symmetry of that system. From a study of crystal habits, it may be possible to say to which crystal system the mineral belongs. The small blue diagram that appears with each mineral represents its crystal system.

selenite

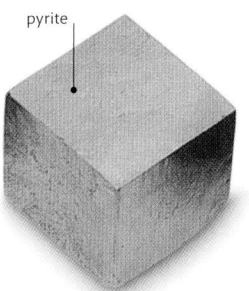
pyrite

Cubic
Essentially cube-shaped crystals, though this category also includes octahedral-shaped (8-sided) and dodecahedral-shaped (12-sided) crystals.

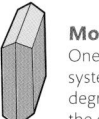

Monoclinic
One of the commonest systems, this has a lower degree of symmetry than the cubic system.

axinite

Triclinic
The least symmetrical of the crystal systems.

vesuvianite

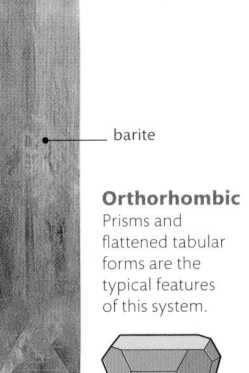
barite

Orthorhombic
Prisms and flattened tabular forms are the typical features of this system.

Hexagonal/Trigonal
Two systems grouped together here because their symmetry is similar.

beryl

Tetragonal
A form that is usually more elongated than the cube.

HABIT
The habit is the characteristic appearance of a mineral that is determined by its predominant form. Several descriptive terms to identify a mineral's habit are defined below.

copper

Dendritic
Plantlike shape.

actinolite

Bladed
Looks like the blade of a knife.

beryl

Prismatic
Shows a uniform cross-section.

scolecite

Acicular
Slender needlelike masses.

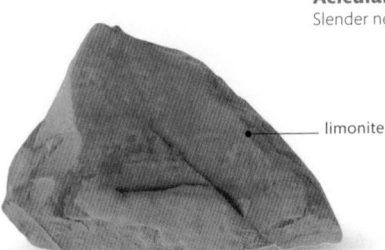

limonite

Massive
Indicates no definitive shape.

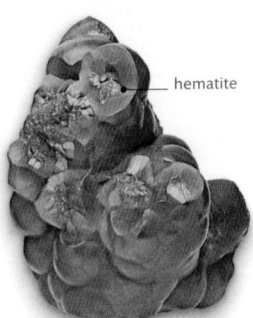

hematite

Reniform
Rounded kidney-shaped masses.

TWINNING
Twinning refers to a nonparallel, symmetrical intergrowth of two or more crystals of the same mineral. Twinning can occur by contact or interpenetration. Multiple and polysynthetic twins involve more than two individual crystals.

cerussite

Contact twins
Radiating intergrown crystals.

staurolite

Penetration twins
Showing two crystals that have intergrown.

CLEAVAGE

Cleavage is the way that a mineral breaks along well-defined planes of weakness. Often these planes are between layers of atoms or other places where the atomic bonding is weakest. Cleavage surfaces are not perfectly smooth like crystal faces, though they are very consistent and reflect light evenly. Cleavage is described as perfect, distinct, indistinct, or none.

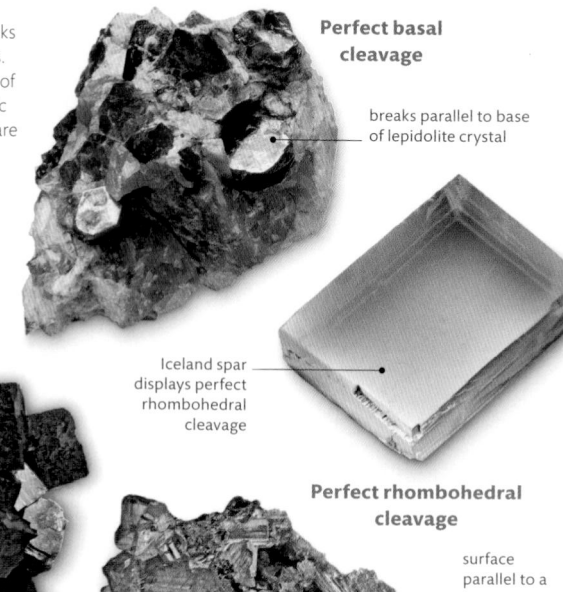

Perfect basal cleavage

breaks parallel to base of lepidolite crystal

Iceland spar displays perfect rhombohedral cleavage

Perfect rhombohedral cleavage

cube-shaped break in galena

surface parallel to a prism face in cerussite

Perfect cubic cleavage

Perfect prismatic cleavage

FRACTURE

If a mineral is struck with a geologist's hammer and it breaks, leaving surfaces that are rough and uneven, it is said to fracture. (Cleavage surfaces are usually flat, and exactly the same shape may be produced by repeated hammer blows.) Most minerals fracture and cleave, but some will only fracture. Common fracture terms are uneven, conchoidal (shell-like), hackly (jagged), and splintery.

Conchoidal

curved fracture in opal

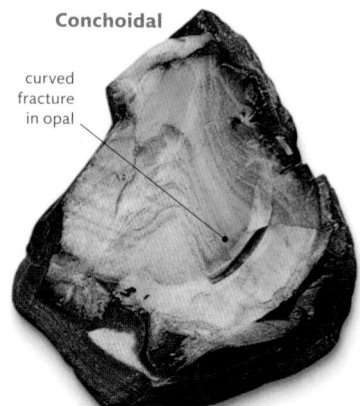

rough, uneven surfaces of rock crystal

Uneven fracture

HARDNESS

A useful aid for identifying a mineral is the hardness test. The hardness of a mineral is its resistance to being scratched. The scale of hardness from 1 (talc) to 10 (diamond) was devised by Friedrich Mohs. Minerals with higher Mohs numbers will scratch those lower down the scale. Thus calcite will scratch gypsum but not fluorite. Minerals can also be tested with everyday objects: a mineral scratched with a coin will have a hardness of less than 3½.

Thumbnail: 2½

Copper coin: 3½

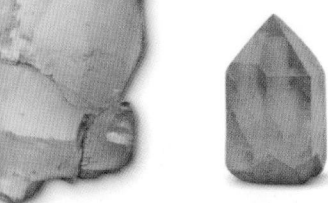

Knife blade: 5½

Glass: 6

Quartz: 7

MOHS SCALE OF HARDNESS

1	2	3	4	5	6	7	8	9	10
Talc	Gypsum	Calcite	Fluorite	Apatite	Orthoclase	Quartz	Topaz	Corundum	Diamond

SPECIFIC GRAVITY

Comparing the weight of a mineral with the weight of an equal volume of water gives a mineral's specific gravity. This is shown numerically: an SG of 2.5 indicates that the mineral is two-and-a-half times as heavy as water. The quartz specimen (below) is larger than the galena but weighs less, as it has a lower SG.

**Quartz
SG: 2.65**

**Galena
SG: 7.5**

COLOR

The color of a mineral—as seen in natural light—is an obvious and useful identification feature. Although it helps to identify those minerals with characteristic colors, there are pitfalls in relying solely on this feature. Many minerals—quartz, for example—occur in a variety of colors, while a large number of minerals are white or colorless. The selection of quartz below, indicates the range of colors found in minerals.

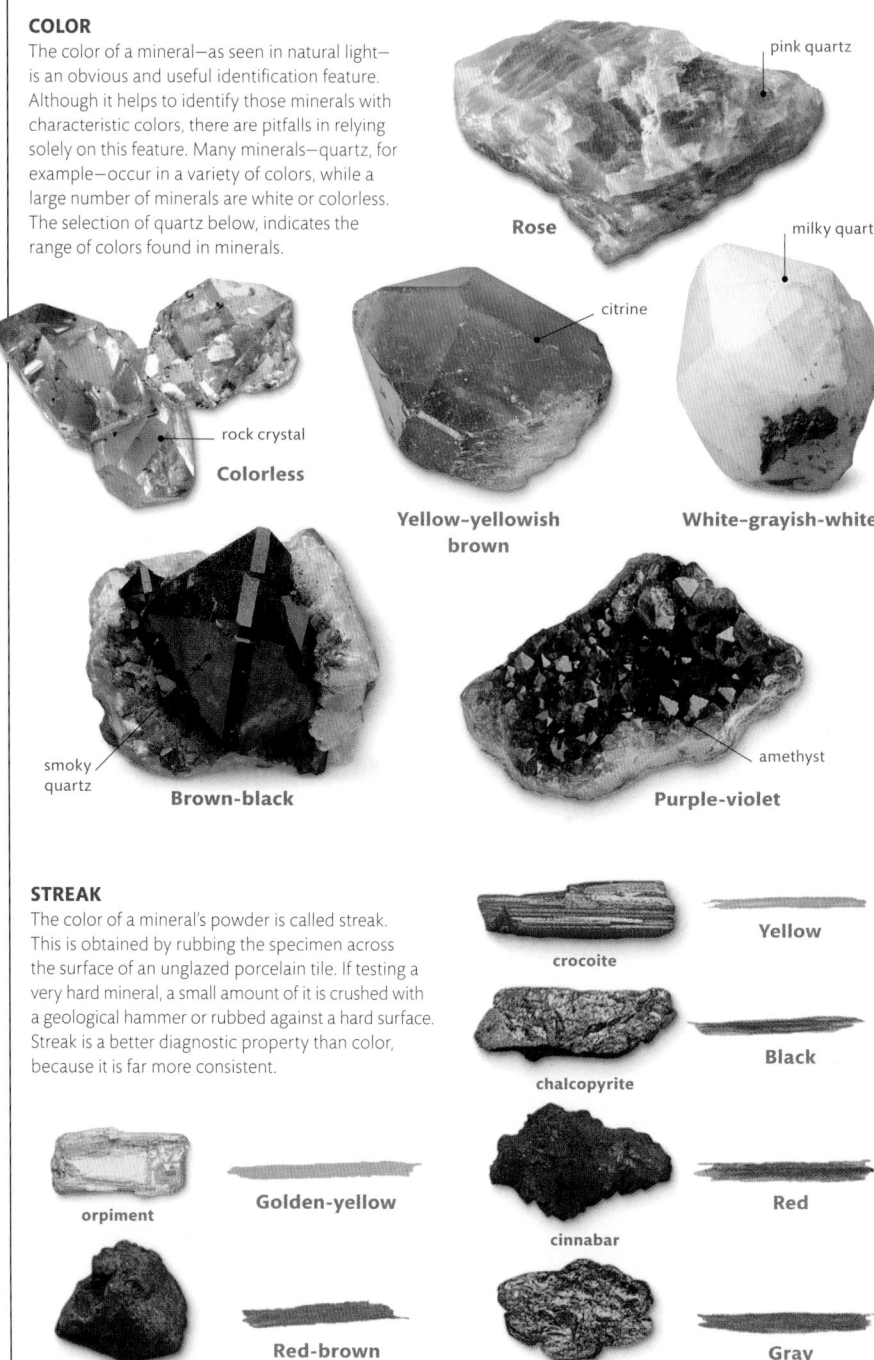

pink quartz

Rose

milky quartz

citrine

rock crystal

Colorless

Yellow–yellowish brown

White–grayish-white

smoky quartz

Brown-black

amethyst

Purple-violet

STREAK

The color of a mineral's powder is called streak. This is obtained by rubbing the specimen across the surface of an unglazed porcelain tile. If testing a very hard mineral, a small amount of it is crushed with a geological hammer or rubbed against a hard surface. Streak is a better diagnostic property than color, because it is far more consistent.

crocoite

Yellow

chalcopyrite

Black

orpiment

Golden-yellow

cinnabar

Red

hematite

Red-brown

molybdenite

Gray

TRANSPARENCY

Transparency refers to the way in which light passes through a mineral specimen. It depends on the way mineral atoms are bonded. Mineral specimens that allow objects to be seen through them are transparent. If light passes through, but the object cannot be clearly seen, then the specimen is translucent. When light does not pass through a specimen, even when cut very thin, it is opaque.

Transparent

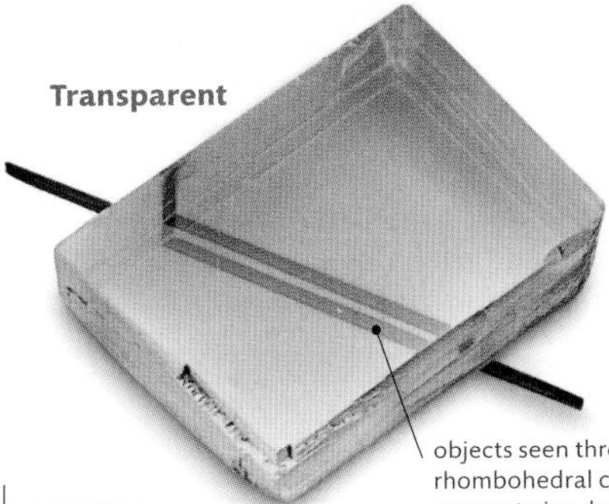

objects seen through rhombohedral calcite appear twice due to double refraction

aquamarine allows light to pass through it

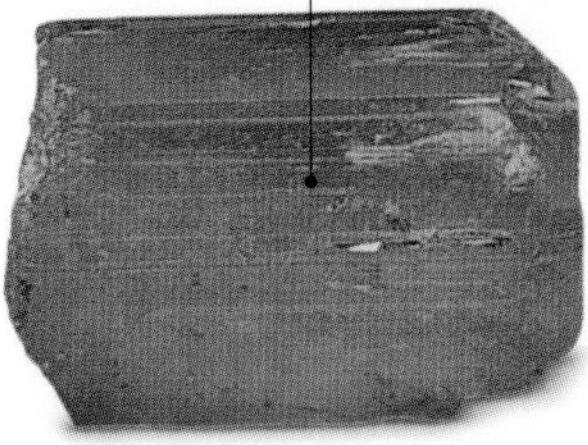

Translucent

Opaque

gold allows no light to pass through it

LUSTER

Luster describes the way light is reflected off a mineral's surface. The type and intensity of luster vary according to the nature of the mineral surface and the amount of light absorbed. Well-recognized, mainly self-explanatory terms are used to describe luster. They include dull, metallic, pearly, vitreous (glassy), greasy, and silky.

greasy luster on halite surface

Greasy

glasslike surface on yellow fluorite crystal

dull luster on hematite

Vitreous

silky surface on "satin spar" gypsum

Dull

metallic luster on galena surface

Silky

Metallic

MINERAL IDENTIFICATION

TO HELP WITH mineral identification, the minerals are listed according to hardness, and other selected properties are included alongside them.

KEY TO ABBREVIATIONS:
con.-conchoidal; dis.-distinct; imp.-imperfect; ind.-indistinct; not det.-not determined; per.-perfect; subcon.-subconchoidal; un.-uneven; <-less than or equal to; >-more than. (Note: average SG = 3)

MINERAL	SG	CLEAVAGE	FRACTURE
Hardness <2½			
Acanthite	7.22	none	uneven
Annabergite	3.07	perfect	uneven
Artinite	2.02	perfect	uneven
Aurichalcite	3.96	perfect	uneven
Autunite	3.05–3.20	per. basal	uneven
Bismuth	9.70–9.83	per. basal	uneven
Bismuthinite	6.78	perfect	uneven
Borax	1.70	perfect	conchoidal
Brucite	2.39	perfect	uneven
Carnallite	1.60l	none	conchoidal
Carnotite	4.70	per. basal	uneven
Chalcanthite	2.29	imperfect	conchoidal
Chlorargyrite	5.55	none	un.–subcon.
Chrysotile	2.53–2.61	none	uneven
Cinnabar	8.08	perfect	con.–un.
Clinochlore	2.60–3.02	perfect	uneven
Covellite	4.68	per. basal	uneven
Cryolite	2.97	none	uneven
Cyanotrichite	2.76	none	uneven
Diaboleite	3.41–3.43	perfect	conchoidal
Epsomite	1.68	perfect	conchoidal
Erythrite	3.06	perfect	uneven
Galena	7.58	per. cubic	subcon.
Glauconite	2.40–2.95	perfect	uneven
Graphite	2.09–2.23	per. basal	uneven
Gypsum	2.32	perfect	splintery
Gyrolite	2.45–2.51	perfect	uneven
Halite	2.17	perfect	un.–con.
Hydrozincite	3.50–4.00	perfect	uneven
Jamesonite	5.63	good basal	un.–con.
Kaolinite	2.63	per. basal	uneven
Kernite	1.91	perfect	splintery
Linarite	5.35	perfect	conchoidal
Molybdenite	4.62–5.06	per. basal	uneven
Muscovite	2.77–2.88	perfect	uneven
Nepouite	3.24	none	splintery
Nitratine	2.27	perfect	conchoidal
Orpiment	3.49	perfect	uneven
Proustite	5.55–5.64	distinct	con.–un.
Pyrargyrite	5.85	distinct	con.–un.
Pyrophyllite	2.65–2.90	perfect	uneven
Realgar	3.56	good	conchoidal
Sepiolite	2.00–2.20	none	uneven
Stephanite	6.26	imperfect	un.–subcon.
Stibnite	4.63–4.66	perfect	un.–subcon.
Sulfur	2.07	imp. basal	un.–con.
Sylvanite	8.16	perfect	uneven
Sylvite	1.99	perfect	uneven
Talc	2.58–2.83	perfect	uneven
Torbernite	3.22	per. basal	uneven
Trona	2.14	perfect	uneven
Tungstite	5.50	perfect	uneven
Tyuyamunite	3.57–4.35	per. basal	uneven
Ulexite	1.95	perfect	uneven
Vermiculite	2.30	perfect	uneven
Vivianite	2.67–2.69	perfect	uneven
Hardness <3½			
Adamite	4.32–4.48	good	subcon.–un.
Anglesite	6.37–6.39	good	con.
Anhydrite	2.98	perfect	un.–splintery
Antimony	6.69	per. basal	uneven
Arsenic	5.72–5.73	per. basal	uneven
Astrophyllite	3.20–3.40	perfect	uneven
Atacamite	3.76	perfect	conchoidal

MINERAL	SG	CLEAVAGE	FRACTURE
Barite	4.50	perfect	uneven
Bauxite	2.30–2.70	none	uneven
Biotite	2.70–3.40	per. basal	uneven
Boleite	5.05	perfect	uneven
Bornite	5.08	very poor	un.–con.
Boulangerite	6.20	good	uneven
Bournonite	5.83	imperfect	subcon.–un.
Calcite	2.71	perfect	subcon.
Celestine	3.96–3.98	perfect	uneven
Cerussite	6.55	distinct	conchoidal
Chalcocite	5.50–5.80	indistinct	conchoidal
Chamosite	3.12	not det.	uneven
Chrysocolla	1.93–2.40	none	un.–con.
Clinoclase	4.38	perfect	uneven
Copiapite	2.08–2.17	perfect	uneven
Copper	8.94	none	hackly
Crocoite	5.97–6.02	distinct	con.–un.
Descloizite	6.20	none	un.–con.
Enargite	4.45	perfect	uneven
Gibbsite	2.40	perfect	uneven
Glauberite	2.75–2.85	perfect	conchoidal
Gold	19.30	none	hackly
Greenockite	4.82	distinct	conchoidal
Heulandite-Na	2.20	perfect	uneven
Jarosite	2.90–3.26	distinct	uneven
Leadhillite	6.55	per. basal	conchoidal
Lepidolite	2.80–2.90	perfect	uneven
Millerite	5.30–5.50	perfect	uneven
Olivenite	4.46	indistinct	un.–con.
Phlogopite	2.78–2.85	perfect	uneven
Polybasite	6.10	imp. basal	uneven
Polyhalite	2.78	perfect	uneven
Silver	10.50	none	hackly
Strontianite	3.78	perfect	uneven
Thenardite	2.66	perfect	uneven
Vanadinite	6.88	none	con.–un.
Volborthite	3.50–3.80	per. basal	uneven
Witherite	4.29	distinct	uneven
Wulfenite	6.50–7.50	dis. pyramidal	subcon.
Hardness <5½			
Alunite	2.60–2.90	dis. basal	conchoidal
Analcime	2.24–2.29	very poor	subcon.
Ankerite	2.93–3.10	perfect	hackly
Antigorite	2.50–2.60	perfect	con.–splintery
Apatite	3.10–3.20	poor	con.–un.
Aragonite	2.95	distinct	subcon.
Azurite	3.77	perfect	conchoidal
Bayldonite	5.24–5.65	none	uneven
Barytocalcite	3.66–3.71	perfect	subcon.–un.
Brochantite	3.97	perfect	con.–un.
Chabazite	2.05–2.20	indistinct	uneven
Chalcopyrite	4.35	poor	un.–con.
Chromite	4.50–4.80	none	uneven
Cobaltite	6.33	perfect	uneven
Colemanite	2.42	perfect	un.–con.
Cuprite	6.14	poor	con.–un.
Datolite	2.96–3.00	none	un.–con.
Dioptase	3.28–3.35	perfect	un.–con.
Dolomite	2.85	perfect	subcon.
Fluorapophy-llite-(K)	2.33–2.37	perfect	uneven
Fluorite	3.18–3.56	perfect	conchoidal
Glaucodot	6.06	perfect	uneven
Goethite	4.27–4.29	perfect	uneven
Harmotome	2.41–2.47	distinct	un.–subcon.

MINERAL	SG	CLEAVAGE	FRACTURE
Hauerite	3.46	perfect	subcon.–un.
Hausmannite	4.83–4.85	good	uneven
Hemimorphite	3.47	perfect	un.–con.
Herderite	3.02	poor	subcon.
Jarlite	3.78–3.93	not det.	uneven
Laumontite	2.23–2.41	perfect	uneven
Lazurite	2.38–2.45	imperfect	uneven
Lepidocrocite	4.05–4.13	perfect	uneven
Limonite	2.70–4.30	none	uneven
Magnesite	3.00–3.10	perfect	con.–un.
Malachite	4.05	perfect	subcon.–un.
Manganite	4.33	perfect	uneven
Mesolite	2.26	perfect	uneven
Mimetite	7.24	none	subcon.–un.
Monazite	4.60–5.50	distinct	con.–un.
Natrolite	2.20–2.26	perfect	uneven
Nickel-iron	7.30–8.20	poor cubic	hackly
Nickeline	7.78	none	uneven
Nickelskutte-rudite	6.50	distinct	uneven
Nosean	2.30–2.40	indistinct	un.–con.
Pectolite	2.84–2.90	perfect	uneven
Pentlandite	4.60–5.00	none	conchoidal
Perovskite	4.01	imperfect	subcon.–un.
Phillipsite-K	2.20	distinct	uneven
Platinum	21.44	none	hackly
Pyrochlore group	4.48–6.40	distinct	subcon.–un.
Pyromorphite	7.04	very poor	un.–subcon.
Pyrrhotite	4.53–4.77	none	subcon.–un.
Rhodochrosite	3.70	perfect	un.–con.
Riebeckite	3.32–3.38	perfect	uneven
Scheelite	6.10	distinct	subcon.–un.
Scolecite	2.25–2.29	perfect	uneven
Scorodite	3.27	imperfect	subcon.
Siderite	3.96	perfect	uneven
Smithsonite	4.42–4.44	perfect	subcon.–un.
Sphalerite	3.90–4.10	perfect	conchoidal
Stilbite-Ca	2.19	perfect	uneven
Tennantite	4.62	none	un.–subcon.
Tetrahedrite	4.97	none	un.–subcon.
Thomsonite-Ca	2.23–2.29	perfect	un.–subcon.
Titanite	3.48–3.60	distinct	conchoidal
Variscite	2.57–2.61	perfect	con. or un.–splintery
Wavellite	2.36	perfect	subcon.–un.
Willemite	3.89–4.19	distinct	uneven
Wolframite	7.10–7.50	perfect	uneven
Wollastonite	2.86–3.09	perfect	splintery
Xenotime-(Y)	4.40–5.10	perfect	uneven
Zincite	5.68	perfect	conchoidal
Hardness <6			
Actinolite	3.03–3.24	good	splintery
Aegirine	3.50–3.60	good	uneven
Akermanite	2.94	distinct	un.–con.
Amblygonite	3.04–3.11	perfect	uneven
Anatase	3.79–3.97	per. basal	subcon.
Anthophyllite	2.85–3.57	perfect	conchoidal
Arfvedsonite	3.30–3.50	perfect	uneven
Arsenopyrite	6.07	indistinct	uneven
Augite	3.19–3.56	good	un.–con.
Brookite	4.08–4.18	poor	subcon.–un.
Cancrinite	2.42–2.51	perfect	uneven
Columbite series	5.20–6.65	distinct	subcon.–un.
Enstatite	3.20–3.90	good	uneven
Epidote	3.38–3.49	perfect	uneven
Eudialyte	2.74–3.10	perfect	uneven
Gehlenite	3.04	distinct	un.–con.
Glaucophane	3.08–3.15	good	un.–con.
Grunerite	3.44–3.60	good	uneven
Hauyne	2.44–2.50	indistinct	un.–con.
Hematite	5.26	none	un.–subcon.
Hornblende	3.00–3.40	perfect	uneven
Humite	3.20–3.32	poor	uneven
Hypersthene	3.40–3.80	good	uneven
Ilmenite	4.72	none	con.–un.

MINERAL	SG	CLEAVAGE	FRACTURE
Ilvaite	3.99–4.05	distinct	uneven
Jadeite	3.25–3.35	good	splintery
Lazulite	3.12–3.24	indistinct	un.–splintery
Leucite	2.45–2.50	very poor	conchoidal
Milarite	2.46–2.61	none	con.–un.
Nepheline	2.55–2.66	indistinct	conchoidal
Neptunite	3.19–3.23	perfect	conchoidal
Orthoclase	2.55–2.63	perfect	un.–con.
Richterite	3.10	perfect	uneven
Romanechite	3.30–4.70	none	uneven
Samarskite-(Y)	5.00–5.69	indistinct	conchoidal
Sanidine	2.56–2.62	perfect	con.–un.
Scapolite group	2.50–2.78	distinct	un.–con.
Skutterudite	6.50	distinct	uneven
Sodalite	2.27–2.33	poor	un.–con.
Tremolite	2.99–3.03	perfect	splintery
Turquoise	2.60–2.80	perfect	subcon.–un.
Uraninite	10.63–10.95	indistinct	con.–un.
Hardness <7			
Albite	2.60–2.65	perfect	un.–con.
Andesine	2.66–2.68	perfect	un.–con.
Anorthite	2.74–2.76	perfect	con.–un.
Anorthoclase	2.56–2.62	perfect	uneven
Axinite	3.25–3.28	good	un.–con.
Benitoite	3.65	indistinct	con.–un.
Bytownite	2.72–2.74	perfect	un.–con.
Cassiterite	6.99	poor	subcon.–un.
Chalcedony	2.60	none	conchoidal
Chloritoid	3.40–3.80	perfect	uneven
Chondrodite	3.16–3.26	poor	uneven
Clinozoisite	3.30–3.40	perfect	uneven
Diaspore	3.20–3.50	perfect	conchoidal
Diopside	3.22–3.38	good	un.–con.
Franklinite	5.07–5.22	none	un.–subcon.
Gadolinite-(Y)	4.36–4.77	none	conchoidal
Grossular garnet	3.59	none	un.–con.
Hedenbergite	3.56	good	un.–con.
Kyanite	3.53–3.67	perfect	uneven
Labradorite	2.69–2.72	perfect	un.–con.
Magnetite	5.17	none	subcon.–un.
Marcasite	4.92	distinct	uneven
Microcline	2.54–2.57	perfect	uneven
Oligoclase	2.63–2.66	perfect	un.–con.
Olivine	3.27–4.32	imperfect	conchoidal
Opal	1.99–2.25	none	con.–un.
Petalite	2.41–2.42	perfect	subcon.
Prehnite	2.80–2.95	distinct	uneven
Pyrite	5.00–5.03	indistinct	con.–un.
Pyrolusite	5.06	perfect	uneven
Quartz	2.65–2.66	none	con.–un.
Rhodonite	3.57–3.76	perfect	con.–un.
Rutile	4.23	distinct	con.–un.
Spodumene	3.10–3.20	perfect	un.–con.
Stibiconite	3.50–5.50	not det.	uneven
Tourmaline	2.90–3.10	very ind.	un.–con.
Vesuvianite	3.32–3.43	indistinct	un.–con.
Wad	2.80–4.40	none	uneven
Zoisite	3.15–3.36	perfect	un.–con.
Hardness >7			
Almandine garnet	4.32	none	un.–con.
Andalusite	3.13–3.21	distinct	un.–subcon.
Beryl	2.63–2.92	indistinct	un.–con.
Chrysoberyl	3.75	distinct	con.–un.
Cordierite	2.60–2.66	distinct	conchoidal
Corundum	4.00–4.10	none	con.–un.
Diamond	3.51	perfect	conchoidal
Dumortierite	3.21–3.41	good	uneven
Euclase	2.99–3.10	perfect	conchoidal
Phenakite	2.96–3.00	distinct	conchoidal
Pyrope garnet	3.58	none	conchoidal
Sillimanite	3.23–3.27	perfect	uneven
Spinel	3.58	none	con.–un.
Staurolite	3.74–3.83	distinct	un.–subcon.
Topaz	3.40–3.60	perfect	subcon.–un.
Zircon	4.60–4.70	imperfect	con.–un.

HOW ROCKS ARE FORMED

ROCKS ARE created and destroyed in many ways within the Earth and on its surface. Upon cooling, rising magma may form large masses, plutons (1) or smaller intrusions, dikes (2). Magma becomes lava on the surface. Igneous rocks form when magmas or lavas cool and crystallize. Rocks are exposed to weathering and erosion by ice, water, and wind and broken down into particles, which are transported by glaciers (3), rivers (4), and wind.

Rock cycle
The rock-making cycle, shown below, spans over millions of years.

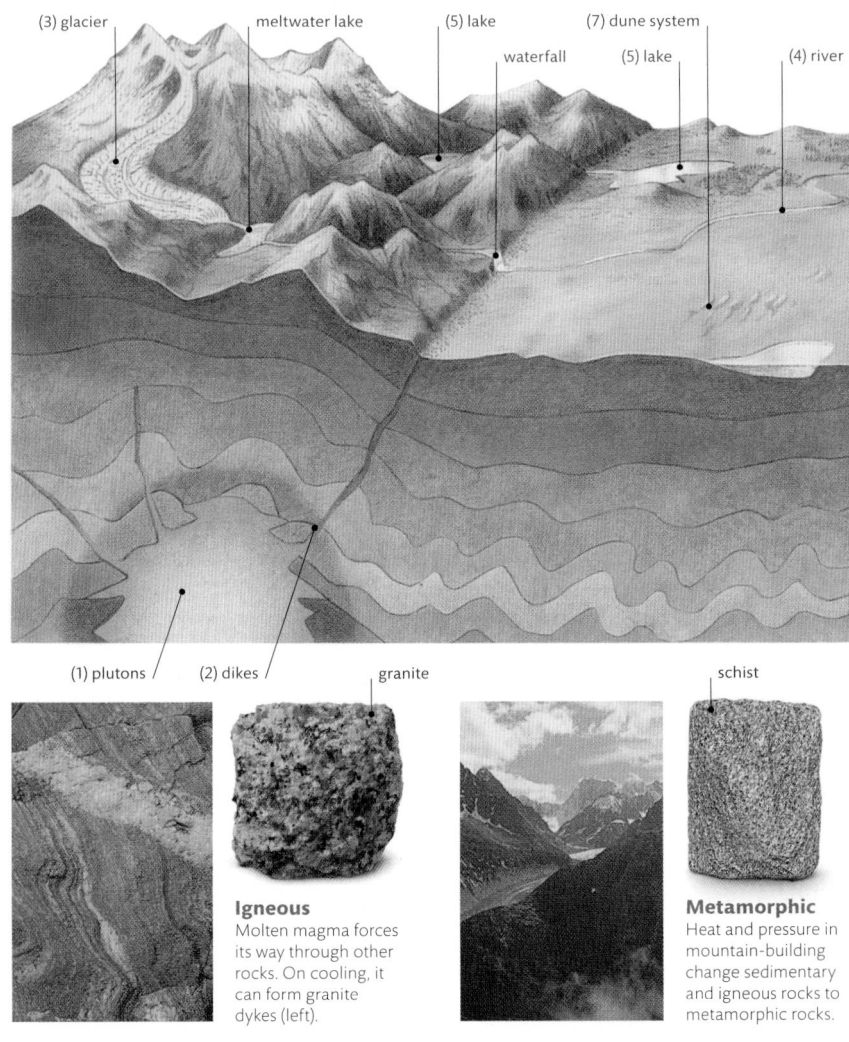

(3) glacier
meltwater lake
(5) lake
(7) dune system
waterfall
(5) lake
(4) river
(1) plutons
(2) dikes
granite
schist

Igneous
Molten magma forces its way through other rocks. On cooling, it can form granite dykes (left).

Metamorphic
Heat and pressure in mountain-building change sedimentary and igneous rocks to metamorphic rocks.

These particles are deposited as sedimentary layers in lakes (5), deltas (6), dunes (7), and on the sea bed to form sedimentary rocks, such as clay or shale (8). A lot of sediment is deposited on the continental shelf (9), and some is carried to the greater depths of the ocean floor by dense currents channeled by ocean canyons (10).

When sedimentary and igneous rocks are subjected to intense heat and pressure during large-scale mountain-building, they become metamorphic rocks, such as schist and gneiss. Further increases in temperature and pressure may cause the rock to become molten, and the rock cycle is completed.

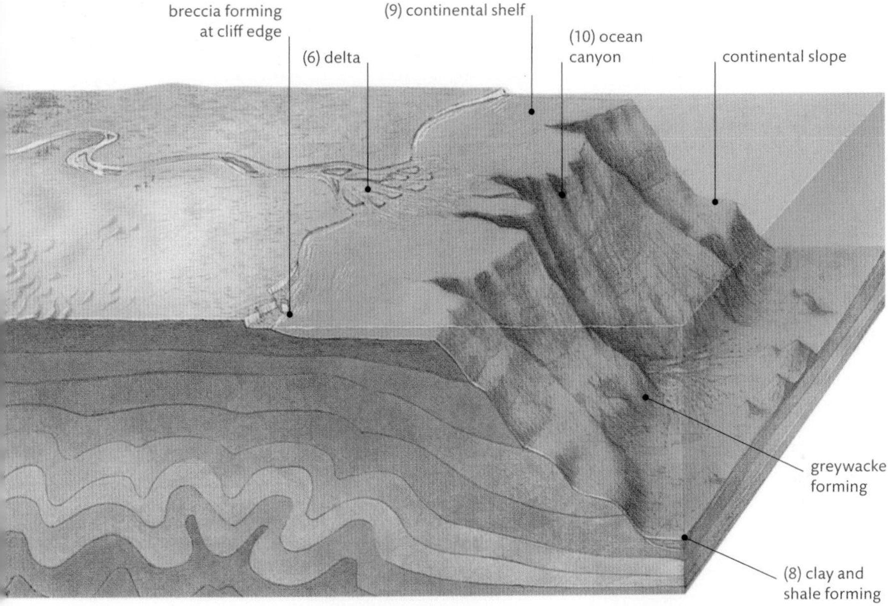

breccia forming at cliff edge

(9) continental shelf

(6) delta

(10) ocean canyon

continental slope

greywacke forming

(8) clay and shale forming

sandstone

Sedimentary

Sandstones consist of particles of quartz, worn from preexisting rocks, which have then been deposited on sea or river beds. After burial and compression, sandstones may be folded, as seen on the sea cliff (left).

IGNEOUS ROCK CHARACTERISTICS

IGNEOUS ROCKS crystallize from molten magma or lava. The starting composition of the magma, the manner in which it travels toward the Earth's surface, and the rate at which it cools all help determine its composition and resulting characteristics. These characteristics include grain size, crystal shape, mineral content, chemical composition, and overall color.

coarse-grained gabbro, a plutonic-igneous rock with large crystals

ORIGIN

Origin indicates whether the rock is intrusive (magma crystallized beneath the Earth's surface) or extrusive (lava crystallized at the Earth's surface).

augite, a ferro-magnesian mineral

OCCURRENCE

This describes the form of the molten mass when it cooled. A pluton, for instance, is a very large, deep intrusion that can measure many miles across; a dyke is a narrow, discordant sheet of rock; while a sill is a concordant sheet.

Granite intrusion
This huge intrusive mass of igneous rock was exposed by glacial erosion.

MINERAL CONTENT

Rocks are aggregates of minerals. Feldspars (right), micas, quartz, and ferromagnesian minerals (above) make up the bulk of igneous rocks. "Composition" describes how minerals affect the rock's chemistry.

labradorite, a feldspar

GRAIN SIZE

This indicates whether a rock is coarse-grained or fine-grained. Coarse-grained igneous rocks such as gabbro have crystals over 3/16 in (5 mm) in diameter; medium-grained rocks like dolerite have crystals 1/48–3/16 in (0.5–5 mm) in size; and fine-grained rocks, such as basalt, have crystals that are less than 1/48 in (0.5 mm) in size.

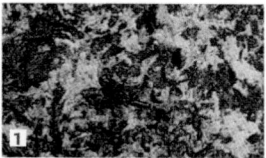

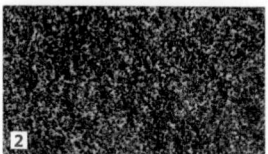

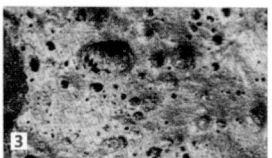

Seeing the grains
Individual grains of gabbro (1) can be seen with the naked eye, but a hand lens is needed to see the separate grains in dolerite (2). Basalt (3) is fine-grained, requiring the use of a microscope.

CRYSTAL SHAPE

With room to grow and ideal conditions, well-formed (euhedral) crystals are formed. When growing crowded together, crystal shapes are poorly formed (anhedral).

TEXTURE

Texture refers to the way the grains or crystals are arranged and their size relative to one another. For instance, equigranular rocks have equal-sized crystals.

Euhedral crystals
Highly magnified section of dolerite (left) with well-formed crystals.

COLOR

Color is generally an accurate indicator of chemistry, reflecting mineral content. Light color indicates a felsic rock, with over 65 percent silica. Mafic rocks are dark-colored, with a low silica content, and a high proportion of dark, dense ferromagnesian minerals such as augite.

COMPOSITION

Igneous rocks are arranged into groups according to chemical composition: felsic rocks, with over 65 percent total silica content (including over 10 percent quartz); intermediate rocks, with 55–65 percent silica content; mafic rocks, with 45–55 percent total silica content (less than 10 percent quartz). Ultramafic rocks have less than 45 percent total silica content.

Light color
Rhyolite, a felsic lava, has over 65 percent silica and over 10 percent quartz.

Medium color
Andesite, an intermediate rock with 55–65 percent total silica content.

Dark color
Basalt, a mafic rock with 45–55 percent silica content.

TYPES OF METAMORPHISM

METAMORPHIC ROCKS are rocks that have been changed considerably from their original igneous, sedimentary, or earlier metamorphic structure and composition. The rocks are formed by the application of heat and pressure (greatest near mountain-building) to a preexisting rock.

REGIONAL METAMORPHISM

When rock in a mountain-building region is transformed by both heat and pressure, it becomes regionally metamorphosed rock. The metamorphosed area can cover thousands of square miles. The sequence below demonstrates how the nature of a rock changes as the heat and pressure intensify.

Metamorphic landscape
Gneiss, a rock altered by a high degree of regional metamorphism, forms a rugged landscape.

Shale

1. No pressure
Fossiliferous shale, a fine-grained sedimentary rock rich in clay minerals and quartz, with fossil bivalve mollusc shells, unaffected by metamorphism.

Slate

2. Low pressure
When fossiliferous shale is subjected to low pressure, the fossils may be distorted or destroyed. The resulting rock is slate.

Schist

4. High pressure
At the highest pressures and temperatures, and where active fluids may be circulating through the rocks, gneiss, a coarse-grained rock, is formed. Any rock can be altered by these conditions.

3. Moderate pressure
Slate, as well as many other rocks, forms medium-grained schist when subjected to moderate increases in temperature and pressure.

Gneiss

CONTACT METAMORPHISM

Rocks in the metamorphic aureole, the area surrounding an igneous intrusion or near a lava flow, may be altered by direct heat alone. These rocks are called contact metamorphic rocks. The heat may change the minerals in the original rock so that the resulting metamorphic rock is more crystalline, and features such as fossils may disappear. The extent of the metamorphic aureole is determined by the magma's or lava's temperature and the size of the intrusion.

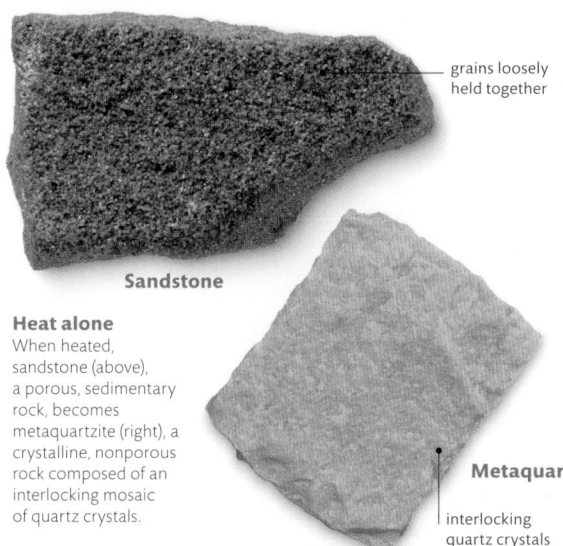

grains loosely held together

Sandstone

Magma intrusion
A mass of dark-colored dolerite (at the base of the cliff) has intruded and heated layers of originally black shale, metamorphosing them to a lighter rock (hornfels).

Heat alone
When heated, sandstone (above), a porous, sedimentary rock, becomes metaquartzite (right), a crystalline, nonporous rock composed of an interlocking mosaic of quartz crystals.

Metaquartzite

interlocking quartz crystals

DYNAMIC METAMORPHISM

When large-scale movements take place in the Earth's crust, especially along fault lines, dynamic metamorphism (thrusting) occurs. Great masses of rock are forced over other rocks. Where these rock masses come into contact with each other, a crushed and powdered metamorphic rock called mylonite forms.

Mylonite
highly altered and distorted by forces of thrust movement

Movement of rock masses
A low-angled thrust fault halfway up the cliff.

METAMORPHIC ROCK CHARACTERISTICS

METAMORPHIC ROCKS exhibit certain typical features that provide clues to their origin and specific identity. The minerals of which they are made usually occur as crystals and studying the characteristics of these reveals a lot of information about the rock. For example, crystal orientation is determined by whether the rock formed as a result of both heat and pressure, or heat alone. Crystal size reflects the degree of heat and pressure to which the rock was subjected.

STRUCTURE

This indicates the way minerals are oriented in a rock. Contact metamorphic rocks have a crystalline structure in which the minerals are usually randomly arranged. Regional metamorphic rocks, however, are foliated: the pressure forces certain minerals to become aligned.

foliated gneiss shows bands of dark biotite mica

Foliated

mass of randomly organized, fused crystals in blue-veined marble

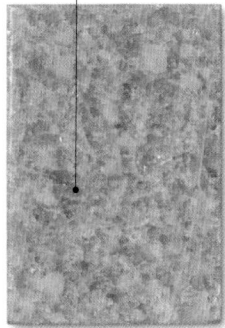

kyanite schist has foliated structure, but alignment here is less evident than in gneiss

Crystalline

GRAIN SIZE

Grain size indicates the temperature and pressure conditions to which the rock was subjected: generally, the higher the pressure and temperature, the coarser the grain size. Slate, which forms under low pressure, is fine-grained; schist, formed by moderate temperature and pressure, is medium-grained; and gneiss, formed at high temperatures and pressures, is coarse-grained.

gneiss

schist

black slate

Coarse-grained   **Medium-grained**   **Fine-grained**

mica

quartz

PRESSURE AND TEMPERATURE

Medium- to high-grade metamorphism occurs at a minimum temperature of approximately 482°F (250°C)—temperatures in some metamorphic rocks can be much lower. Above 1382°F (750°C), metamorphic rocks begin to melt, starting the process of igneous rock creation. Metamorphic rocks typically form at pressures ranging from 2,000 kilobars to 10,000 kilobars.

Gneiss
Under a microscope, gneiss reveals quartz and mica (above).

MINERAL CONTENT

The presence of certain minerals in metamorphic rocks can help the identification process. Garnet and kyanite occur in gneiss and schists, while crystals of pyrite are frequently set into the cleavage surfaces of slate. Minerals such as brucite are often found in marble.

found in metaquartzite and gneiss

Milky quartz

occurs in gneiss and schist

occurs in gneiss and schist

Orthoclase feldspar   **Muscovite**

SEDIMENTARY ROCK CHARACTERISTICS

AS SEDIMENTARY ROCKS form in layers, or strata, they can be distinguished from igneous and metamorphic rocks in the field. A hand specimen usually breaks along the surfaces of these layers. Another key feature that sets them apart is their fossil content—fossils are never found in crystalline igneous rocks and only rarely in metamorphic rocks. The origins of the particles that make up sedimentary rocks determine their appearance and give clues to their identity.

ORIGIN
Sedimentary rocks form at or very near the Earth's surface, where rock particles transported by wind, water, and ice are deposited on dry land; on the beds of rivers and lakes; and in marine environments: beaches, deltas, and the sea.

quartz conglomerate

Layers of sediment
The pebbles and sand collecting on this beach may eventually form sedimentary rocks.

FOSSIL CONTENT
Fossils mainly occur in sedimentary rocks. They are the remains of animals and plants preserved in layers of sediment. The type of fossil found in a rock gives an indication of the rock's origin. A marine fossil, for instance, suggests that the rock formed from sediments deposited in the sea. Rocks especially rich in fossils include limestone.

brachiopod fossils in shelly limestone

GRAIN SIZE

Although the classification of grain size in sedimentary rocks can be complex, the terms coarse-, medium-, and fine-grained are usually used. Grains may range in size from boulders to minute particles of clay. Coarse-grained rocks composed of fragments easily seen with the naked eye include conglomerate, breccia, and some sandstones. Medium-grained rocks, the grains of which can be seen with a hand lens, include other sandstones. Fine-grained rock includes shale, clay, and mudstone.

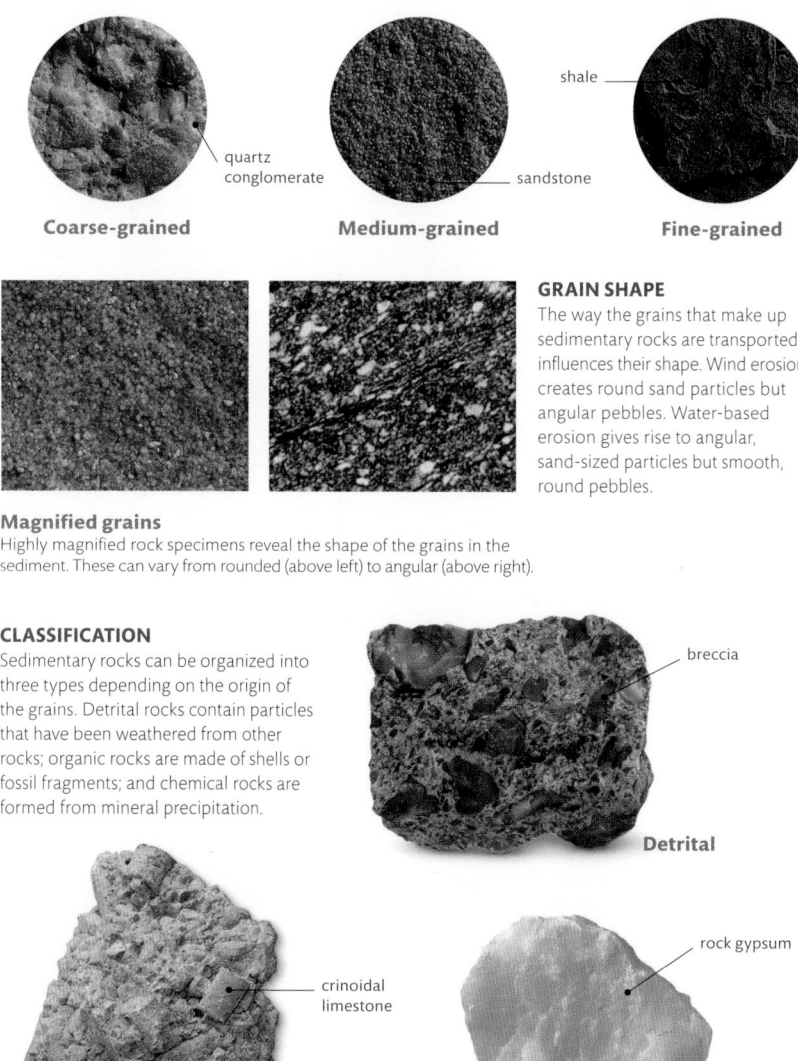

quartz
conglomerate

shale

sandstone

Coarse-grained   **Medium-grained**   **Fine-grained**

GRAIN SHAPE

The way the grains that make up sedimentary rocks are transported influences their shape. Wind erosion creates round sand particles but angular pebbles. Water-based erosion gives rise to angular, sand-sized particles but smooth, round pebbles.

Magnified grains

Highly magnified rock specimens reveal the shape of the grains in the sediment. These can vary from rounded (above left) to angular (above right).

CLASSIFICATION

Sedimentary rocks can be organized into three types depending on the origin of the grains. Detrital rocks contain particles that have been weathered from other rocks; organic rocks are made of shells or fossil fragments; and chemical rocks are formed from mineral precipitation.

breccia

Detrital

crinoidal
limestone

rock gypsum

Organic   **Chemical**

ROCK IDENTIFICATION KEY

THIS KEY IS DESIGNED to help identify your rock specimens. In Stage 1, decide whether the rock is igneous, metamorphic, or sedimentary. In Stage 2, determine the grain size—follow the key to direct you to the correct category: an eye represents coarse-grained; a hand lens represents medium-grained; and a microscope suggests fine-grained. In Stage 3 (see pages 42–45), you have to take into consideration other rock properties (color, structure, and mineral content) to lead you finally to specific rock entries in this book.

STAGE 1

IGNEOUS?

If you have an igneous rock, it will show a crystalline structure—that is, it will be composed of an interlocking mosaic of mineral crystals. These crystals may be randomly set into the rock, or they may show some form of alignment. They lack structures like bedding planes (sedimentary rocks) and foliation (metamorphic rocks). Some lavas may be full of small gas-bubble hollows. No fossils will be evident.

randomly oriented crystals

interlocking crystals cannot be easily broken from the rock

METAMORPHIC?

A metamorphic rock may be one of two major types. A regionally metamorphosed rock will have a characteristic structure, or foliation. This foliation is often wavy, not flat like the bedding planes of a sedimentary rock. Contact metamorphism produces a more random arrangement.

foliated gneiss with wavy bands

SEDIMENTARY?

If your specimen is a sedimentary rock, layers may be evident in it. Grains can be poorly held together, and you may be able to rub them off with your fingers. Quartz is a dominant mineral in many sediments, and calcite is present in limestones. The occurrence of fossils also helps distinguish sedimentary rocks from igneous or metamorphic specimens.

grains of quartz, weakly cemented together

STAGE 2

Once you have established the formation of the rock, the next step is to categorize it by grain size. This refers to the size of the grains in the body of rock, not to the odd large crystal that may be set into it.

Visible to naked eye

Hand lens needed

Microscope needed

IGNEOUS

 **Coarse-grained**   Medium-grained    **Fine-grained**

METAMORPHIC

Coarse-grained   **Medium-grained**   **Fine-grained**

SEDIMENTARY

Coarse-grained   **Medium-grained**   **Fine-grained**

STAGE 3

You have decided whether the rock is igneous, sedimentary, or metamorphic, and you have identified its grain size. If you have an igneous rock, next look at its color. Felsic rocks, rich in low-density, pale silicates, are light-colored. Mafic and ultramafic rocks, rich in heavy ferromagnesian minerals, are dark. The intermediate rocks, as the description implies, lie

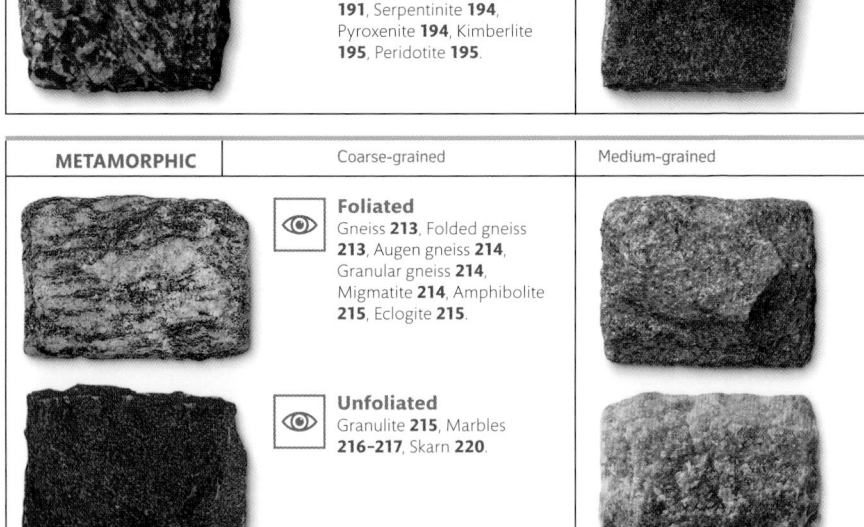

IGNEOUS	Coarse-grained	Medium-grained
	Light color Pink granite **180**, White granite **180**, Porphyritic granite **181**, Graphic granite **181**, Adamellite **182**, Pegmatite **185**, White granodiorite **187**, Syenite **188**, Anorthosite **191**.	
	Medium color Hornblende granite **181**, Granodiorite **187**, Diorite **187**, Syenite **188**, Nepheline syenite **188**, Agglomerate **204**.	
	Dark color Gabbro **189**, Larvikite **189**, Olivine gabbro **190**, Bojite **191**, Serpentinite **194**, Pyroxenite **194**, Kimberlite **195**, Peridotite **195**.	

METAMORPHIC	Coarse-grained	Medium-grained
	Foliated Gneiss **213**, Folded gneiss **213**, Augen gneiss **214**, Granular gneiss **214**, Migmatite **214**, Amphibolite **215**, Eclogite **215**.	
	Unfoliated Granulite **215**, Marbles **216–217**, Skarn **220**.	

between the above two categories in mineral content and, therefore, color. If you have a metamorphic rock, examine whether it is foliated (some minerals aligned) or unfoliated (crystalline, with no apparent structure). Decide which of these categories your specimen falls into, then refer to the pages indicated for further identification information.

Fine-grained

 Light color
Microgranite **183**,
Quartz porphyry **184**,
Granophyre **186**,
Leucogabbro **190**.

 Light color
Rhyolite **196**, Ignimbrite **206**,
Volcanic bomb **206**.

 Medium color
Lamprophyre **199**,
Rhomb porphyry **201**.

 Medium color
Dacite **197**, Lamprophyre
199, Andesite **199**, Trachyte
201, Pumice **205**, Tuff **205**,
Ignimbrite **206**, Volcanic
bomb **206**.

 Dark color
Dolerite **192**, Norite
192, Troctolite **193**.

 Dark color
Xenolith **184**, Dunite **193**,
Obsidian **197**, Pitchstone
198, Basalt **202**, Spilite **203**,
Tuff **204**, Volcanic bomb
206, Ropy lava **207**.

Fine-grained

 Foliated
Phyllite **210**, Garnet schist
210, Folded schist **211**,
Muscovite schist **211**,
Biotite schist **212**,
Kyanite schist **212**.

 **Foliated**
Green slate **208**, Black
slate **208**, Slate with pyrite
209, Fossiliferous slate **209**,
Phyllite **210**.

 Unfoliated
Marbles **216–217**,
Hornfels **218–219**,
Chiastolite hornfels
219, Spotted slate **219**,
Metaquartzite **220**,
Skarn **220**.

 Unfoliated
Marbles **216–217**,
Spotted slate **219**,
Skarn **220**, Halleflinta
221, Mylonite **221**.

STAGE 3 *continued*

If you have a sedimentary rock, look at its mineral composition. Is it made up mainly of rock fragments? Or is it composed mainly of quartz? Quartz is easily recognizable, as it is usually gray in color and very hard. You may have a limestone, rich in calcium carbonate, identifiable by its pale color

SEDIMENTARY	Coarse-grained	Medium-grained

Mainly rock fragments
Polygenetic conglomerate **222**, Breccia **223**.

Mainly quartz fragments
Quartz conglomerate **222**.

Calcium carbonate dominant
Limestone breccia **223**, Pisolitic limestone **236**, Crinoidal limestone **238**.

Other minerals
No rocks in this category.

and its effervescing reaction with dilute hydrochloric acid. Or your sedimentary rock specimen may be composed mainly of minerals other than calcium carbonate and quartz. Decide which of these four categories your specimen falls into, then refer to the pages indicated for further identification information.

Fine-grained

Mainly rock fragments
Greywacke **229**.

Mainly rock fragments
No rocks in this category.

Mainly quartz fragments
Loess **224**, Shale **231**, Siltstone **232**, Mudstone **232**, Clay **233**.

Mainly quartz fragments
Sandstone **225**,
Red sandstone **226**,
Millet-seed sandstone **226**,
Micaceous sandstone **227**,
Limonitic sandstone **227**,
Orthoquartzite (pink and gray) **228**, Arkose **229**.

Calcium carbonate dominant
Calcareous mudstone **233**,
Marl **234**, Chalk **237**,
Coral limestone **238**,
Bryozoan limestone **239**,
Shelly limestone **239**,
Nummulitic limestone **240**.

Calcium carbonate dominant
Oolitic limestone **236**,
Shelly limestone **239**,
Tufa **241**, Stalactite **242**,
Travertine **242**.

Other minerals
Boulder clay **224**, Loess **224**, Clay **233**, Dolomite **241**, Ironstone **243**, Anthracite **244**, Coal **244**, Lignite **244**, Peat **245**, Jet **245**, Amber **246**, Chert **246**, Flint **246**.

Other minerals
Rock salt **235**, Rock gypsum **235**, Potash rock **235**, Dolomite **241**, Ironstone **243**.

MINERALS

NATIVE ELEMENTS

NATIVE ELEMENTS are free, uncombined elements which are classified into three groups: metals such as gold, silver, and copper; semimetals such as arsenic and antimony; and nonmetals, including carbon and sulfur. Metallic elements are very dense, soft, malleable, ductile, and opaque. Massive, dendritic, and wirelike habits are common. Distinct crystals are rare. Unlike metals, semimetals are poor conductors of electricity, and they usually occur in nodular masses. Nonmetallic elements can be transparent to translucent, do not conduct electricity, and tend to form distinct crystals.

Group: NATIVE ELEMENTS	Composition: Au	Hardness: $2\frac{1}{2}$–3

Gold

Crystals form as cubes or octahedra but are rare. The usual habits are as grains, flakes, nuggets, and dendritic masses. The bright yellow color is resistant to tarnishing. Gold is often rich in silver, when it is paler in color. The streak is golden-yellow. Gold is opaque, and its luster is metallic.

FORMATION Forms mainly in hydrothermal veins, often associated with quartz and sulfides. It also occurs in placer deposits of unconsolidated sand and in sandstone and conglomerate. It is possible to find alluvial gold as grains or nuggets in stream beds. Panning for gold by sifting the sediment is an age-old method of looking for this rare and valuable mineral. Gold can be confused with pyrite and chalcopyrite at first, but only a few tests are needed to identify it.

TESTS Insoluble in all single acids; soluble in aqua regia.

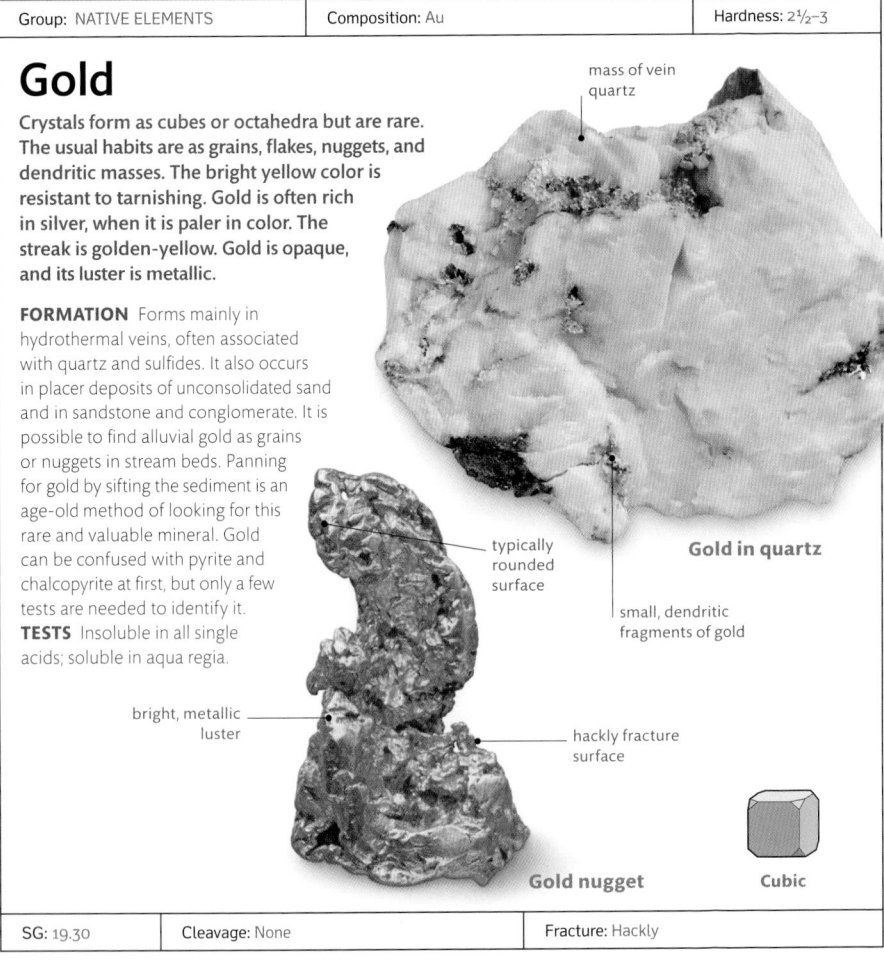

mass of vein quartz

typically rounded surface

Gold in quartz

small, dendritic fragments of gold

bright, metallic luster

hackly fracture surface

Gold nugget

Cubic

SG: 19.30	Cleavage: None	Fracture: Hackly

Group: NATIVE ELEMENTS	Composition: Ag	Hardness: 2½–3

Silver

Crystals are rare, forming as cubes and octahedra, sometimes in parallel bands. The usual habits are as wires, scales, dendrites, and massive. Silver is silver white in color, though it tarnishes on exposure to the atmosphere. It produces a silvery white streak. Silver is opaque, and the luster is metallic.

FORMATION Forms in hydrothermal veins and in the oxidized regions of ore deposits, with other silver minerals, gold, and metallic sulfides. Silver forms 20 to 25 percent of the gold and silver alloy, called electrum.

TESTS Silver is soluble in nitric acid and is fusible. It tarnishes if exposed to the fumes of hydrogen sulfide. It is the best conductor of electricity and heat.

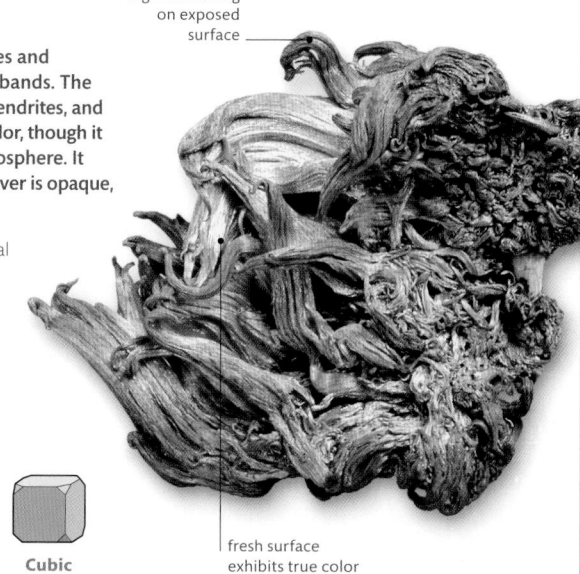

slight tarnishing on exposed surface

fresh surface exhibits true color

Cubic

SG: 10.50	Cleavage: None	Fracture: Hackly

Group: NATIVE ELEMENTS	Composition: Pt	Hardness: 4–4½

Platinum

Crystals take the form of cubes but are uncommon. Usually found as grains, nuggets, and scales, platinum is silvery gray to white in color. The streak is white to silvery gray. Platinum is opaque and has a metallic luster. This luster is not altered by tarnishing if the mineral is exposed to the atmosphere.

FORMATION Originally formed in mafic and ultramafic igneous rocks, and rarely in contact aureoles, platinum also occurs in placer sediments because of its very high specific gravity.

TESTS When there are iron impurities present, platinum can be weakly magnetic. It is insoluble in all acids except aqua regia.

uneven surface

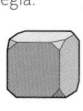

Cubic

SG: 21.44	Cleavage: None	Fracture: Hackly

Group: NATIVE ELEMENTS	Composition: Cu		Classification: 2½–3

Copper

It is rare for copper to form crystals; when it does, they take the form of cubes, octahedra, or dodecahedra. The usual habits are dendritic and massive. Copper can also form in wires. Color is a key identification feature and is copper-red or pale rose-red on fresh surfaces. It tarnishes to copper-brown. The streak is copper-red. Copper is an opaque mineral. Its luster is metallic.

FORMATION Forms chiefly in the regions where veins containing copper sulfides have been altered.
TESTS It is soluble in nitric acid.

dendritic copper

Copper on limonite

limonite groundmass

copper

metallic luster on fresh surfaces

Dendritic copper

Cubic

SG: 8.94	Cleavage: None		Fracture: Hackly

Group: NATIVE ELEMENTS	Composition: Bi	Hardness: 2–2½

Bismuth

This mineral forms indistinct crystals, which are often twinned. Habits are usually massive, foliated, dendritic, reticulated, lamellar, and granular. It is silvery white, with a reddish or iridescent tarnish. The streak is silvery white. Bismuth is opaque, with a metallic luster.

FORMATION Forms in hydrothermal veins and pegmatites.
TESTS Fuses at low temperatures and dissolves easily in nitric acid.

lamellar habit

metallic luster

Trigonal/ Hexagonal

SG: 9.70–9.83	Cleavage: Perfect basal	Fracture: Uneven

Group: NATIVE ELEMENTS	Composition: As	Hardness: 3½

Arsenic

On rare occasions, arsenic forms rhombohedral crystals. It commonly occurs as granular, botryoidal, or stalactitic masses. It is pale gray and tarnishes to dark gray. The streak is pale gray. Arsenic is an opaque mineral, and it has a metallic luster.

FORMATION Forms mainly in hydrothermal veins.
TESTS Heated, arsenic gives off fumes smelling of garlic.

Trigonal/ Hexagonal

metallic luster

botryoidal habit

SG: 5.72–5.73	Cleavage: Perfect basal	Fracture: Uneven

Group: NATIVE ELEMENTS	Composition: Sb	Hardness: 3–3½

Antimony

Crystals, though rare, are pseudocubic or tabular and often twinned. Usual habits are massive, lamellar, granular, or acicular. It is pale silvery gray, with a gray streak. It is opaque, and the luster is brilliant metallic.

FORMATION Forms in hydrothermal veins with arsenic and silver, as well as galena, sphalerite, pyrite, and stibnite.
TESTS Burns white fumes in the air; turns flame greenish blue.

crystal apparent

Trigonal/ Hexagonal

massive habit

SG: 6.69	Cleavage: Perfect basal	Fracture: Uneven

Group: NATIVE ELEMENTS	Composition: S	Hardness: 1½–2½

Sulfur

The crystal forms of this mineral are tabular and bipyramidal. Sulfur also occurs in massive, encrusting, powdery, and stalactitic habits. It is bright lemon-yellow to yellowish brown, and the streak is white. Sulfur is transparent to translucent and has a resinous to greasy luster.

FORMATION Forms around volcanic craters and hot springs.
TESTS Fuses at low temperatures, giving off sulfur dioxide.

tabular crystal

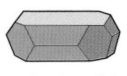

resinous luster

Orthorhombic

bipyramidal crystal

SG: 2.07	Cleavage: Imperfect basal	Fracture: Uneven to conchoidal

Group: NATIVE ELEMENTS	Composition: Hg		Hardness: Liquid

Mercury

This mineral is classified in the trigonal/hexagonal system, but it shows a rhombohedral crystal habit only below -38.2°F (-39°C). It occurs as a liquid at normal temperatures, forming as small globules. It is pale silvery white. There is no streak. Mercury is opaque and has a brilliant metallic luster.

FORMATION Around volcanic vents, often with cinnabar.
TESTS Mercury dissolves when placed in nitric acid.

mercury in cavities in rock groundmass

opaque

Mercury in close-up

rock groundmass

Trigonal/ Hexagonal

SG: 14.38	Cleavage: None	Fracture: None

Group: NATIVE ELEMENTS	Composition: Ni,Fe		Hardness: 4–5

Nickel-Iron

This uncommon mineral forms in massive and granular habits. It is steel gray, dark gray, or blackish in color. The streak is steel gray. Nickel-iron is opaque and has a metallic luster on fresh surfaces.

FORMATION Nickel-iron forms in some altered basalts. It occurs when iron-rich minerals in the basalt are chemically reduced. Some varieties occur in ultramafic rocks that have been altered by serpentinization. Nickel-iron is very common in meteorites as kamacite-taenite masses; it is a rare terrestrial material, though it is believed that much of the earth's core contains both iron and nickel.
TESTS Nickel-iron is strongly magnetic.

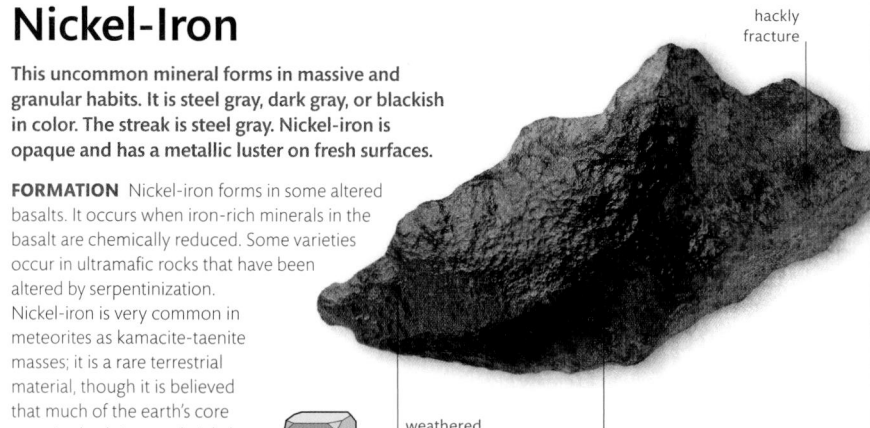

hackly fracture

weathered iron meteorite

opaque

Cubic

SG: 7.30–8.20	Cleavage: Poor cubic	Fracture: Hackly

Group: NATIVE ELEMENTS	Composition: C		Hardness: 10

Diamond

The crystals form as octahedra, cubes, dodecahedra, and tetrahedra, often with curved faces. Diamond also occurs in rounded masses with a radiating structure (bort) and as microcrystalline masses (carbonado). It may be colorless, white, gray, orange, yellow, brown, pink, red, blue, green, or black. The streak is white. Diamond is transparent to opaque and has an adamantine to greasy luster. It is used chiefly as an industrial abrasive and is also a highly valued and sought-after gem.

rock groundmass

transparent crystal

Transparent diamond

FORMATION Found in ultramafic rocks (kimberlites), forming pipelike intrusions.

TESTS The hardest of all the known minerals—it cannot be scratched by any other mineral.

yellowish octahedral crystal in rock groundmass

Yellow diamond

adamantine luster

Cubic

SG: 3.51	Cleavage: Perfect octahedral	Fracture: Conchoidal

Group: NATIVE ELEMENTS	Composition: C		Hardness: 1–2

Graphite

The crystals form as flattened, tabular, hexagonal plates. Graphite also occurs in massive, foliated, granular, and earthy habits. It is dark gray to black and has a dark gray or black streak. This is an opaque mineral. Its luster is dull metallic.

FORMATION Forms in metamorphic rocks, including slate and schist.

TESTS Feels greasy. If rubbed on paper, a gray mark is left.

perfect cleavage

metallic luster

massive habit

Trigonal/ Hexagonal

SG: 2.09–2.23	Cleavage: Perfect basal	Fracture: Uneven

SULFIDES AND SULFOSALTS

SULFIDES ARE chemical compounds in which sulfur has combined with metallic and semimetallic elements. When tellurium sulfide substitutes for sulfur, the resultant compound is a telluride; if arsenic substitutes, arsenide is formed. The properties of sulfides, tellurides, and arsenides are somewhat variable.

Many sulfides have metallic lusters and are soft and dense (such as galena and molybdenite). Some are nonmetallic (orpiment, realgar), or relatively hard (marcasite, cobaltite). Well-formed, highly symmetrical crystals are the rule.

Sulfides are very important ores of lead, zinc, iron, and copper. They form in hydrothermal veins below the water table as they are easily oxidized to sulfates. Sulfosalts are compounds in which metallic elements combine with sulfur plus a semimetallic element (for example, antimony and arsenic). Their properties are similar to sulfides.

Group: SULFIDES	Composition: PbS	Hardness: 2½

Galena

This very common ore mineral forms cubes, octahedra, or cubo-octahedral crystals and also occurs in massive, granular, and fibrous habits. Both the color and streak are lead gray. Galena is opaque, with a metallic luster.

FORMATION Galena forms in hydrothermal veins when hot fluids find their way to higher levels in the earth's crust. It can occur with several other minerals, including fluorite, quartz, calcite, sphalerite, and pyrite.

TESTS This mineral is soluble in hydrochloric acid, producing the "bad eggs" smell of hydrogen sulfide.

twinning

Cubic

Galena

bright metallic luster

Cubic galena

"stepped" pattern of cleavage

SG: 7.58	Cleavage: Perfect cubic	Fracture: Subconchoidal

Group: SULFIDES	Composition: HgS	Hardness: 2½

Cinnabar

This mineral forms as thick tabular, rhombohedral, and prismatic crystals, which are commonly twinned. It also occurs in massive, encrusting, or granular habits. The color is typically brownish red or scarlet. The streak is scarlet. Cinnabar is transparent to opaque and has an adamantine, submetallic, or dull luster.

Trigonal/ Hexagonal

FORMATION Forms with realgar and pyrite around volcanic vents and hot springs. Other associated minerals include native mercury, marcasite, opal, quartz, stibnite, and calcite. It may also occur in mineral veins and in sedimentary rocks associated with recent volcanic activity.

TESTS Does not alter when exposed to the atmosphere.

mass of small crystals

adamantine luster

SG: 8.08	Cleavage: Perfect prismatic	Fracture: Conchoidal to uneven

---

Group: SULFIDES	Composition: CdS	Hardness: 3–3½

Greenockite

This mineral occurs as tabular, pyramidal, and prismatic crystals, but more often as earthy coatings on other minerals. It is yellow, orange-yellow, orange, or red in color, and the streak is orange-yellow to brick red. It is a transparent to translucent mineral. It has a resinous or adamantine luster.

resinous luster

coating of greenockite on rock surface

Trigonal/ Hexagonal

conchoidal fracture

FORMATION Greenockite occurs as a replacement and alteration product of sphalerite when the sphalerite is cadmium-rich. Although it is not a common mineral, greenockite sometimes forms as minute crystals with other minerals, including prehnite and zeolites.

TESTS Greenockite is soluble in hydrochloric acid, producing hydrogen sulfide, which gives off a "bad eggs" smell.

SG: 4.82	Cleavage: Distinct	Fracture: Conchoidal

Group: SULFIDES	Composition: Ag₂S	Hardness: 2–2½

Acanthite

This mineral forms as prismatic crystals. Acanthite is typically gray to iron black and has a black streak. The mineral is opaque and has a metallic luster. It is dimorphous with argentite; this means that, over a certain temperature, acanthite alters from a single mineral into another mineral form, which is known as argentite.

FORMATION Forms in hydrothermal mineral veins; associated with native silver, proustite, pyrargyrite, and other sulfides, such as galena.

TESTS Acanthite is soluble in dilute nitric acid. It fuses easily, releasing sulfurous fumes.

uneven fracture surface

luster less brilliant on exposed surfaces

metallic luster

Monoclinic

SG: 7.22	Cleavage: None	Fracture: Uneven

Group: SULFIDES	Composition: CoAsS	Hardness: 5½

Cobaltite

This mineral commonly forms as octahedral or pseudocubic crystals. Crystal faces are usually striated. Other habits include massive, granular, and compact. The color varies from grayish black to silvery white. When tested for streak, a grayish-black powder is produced. Cobaltite is opaque; light is unable to pass through it, even when it is in thin pieces. It has a metallic luster on fresh crystal, or broken, surfaces.

FORMATION Forms in hydrothermal veins (fractures in the earth's crust through which hot fluids circulate, depositing minerals as they cool) and also in metamorphic rocks with other arsenides and sulfides.

TESTS Fuses quite easily, forming a globule that is slightly magnetic. Cobaltite is soluble in nitric acid.

striations on crystal face

pseudocubic cobaltite crystal

metallic luster

chalcopyrite, an associated mineral

Orthorhombic

SG: 6.33	Cleavage: Perfect	Fracture: Uneven

Group: SULFIDES	Composition: ZnS	Hardness: 3½–4

Sphalerite

This mineral, also known as blende or black jack, forms tetrahedral and dodecahedral crystals; it often exhibits curved crystal faces. Other habits include massive, granular, concretionary, and botryoidal. The color ranges from black, brown, yellow, and red to green, gray, and white. It can also be colorless. The streak is pale brown to colorless. Sphalerite varies from translucent to transparent. It has a resinous to adamantine luster.

FORMATION Common in hydrothermal veins, it occurs with minerals such as dolomite, quartz, pyrite, galena, fluorite, barite, and calcite.

TESTS The addition of dilute hydrochloric acid to sphalerite produces a smell reminiscent of hydrogen sulfide ("rotten eggs"). If pure, it is infusible, but as the iron content of sphalerite rises, the mineral specimen melts with increasing ease.

typical resinous luster

Massive sphalerite

groundmass of rock and pale dolomite

Crystalline sphalerite

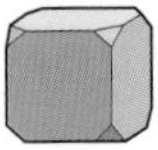

Cubic

SG: 3.90–4.10	Cleavage: Perfect	Fracture: Conchoidal

Group: SULFIDES	Composition: Sb_2S_3	Hardness: 2

Stibnite

This mineral forms as prismatic crystals, which often have longitudinal striations. Other habits are columnar, granular, compact, and bladed. Both color and streak are lead gray. Stibnite is opaque. It has a metallic luster.

FORMATION Forms in hydrothermal veins and deposits where a preformed rock is wholly or partly replaced with new material from circulating fluids.

TESTS Stibnite is fusible in a match flame, and it is soluble in hydrochloric acid.

prismatic stibnite crystals in radiating groups

quartz and barite groundmass

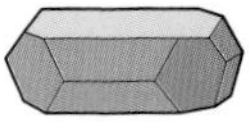

Orthorhombic

SG: 4.63–4.66	Cleavage: Perfect	Fracture: Uneven to subconchoidal

Group: SULFIDES	Composition: Cu_5FeS_4	Hardness: 3

Bornite

The crystals formed by bornite are cubic, octahedral, or dodecahedral, and they often have curved or rough faces. More commonly, it forms in compact, granular, or massive habits. Bornite can be coppery red, coppery brown, or bronze, tarnishing to iridescent blue, purple, and red—leading to its common name, "peacock ore." The streak is grayish black. Bornite is opaque, with a metallic luster.

FORMATION Forms in hydrothermal veins with minerals such as quartz, chalcopyrite, and galena. It also forms in some igneous rocks. The oxidation zone of copper veins can contain bornite.

TESTS Bornite is soluble in nitric acid.

rough crystal faces

metallic luster

iridescence

uneven fracture

Cubic

SG: 5.08	Cleavage: Very poor	Fracture: Uneven to conchoidal

Group: SULFIDES	Composition: $CuFeS_2$	Hardness: $3\frac{1}{2}$–4

Chalcopyrite

Forming pseudotetrahedral crystals, often with striated faces and commonly twinned, chalcopyrite can also occur in compact, massive, reniform, or botryoidal habits. It is brassy yellow in color, often with an iridescent tarnish. There is a greenish-black streak. The mineral has a metallic luster and is opaque.

FORMATION One of the most important ores of copper, chalcopyrite forms in sulfide ore deposits. These are often hydrothermal veins, where it may occur with pyrrhotite, quartz, calcite, pyrite, sphalerite, and galena. It is also present where copper deposits have been altered.

TESTS It is soluble in nitric acid and colors a flame green.

metallic luster

twinned chalcopyrite crystals

quartz crystals

Tetragonal

SG: 4.35	Cleavage: Poor	Fracture: Uneven to conchoidal

Group: SULFIDES	Composition: Cu_2S	Hardness: 2½–3

Chalcocite

On rare occasions, chalcocite occurs as pseudohexagonal prisms formed by twinning. It may also form in short, prismatic or tabular crystals, but the usual habit is massive. Both the color and streak are dark gray. It is an opaque mineral, and it has a metallic luster.

FORMATION Forms in hydrothermal veins with other minerals, such as bornite, quartz, calcite, covellite, chalcopyrite, galena, and sphalerite.
TESTS This mineral is soluble in nitric acid and is also fusible. When it is burned, chalcocite colors a flame green and also produces sulfur dioxide fumes.

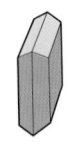

Monoclinic

pseudohexagonal crystals

twinning

dolomite groundmass

metallic luster

SG: 5.50–5.80	Cleavage: Indistinct	Fracture: Conchoidal

Group: SULFIDES	Composition: CuS	Hardness: 1½–2

Covellite

This mineral occurs as thin, tabular, hexagonal plates, but more commonly it forms in a massive, foliated habit. It is indigo-blue in color, often tinged with purple iridescence. There is a dark gray to black streak. Covellite is an opaque mineral and has a submetallic to dull luster. If broken, a perfect basal cleavage into thin, flexible laminae is produced.

FORMATION Occurs in the parts of copper veins that have been altered— often by secondary enrichment, due to fluids seeping through the vein.
TESTS Covellite fuses very easily, producing a blue-colored flame. It dissolves in hydrochloric acid.

Trigonal/ Hexagonal

foliated habit

thin, tabular covellite crystals

iridescence

clay groundmass

SG: 4.68	Cleavage: Perfect basal	Fracture: Uneven

Group: SULFIDES	Composition: As_2S_3	Hardness: $1\frac{1}{2}$–2

Orpiment

This mineral forms small, prismatic crystals, though only rarely. More frequently, it occurs as chin, foliated masses or in massive or columnar habits. The color is usually a rich lemon-yellow, though it can be brownish yellow. The streak is pale yellow. Orpiment is transparent to translucent. On fresh surfaces, the luster is resinous, but the cleavage surfaces are pearly.

FORMATION This mineral is found in low-temperature hydrothermal veins, often with stibnite and realgar. Orpiment also forms in the crusts deposited around hot springs.

TESTS This mineral fuses quite easily. When heated, it gives off a very strong smell of garlic, typical for a mineral rich in arsenic. Orpiment also dissolves in nitric acid, leaving behind traces of yellow sulfur on the liquid surface.

uneven fracture

pearly luster on cleavage surface

typical foliated appearance

Monoclinic

SG: 3.49	Cleavage: Perfect	Fracture: Uneven

Group: SULFIDES	Composition: AsS	Hardness: $1\frac{1}{2}$–2

Realgar

This mineral forms as short, prismatic, striated crystals and also as massive, compact, and granular aggregates. The color is bright red to orange-red. The streak is orange-yellow to orange-red. Realgar is transparent to translucent. It has a resinous to greasy luster.

FORMATION Forms in hydrothermal veins and also around hot springs. It can be found with stibnite and orpiment, as well as with minerals of lead, silver, and antimony.

TESTS As with other arsenic minerals, realgar gives off a strong smell of garlic when heated.

gray quartz

rock groundmass

prismatic realgar crystals

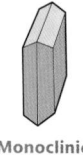

Monoclinic

SG: 3.56	Cleavage: Good	Fracture: Conchoidal

Group: SULFIDES	Composition: MoS_2	Hardness: $1–1\frac{1}{2}$

Molybdenite

This mineral usually forms as tabular or barrel-shaped crystals. It can also occur as foliated masses, scales, or grains. The color is gray. There is also a gray streak. Molybdenite is an opaque mineral, and it has a metallic luster.

FORMATION Forms in hydrothermal veins. This mineral also forms in granitic rocks.
TESTS Molybdenite can feel quite greasy to the touch.

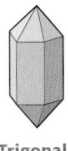

Trigonal/ Hexagonal

metallic luster

hexagonal foliated mass

granite groundmass

SG: 4.62–5.06	Cleavage: Perfect basal	Fracture: Uneven

Group: SULFIDES	Composition: MnS_2	Hardness: 4

Hauerite

Crystals are octahedral to cubo-octahedral. It can also occur in a massive habit or as globular aggregates. The color is reddish brown to brownish or black, and hauerite has a brownish-red streak. This mineral is opaque, with a metallic to dull luster.

FORMATION Forms in caps of salt domes by alteration in evaporites.
TESTS It is soluble in hydrochloric acid.

octahedral habit

Cubic

opaque   dull luster

SG: 3.46	Cleavage: Perfect	Fracture: Subconchoidal to uneven

Group: SULFIDES	Composition: Bi_2S_3	Hardness: 2

Bismuthinite

Crystals are prismatic or acicular. Bismuthinite also occurs in massive, fibrous, or foliated habits. The color is lead gray to silvery white, and the streak is lead gray. It is opaque, with a metallic luster.

FORMATION Forms in high-temperature hydrothermal veins and in granitic rocks. It occurs with native bismuth and various sulfides.
TESTS It is soluble in nitric acid, leaving flaky particles of sulfur on the surface.

mass of small, bismuthinite, acicular crystals

rock groundmass

Orthorhombic

SG: 6.78	Cleavage: Perfect	Fracture: Uneven

Group: SULFIDES	Composition: FeS$_2$	Hardness: 6–6½

Pyrite

This mineral forms as cubic, pyritohedral, or octahedral crystals; twinning is common. The crystal faces are frequently striated. Pyrite can be massive, granular, reniform, stalactitic, botryoidal, and nodular. The pale yellow color gives rise to its nickname, "fool's gold." It has a greenish-black streak. Pyrite is opaque and has a metallic luster.

FORMATION Pyrite is a common accessory mineral in igneous, sedimentary, and metamorphic rocks.
TESTS Gives off sparks if struck with a hard metal object. Fuses quite easily.

striated pyrite crystal face

quartz crystal

perfect octahedral pyrite crystal

Octahedral pyrite

Nodular pyrite

Cubic

SG: 5.00–5.03	Cleavage: Indistinct	Fracture: Conchoidal to uneven

Group: SULFIDES	Composition: FeS	Hardness: 3½–4½

Pyrrhotite

This mineral forms as tabular or platy crystals. Other habits are massive and granular. The color varies from bronze-yellow to a coppery bronze-red; the mineral tarnishes to brown, often with iridescence. The streak is dark gray to black. Pyrrhotite is an opaque mineral and has a metallic luster.

FORMATION Commonly forms in magmatic igneous deposits, especially those of mafic and ultramafic composition. It occurs with pyrite, galena, sphalerite, and other sulfides.
TESTS Pyrrhotite is magnetic.

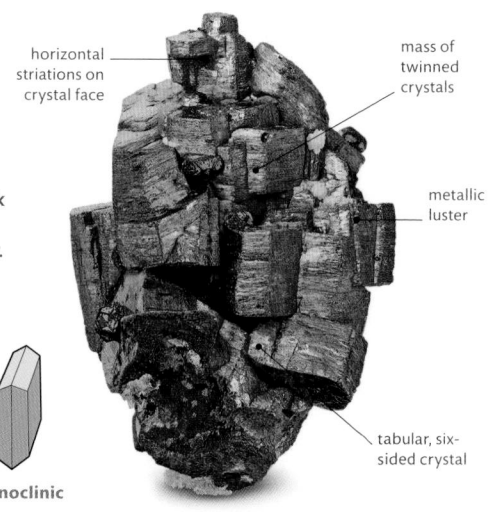

horizontal striations on crystal face

mass of twinned crystals

metallic luster

tabular, six-sided crystal

Monoclinic

SG: 4.53–4.77	Cleavage: None	Fracture: Subconchoidal to uneven

| Group: SULFIDES | Composition: FeAsS | Hardness: 5½–6 |

Arsenopyrite

This mineral forms as prismatic crystals, often twinned. It also exhibits massive, columnar, and granular habits. Typically silvery white, arsenopyrite tarnishes to pink, brown, and copper shades, with iridescence. The streak is black to gray. It is opaque and has a metallic luster.

FORMATION Forms in hydrothermal veins, in metamorphic rocks, and in mafic igneous rocks.

TESTS When a specimen is heated, or if it is struck with a hard object, arsenopyrite produces a smell reminiscent of garlic.

metallic luster on crystal face

striated crystal face

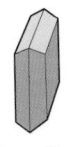

Monoclinic

| SG: 6.07 | Cleavage: Indistinct | Fracture: Uneven |

| Group: SULFIDES | Composition: FeS$_2$ | Hardness: 6–6½ |

Marcasite

This mineral forms crystals in a variety of shapes, including tabular and pyramidal. These crystals commonly have curved faces and form spear-shaped or cockscomb aggregates as a result of twinning. Marcasite also occurs in massive, stalactitic, and reniform habits. Nodules of marcasite have a radiating internal structure. Its brassy yellow color is paler than that of pyrite and darkens with exposure. The streak is greenish black. It is an opaque mineral, and it has a metallic luster.

FORMATION Commonly forms from acidic solutions permeating beds of shale, clay, limestone, and chalk.

TESTS Decomposes readily on exposure to the air. Pyrite, which is chemically identical to marcasite, does not decompose as easily. It will dissolve in nitric acid, but with difficulty.

marcasite crystal aggregates with a spear-shaped habit

chalk groundmass

marcasite color change due to exposure

Orthorhombic

| SG: 4.92 | Cleavage: Distinct | Fracture: Uneven |

Group: SULFIDES	Composition: NiS	Hardness: 3–3½

Millerite

Crystals are usually very thin, often hairlike, and in radiating groups. Millerite can occur in a massive habit. It is brass yellow, and the streak is greenish black. It is opaque, with a metallic luster.

FORMATION Often forms by replacing other nickel minerals. Occurs in limestones, dolomites, serpentines, and veins of carbonate minerals.
TESTS A good conductor of electricity, millerite fuses easily.

Trigonal/ Hexagonal

radiating mass of thin millerite crystals

calcite groundmass

SG: 5.30–5.50	Cleavage: Perfect rhombohedral	Fracture: Uneven

Group: SULFIDES	Composition: (Co,Fe)AsS	Hardness: 5

Glaucodot

This mineral occurs as prismatic, striated crystals, which may be twinned. It also occurs in a massive habit. The color is gray to white. There is a black streak. Glaucodot is an opaque mineral, with a metallic luster.

FORMATION Forms in hydrothermal veins with minerals such as pyrite.
TESTS Glaucodot is soluble in nitric acid and gives off a smell of garlic when heated.

prismatic habit

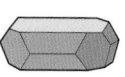

Orthorhombic

SG: 6.055	Cleavage: Perfect	Fracture: Uneven

Group: SULFIDES	Composition: $(Fe_2,Ni)_9S_8$	Hardness: 3½–4

Pentlandite

This mineral forms as massive or granular specimens. It is bronze yellow and has a brown streak. Pentlandite is an opaque mineral, with a metallic luster.

FORMATION Forms in basic igneous rocks, such as norite, as a result of magmatic segregation. It is associated with minerals such as chalcopyrite, pyrrhotite, and arsenides of nickel.
TESTS Fuses very easily, producing a bead of lead gray.

uneven fracture

massive habit

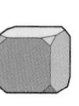

Cubic

SG: 4.60–5.00	Cleavage: None	Fracture: Conchoidal

| Group: TELLURIDES | Composition: AuAgTe$_4$ | Hardness: 1–1½ |

Sylvanite

This mineral forms short, prismatic crystals, which are commonly twinned. Sylvanite also occurs as bladed, columnar, and granular masses. The color is silvery white, gray, or yellow. The streak is silvery white to steel gray. Sylvanite is opaque, and it has a metallic luster.

FORMATION Forms in hydrothermal veins with fluorite, other tellurides, sulfides, carbonates, gold, tellurium, and quartz. Very fine crystals, up to ⅜ in (1 cm) long, have been found with native gold.

TESTS It is soluble in nitric acid, leaving a yellow-gold residue. When heated in concentrated sulfuric acid, the solution becomes reddish in color.

Monoclinic

brilliant metallic luster

twinned sylvanite crystals

calcite groundmass

| SG: 8.16 | Cleavage: Perfect | Fracture: Uneven |

| Group: ARSENIDES | Composition: NiAs | Hardness: 5–5½ |

Nickeline

Crystals rarely form in nickeline; when they occur, it is as small pyramidal specimens. The usual habits are massive, reniform, and columnar. It is very pale copper red, tarnishing to blackish. When tested for streak, a brownish-black powder is produced. It is an opaque mineral and has a metallic luster.

FORMATION Forms in hydrothermal veins and in norites and is associated with ores of silver, nickel, and cobalt.

TESTS Nickeline is soluble in nitric acid, staining the solution green. It smells of garlic when heated. It fuses very easily.

Trigonal/ Hexagonal

massive habit

copper red when fresh

| SG: 7.78 | Cleavage: None | Fracture: Uneven |

Group: ARSENIDES	Composition: $CoAs_{2-3}$	Hardness: $5\frac{1}{2}$–6

Skutterudite

Skutterudite contains variable quantities of iron and nickel in its chemical structure. Members of the skutterudite group that contain a relatively high proportion of nickel are called nickelskutterudite. Skutterudite occurs as cubic or, more rarely, octahedral crystals and has a pale gray or tin-white color, with a black streak. The luster of this opaque mineral is metallic.

FORMATION Skutterudite occurs in hydrothermal mineral veins, where it can be found with silver, arsenopyrite, nickeline, quartz, barite, siderite, calcite, and cobaltite.

TESTS Fumes smelling strongly of garlic are given off when skutterudite is heated or crushed.

octahedral habit

Cubic

opaque

metallic luster

SG: 6.50	Cleavage: Distinct	Fracture: Uneven

Group: ARSENIDES	Composition: $NiAs_{2-3}$	Hardness: $5\frac{1}{2}$–6

Nickelskutterudite

Nickelskutterudite, formerly known as chloanthite, is a member of the skutterudite series. It contains more nickel than cobalt, and forms cubic or octahedral crystals. Nickelskutterudite is tin white in color, with a black streak. This mineral is opaque and has a metallic luster.

FORMATION Nickelskutterudite can be found in hydrothermal mineral veins, where it is mined as an ore of nickel and cobalt. In such veins, it is associated with a variety of minerals, including arsenopyrite, nickeline, cobaltite, annabergite, erythrite, native bismuth, calcite, siderite, quartz, and barite.

TESTS Nickelskutterudite gives off a strong smell of garlic when heated.

octahedral crystals on groundmass

Cubic

metallic luster

opaque

SG: 6.50	Cleavage: Distinct	Fracture: Uneven

Group: SULFOSALTS	Composition: Cu_3AsS_4	Hardness: 3

Enargite

Crystals are prismatic or tabular and often twinned. The crystal faces show vertical striations. Enargite may also form in massive or granular habits. The color and streak are dark gray to black. It is opaque, with a metallic luster.

FORMATION Found in hydrothermal veins or replacement deposits. These mineral veins are formed when hot fluids circulating in the earth's crust move upward, where the elements held in them are precipitated. Enargite is associated with many minerals, such as quartz, and sulfides, including galena, bornite, sphalerite, pyrite, and chalcopyrite. It also occurs in the cap rocks of salt domes, with minerals such as anhydrite.

TESTS When heated, it smells of garlic. It is soluble in nitric acid and melts in a match flame.

twinned crystals with striations

uneven fracture

metallic luster

Orthorhombic

SG: 4.45	Cleavage: Perfect	Fracture: Uneven

Group: SULFOSALTS	Composition: $Pb_4FeSb_6S_{14}$	Hardness: $2\frac{1}{2}$

Jamesonite

This mineral forms as acicular to fibrous crystals and in massive and plumose habits. The color and streak are both dark gray. Jamesonite is an opaque mineral and has a metallic luster.

FORMATION Forms in hydrothermal veins, where hot, chemically rich fluids have permeated joints and fault lines, depositing minerals in the process of cooling. Jamesonite is associated with other sulfosalts, with sulfides, with carbonates, and also with the common mineral quartz.

TESTS Jamesonite is soluble in hydrochloric acid.

rock groundmass

metallic luster

mass of fibrous, twisted jamesonite crystals

Monoclinic

SG: 5.63	Cleavage: Good basal	Fracture: Uneven to conchoidal

Group: SULFOSALTS	Composition: Ag_5SbS_4	Hardness: 2–2½

Stephanite

This mineral forms as short, prismatic or tabular crystals, which are sometimes twinned. The habit can also be massive. Stephanite is typically iron black in color, with a black streak. It is an opaque mineral, and the luster is metallic.

FORMATION Forms in veins with native silver and with sulfides and other sulfosalts, such as acanthite, tetrahedrite, polybasite, proustite, and argentite.

TESTS Stephanite is soluble in nitric acid and produces arsenic and sulfur oxide when this test is carried out. This mineral fuses very easily.

short, tabular crystal

hexagonal crystal outline

metallic luster on fresh faces

twinned crystals

Orthorhombic

SG: 6.26	Cleavage: Imperfect	Fracture: Uneven to subconchoidal

Group: SULFOSALTS	Composition: Ag_3SbS_3	Hardness: 2½

Pyrargyrite

This mineral forms as prismatic or scalenohedral crystals, which may be twinned. Other habits include massive, compact, and disseminated particles. Pyrargyrite is typically dark red to black. The streak is dark red. This is a translucent mineral; the luster is adamantine to submetallic.

FORMATION Forms in hydrothermal veins, where it is associated with other sulfosalts; with silver; and with other minerals, such as pyrite, galena, quartz, dolomite, and calcite.

TESTS This mineral is soluble in nitric acid and fuses easily.

twinned crystals

prismatic crystal showing six sides

submetallic luster

Trigonal/ Hexagonal

SG: 5.85	Cleavage: Distinct rhombohedral	Fracture: Conchoidal to uneven

Group: SULFOSALTS	Composition: $(Ag)_{16}Sb_2S_{11}$	Hardness: $2\frac{1}{2}$–3

Polybasite

This mineral forms as tabular, pseudohexagonal crystals, which often have triangular striations on their faces. It can occur in a massive habit. Polybasite is iron black in color and has a black streak; thin splinters may be dark red. It is an opaque mineral and has a metallic luster on fresh surfaces.

FORMATION Forms in hydrothermal veins with native silver, as well as with other sulfosalts and sulfides, such as galena, argentite, and other silver and lead minerals.
TESTS When it is heated in a flame, this mineral fuses very easily at low temperatures.

striations on crystal faces

uneven fracture surface

tabular crystals

Monoclinic

SG: 6.10	Cleavage: Imperfect basal	Fracture: Uneven

Group: SULFOSALTS	Composition: $PbCuSbS_3$	Hardness: $2\frac{1}{2}$–3

Bournonite

This mineral forms as short, prismatic or tabular crystals, which are commonly twinned and striated. It can also occur in massive, granular, and compact habits. The color is typically steel gray to black. The streak is gray or black. Bournonite is opaque and has a metallic luster.

FORMATION Forms with tetrahedrite, galena, silver, chalcopyrite, siderite, quartz, sphalerite, and stibnite in hydrothermal veins; these are fractures in the earth's crust through which hot fluids circulate, depositing minerals as they cool.
TESTS When heated in a flame, bournonite fuses very easily. It is readily soluble in nitric acid. The presence of copper in bournonite's chemical composition is suggested by the fact that the resultant nitric acid solution is colored green.

prismatic bournonite crystal, showing orthorhombic symmetry

metallic luster on crystal faces

quartz groundmass

uneven fracture

Orthorhombic

SG: 5.83	Cleavage: Imperfect	Fracture: Subconchoidal to uneven

Group: SULFOSALTS	Composition: $Cu_6Cu_4(Fe,Zn)_2Sb_4S_{13}$	Hardness: 3–4½

Tetrahedrite

This mineral forms tetrahedral-shaped crystals, from which it gets its name. The crystals are often twinned and have a mass of triangular faces. Other habits are granular, massive, and compact. The color is gray to black, and the streak is variable, from black or brown to red. It is opaque and has a metallic luster. Tetrahedrite is grouped chemically with tennantite (below).

FORMATION Forms in hydrothermal veins with sulfides, carbonates, quartz, fluorite, and barite.

TESTS Tetrahedrite is soluble in nitric acid.

triangular crystal face

quartz crystals

twinned, tetrahedral crystals

Cubic

SG: 4.97	Cleavage: None	Fracture: Uneven to subconchoidal

Group: SULFOSALTS	Composition: $Cu_6Cu_4(Fe,Zn)_2As_4S_{13}$	Hardness: 3–4½

Tennantite

The tetrahedral crystals formed by tennantite are often modified by other forms. The crystals are frequently twinned. Other habits are massive, granular, and compact. This mineral is dark gray to black in color, and the streak is black, brown, or dark red. Tennantite is opaque. It has a metallic luster, which sometimes can be very bright.

FORMATION Forms in hydrothermal veins in association with many other minerals, such as barite, fluorite, quartz, galena, sphalerite, pyrite, chalcopyrite, calcite, and dolomite. This mineral may also form in high-temperature veins and in contact metasomatic deposits.

TESTS It is soluble in nitric acid and fuses easily.

iridescent crystals

tetrahedral crystal

Cubic

SG: 4.62	Cleavage: None	Fracture: Uneven to subconchoidal

Group: SULFOSALTS	Composition: $Pb_5Sb_4S_{11}$	Hardness: $2\frac{1}{2}$–3

Boulangerite

This mineral forms long, prismatic crystals, which may be acicular. Other habits are massive, fibrous, or plumose. The color is lead gray to bluish gray, and the streak is brownish. Boulangerite is opaque and has a dull or metallic luster.

FORMATION Forms in hydrothermal veins, together with galena, pyrite, and sphalerite; with sulfosalts, including tetrahedrite, tennantite, and proustite; and with other minerals, such as quartz, and various carbonates.

TESTS When it is heated in a flame, boulangerite fuses very easily. It does not react with cold, dilute acids but is soluble in hot, strong acids.

massive habit

dull luster

metallic luster

uneven fracture

Monoclinic

SG: 6.20	Cleavage: Good	Fracture: Uneven

Group: SULFOSALTS	Composition: Ag_3AsS_3	Hardness: 2–$2\frac{1}{2}$

Proustite

The crystals formed by proustite are prismatic, rhombohedral, and scalenohedral. This mineral also forms in massive or compact habits. It is a rich scarlet color and also has a scarlet streak, though it blackens on exposure to light. It is translucent to transparent. The luster of proustite ranges from adamantine to submetallic.

FORMATION Forms in hydrothermal veins, where it is associated with other sulfosalts, including tetrahedrite and tennantite; with sulfides, such as galena; and with quartz.

TESTS Soluble in nitric acid. Fuses easily.

twinned, prismatic crystals

adamantine luster on crystal faces

translucent edge

Trigonal/ Hexagonal

striated face

SG: 5.55–5.64	Cleavage: Distinct rhombohedral	Fracture: Conchoidal to uneven

HALIDES

HALIDES ARE compounds in which metallic elements combine with halogens (the elements chlorine, bromine, fluorine, and iodine). These minerals are common in a number of geological environments. Some, such as halite, are found in evaporite sequences. These are alternating layers of sedimentary rock that contain evaporites such as gypsum, halite, and sylvite in a strict sequence, interbedded with rocks such as marl and limestone. Other halides, like fluorite, occur in hydrothermal veins.

The halides are usually very soft minerals, and many have cubic crystal symmetry. Their specific gravity tends to be low.

Group: HALIDES	Composition: NaCl		Hardness: 2

Halite

The crystals formed by halite are often cube-shaped and frequently have concave faces (hopper crystals). Very rarely, halite occurs as octahedral crystals. Other habits include massive, granular, and compact. In a compact habit, the mineral is known as rock salt, and can be white, colorless, orange, yellow, reddish, blue, purple, or black. The streak, however, is consistently white. Halite is transparent to translucent and has a vitreous luster.

FORMATION This is an evaporite mineral formed by precipitation as the water in a salt lake or a lagoon dries out. Halite is associated with other evaporite minerals, such as sylvite, gypsum, dolomite, and anhydrite.

TESTS There are several very easy tests that can be applied to halite. It has a salty taste. It is also readily soluble in cold water; if some of the resulting solution is left to dry out, small hopper crystals will form by precipitation. Halite feels greasy when handled. It colors a flame yellow. It can contain impurities, which may produce green, orange, or reddish fluorescence.

hopper crystal

Halite crystals

cleavage faces with vitreous luster

Orange halite

Cubic

uneven fracture

SG: 2.17	Cleavage: Perfect	Fracture: Uneven to conchoidal

Group: HALIDES	Composition: KCl	Hardness: $1\frac{1}{2}$–2

Sylvite

The crystals usually form as cubes and, rarely, as octahedra. Sylvite can also occur in crusts and in massive or granular habits. It can be colorless, whitish, gray, bluish, yellow, purple, or red. The streak is white. This is a transparent to translucent mineral that has a vitreous luster.

FORMATION Forms as an evaporite mineral by precipitation from salt solutions. It is associated with minerals such as halite, gypsum, polyhalite, carnallite, and anhydrite.

TESTS Like halite, sylvite is soluble in cold water. It has a bitter taste.

vitreous luster on crystal faces

Interlocking cubic crystals

transparency around crystal margins

well-formed, cube-shaped crystals

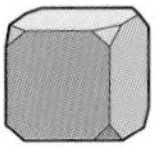

Cubic

SG: 1.99	Cleavage: Perfect	Fracture: Uneven

Group: HALIDES	Composition: AgCl	Hardness: $1\frac{1}{2}$–$2\frac{1}{2}$

Chlorargyrite

Crystals are rare. This mineral usually occurs in massive or flaky habits or as crusts and waxy coatings. Chlorargyrite is colorless when fresh but varies from gray to green or yellow on exposure to light, eventually turning purple-brown. It ranges from transparent to nearly opaque. The luster is resinous to adamantine.

FORMATION Forms as a secondary mineral in oxidation zones of silver deposits.

TESTS Chlorargyrite is malleable at ordinary temperatures and melts in a candle flame. It is soluble in ammonia but not in nitric acid.

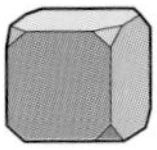

vitreous luster on crystal faces

crusty chlorargyrite

Cubic

limonite groundmass

SG: 5.55	Cleavage: None	Fracture: Uneven to subconchoidal

Group: HALIDES	Composition: KMgCl₃.6H₂O	Hardness: 2½

Carnallite

This mineral rarely forms crystals. When crystals occur, they are pseudohexagonal and have a pyramidal shape. The usual habits are granular or massive. Carnallite is white or colorless, though it can be reddish in color due to minute inclusions of the iron oxide mineral, hematite. Carnallite varies between transparent and translucent. The luster is greasy and has a shiny appearance.

FORMATION Forms in thick sequences of evaporites, including gypsum, anhydrite, halite (rock salt), and sylvite, in association with sedimentary rocks, such as marl, clay, and dolomite.

TESTS Carnallite has a bitter, salty caste and is deliquescent. It fuses easily, turning the flame violet, which indicates the presence of potassium.

massive habit

reddish color due to inclusions of hematite

Orthorhombic

granular surface

greasy luster, with shiny, reflective surfaces

SG: 1.60	Cleavage: None	Fracture: Conchoidal

Group: HALIDES	Composition: Na₃AlF₆	Hardness: 2½

Cryolite

This mineral forms pseudocubic and short, prismatic crystals; twinning is common. It can also occur in massive or granular habits. Cryolite can be colorless, white, yellowish, brown, or reddish. The streak is white. The mineral is transparent to translucent and has a vitreous or greasy luster.

FORMATION Forms in igneous rocks, especially acid pegmatites.

TESTS It is almost invisible in water because it has a similar refractive index. It fuses very easily, the flame being colored yellow, which indicates the presence of sodium. The transparent globule produced by melting becomes opaque as it cools down.

cuboidal outline

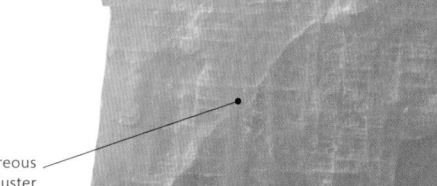

vitreous luster

Monoclinic

transparency at edges

SG: 2.97	Cleavage: None	Fracture: Uneven

Group: HALIDES	Composition: $Pb_{26}Ag_{10}Cu_{24}Cl_{62}(OH)_{48}\cdot 3H_2O$	Hardness: 3–$3\frac{1}{2}$

Boleite

This mineral forms cubic and octahedral crystals in the cubic system. (Some mineralogists put boleite into the tetragonal system.) The color is a deep, rich indigo-blue, and the streak is blue with a greenish tinge. Boleite is a translucent mineral. Although the crystal faces have a vitreous luster, the cleavage surfaces are pearly.

FORMATION Forms with a number of other secondary lead minerals in the leached zone of lead deposits. These minerals include cumengite and pseudoboleite.

TESTS Boleite is soluble in nitric acid. A further aid to identification is that the mineral fuses easily.

gypsum groundmass

twinned boleite crystals

uneven fracture on broken surfaces

cubic boleite crystals

Cubic

SG: 5.05	Cleavage: Perfect	Fracture: Uneven

Group: HALIDES	Composition: $Cu_2Cl(OH)_3$	Hardness: 3–$3\frac{1}{2}$

Atacamite

This mineral forms thin, prismatic and tabular crystals, which are often twinned. The crystal faces are frequently striated. Atacamite can also occur in massive, fibrous, and granular habits. The color varies from bright green to very dark green, and the streak is apple-green. This is a transparent to translucent mineral. It has a vitreous to adamantine luster.

FORMATION Forms in the oxidized regions of copper deposits as a secondary mineral, in association with malachite, azurite, and quartz. Atacamite also forms around volcanic vents.

TESTS Atacamite is soluble in hydrochloric acid without any effervescence. It fuses in a flame easily, coloring the flame blue.

pale quartz, an associated mineral

dark green, prismatic atacamite crystals

bright green malachite, an associated mineral

Orthorhombic

SG: 3.76	Cleavage: Perfect	Fracture: Conchoidal

Group: HALIDES	Composition: CaF$_2$	Hardness: 4

Fluorite

The crystals formed by this mineral are cubes and octahedra and are often twinned. Fluorite may also be in massive, granular, and compact habits. It occurs in a great variety of colors, ranging from purple, green, colorless, white, and yellow to pink, red, blue, and black. The streak is white. Fluorite is a transparent to translucent mineral and has a vitreous luster. If broken, its perfect octahedral cleavage produces triangular shapes at the corners of the cubic crystals.

twinned fluorite crystals showing translucency

Purple fluorite

FORMATION Forms in hydrothermal veins and around hot springs. Fluorite is a fairly common mineral and is associated with quartz, calcite, dolomite, galena, pyrite, chalcopyrite, sphalerite, barite, and various other hydrothermal-vein minerals.

TESTS As its name suggests, it can be strongly fluorescent in ultraviolet light.

transparent

twinned cubes

Green fluorite

vitreous luster

twinning

Yellow fluorite

octahedral crystal

vitreous luster

Pink fluorite

Cubic

alternating light and dark bands

Blue John

SG: 3.18–3.56	Cleavage: Perfect	Fracture: Conchoidal

Group: HALIDES	Composition: $Pb_2CuCl_2(OH)_4$	Hardness: $2\frac{1}{2}$

Diaboleite

This mineral forms as tabular crystals, which often have a square outline and which are usually very small. Diaboleite can also occur in a massive or granular habit and as aggregates of thin plates. It is deep blue in color and has a pale blue-colored streak. Diaboleite is a transparent to translucent mineral with a vitreous luster on fresh surfaces.

FORMATION Diaboleite forms where original minerals have been secondarily altered. This may occur when fluids from the Earth's surface, or rising from below, react with existing rocks and minerals. Its formation is associated with several other similar minerals, such as linarite, boleite, and cerussite.

TESTS Gives off water if heated in a closed tube.

rock groundmass

aggregates of very small diaboleite crystals

Tetragonal

SG: 3.41–3.43	Cleavage: Perfect	Fracture: Conchoidal

Group: HALIDES	Composition: $Na(Sr,Na)_7MgAl_6F_{32}(OH,H_2O)_2$	Hardness: $4–4\frac{1}{2}$

Jarlite

This mineral can sometimes form as very small tabular crystals. More commonly, however, the habit is massive. Jarlite is usually white in color, but it can also be brown, gray, or colorless. The streak is white. It is a transparent to translucent mineral and has a vitreous luster on crystal faces.

FORMATION This unusual mineral forms in two main geological situations. It occurs with another halide, cryolite, in pegmatites, and can also be found in mica schists. These rocks are formed by medium-grade regional metamorphism and are produced at considerable depth in the Earth's crust. Jarlite is also found with topaz and fluorite.

TESTS Gives off water if heated in a closed tube.

Monoclinic

SG: 3.78–3.93	Cleavage: Not determined	Fracture: Uneven

OXIDES AND HYDROXIDES

OXIDES are composed of elements combined with oxygen. A particularly common example is the iron oxide, hematite, which is iron combined with oxygen (O). Oxides form a variable group, occurring in many geological environments and in most rock types. Some, such as hematite, magnetite (another iron oxide), cassiterite (tin oxide), and chromite (chromium oxide), are important ores of metals. Others, like corundum (aluminum oxide), have gemstone varieties, such as ruby and sapphire. The properties of the oxides are varied. The gem varieties and metallic ores are very hard and of high specific gravity. They also vary considerably in color, from the rich red of ruby; the blue of sapphire; and the red, green, and blue of spinel (magnesium, aluminum oxide); to the black of magnetite.

Hydroxides form when a metallic element combines with water and hydroxyl (OH). A common example is brucite (magnesium hydroxide). Hydroxides, formed through a chemical reaction between an oxide and water, are usually of low hardness: brucite, for example, has a hardness of $2\frac{1}{2}$; gibbsite (aluminum hydroxide) is $2\frac{1}{2}$–$3\frac{1}{2}$.

Group: OXIDES	Composition: $MgAl_2O_4$	Hardness: $7\frac{1}{2}$–8

Spinel

This mineral forms as octahedral and sometimes cubic or dodecahedral crystals. Other habits are massive, granular, and compact. The color ranges from red to green, blue, brown, and black. The streak is white. Spinel is transparent to opaque and has a vitreous luster.

FORMATION Forms in a variety of metamorphic rocks, including serpentinites, gneiss, and marble, as well as in igneous rocks of mafic chemistry.

TESTS A characteristic of this mineral is that it is infusible. Picotite is the chromium-rich variety, and pleonaste is the dark, iron-rich variety of spinel.

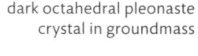
dark octahedral pleonaste crystal in groundmass

quartz groundmass

Pleonaste

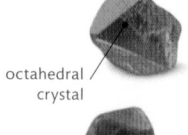

octahedral crystal

Ruby spinel

Cubic

SG: 3.58	Cleavage: None	Fracture: Conchoidal to uneven

Group: OXIDES	Composition: ZnO	Hardness: 4

Zincite

Pyramidal, hemimorphic crystals are formed by this mineral, but only rarely. Usually, zincite occurs in massive, granular, and foliated habits. The color is dark red to orange-yellow. The streak is orange-yellow. Zincite is translucent to transparent, and it has a subadamantine luster.

FORMATION Forms in contact metamorphic rocks and is associated with minerals such as calcite, willemite, franklinite, and tephrite. Zincite is an important zinc mineral, prized by collectors and mineralogists for its rarity.

TESTS Zincite is soluble in hydrochloric acid but shows no effervescence. It is fluorescent and is infusible when placed in a flame.

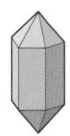

Trigonal/ Hexagonal

mass of foliated zincite crystals

calcite groundmass

SG: 5.68	Cleavage: Perfect	Fracture: Conchoidal

Group: OXIDES	Composition: $ZnFe^{+3}_2O_4$	Hardness: $5\frac{1}{2}$–$6\frac{1}{2}$

Franklinite

This mineral is in the spinel group. It occurs as octahedral crystals, frequently with rounded edges, and in granular or massive habits. The color is black, with a reddish-brown to black streak. Franklinite is opaque, and it has a metallic luster.

FORMATION Forms in zinc deposits in metamorphosed limestones and dolomites. It is associated with a number of other minerals, including calcite, willemite, zincite, rhodonite, and garnet.

TESTS This mineral is weakly magnetic. When heated in a flame, it becomes strongly magnetic and is infusible. It is soluble in hydrochloric acid, with no effervescence.

uneven fracture

calcite groundmass

Cubic

octahedral franklinite crystal

SG: 5.07–5.22	Cleavage: None	Fracture: Uneven to subconchoidal

Group: OXIDES	Composition: Cu_2O	Hardness: $3\frac{1}{2}$–4

Cuprite

Crystals are octahedral, cubic, and dodecahedral; twinning is uncommon. Cuprite also occurs in massive, compact, and granular habits. The color is red, and the streak a brownish red. Cuprite is a translucent to transparent mineral. When exposed to the air, it tarnishes to semiopaque. It has an adamantine, submetallic, or earthy luster.

FORMATION This widespread mineral forms in the oxidized parts of copper deposits, where it is associated with native copper, malachite, azurite, chalcocine, and oxides of iron.
TESTS It is soluble in nitric and other acids. It fuses, turning the flame green.

twinned crystals

adamantine luster on crystal faces

submetallic luster

Cubic

cubo-octahedral crystal

SG: 6.14	Cleavage: Poor octahedral	Fracture: Conchoidal to uneven

---

Group: OXIDES	Composition: $FeCr_2O_4$	Hardness: $5\frac{1}{2}$

Chromite

The crystals are octahedral but rarely occur. The usual habits are massive, granular, or nodular. Chromite is black to brownish black, and the streak is dark brown. This mineral is opaque and has a metallic luster.

FORMATION Forms in igneous rocks, especially ultramafic and mafic rocks; placer deposits often contain chromite.
TESTS Chromite is insoluble in acids and is weakly magnetic. It is infusible when placed in a flame.

nodular chromite

weathered, individual chromite crystals

metallic luster not seen on unbroken surfaces

Cubic

serpentinite groundmass

SG: 4.50–4.80	Cleavage: None	Fracture: Uneven

Group: OXIDES	Composition: Fe_3O_4	Hardness: $5\frac{1}{2}$–$6\frac{1}{2}$

Magnetite

This common oxide mineral forms octahedral and dodecahedral crystals and also occurs in massive and granular habits. The color is black, and so is the streak. Magnetite is an opaque mineral. The luster may be either metallic or dull.

FORMATION Magnetite forms in igneous rocks and also in veins and replacement deposits.
TESTS As the name suggests, this mineral is highly magnetic, attracting iron filings. It will also deflect a compass needle.

granular habit
of small
particles

triangular
crystal face

Cubic

Octahedral crystal

Granular magnetite

SG: 5.17	Cleavage: None	Fracture: Subconchoidal to uneven

Group: OXIDES	Composition: $FeTiO_3$	Hardness: 5–6

Ilmenite

This mineral usually forms thick, tabular crystals; sometimes it forms rhombohedral crystals. Twinning is common. Other habits are lamellar, massive, compact, and granular. It is black or brownish black, with a black to brownish-red streak. It is opaque. Ilmenite has a luster ranging from metallic to dull.

FORMATION Forms in many igneous rocks as an accessory mineral, including pegmatites, and in mineral veins. It is also found as a placer in black sands.
TESTS Soluble in concentrated hydrochloric acid if powdered first. Weakly magnetic when cold.

lamellar ilmenite

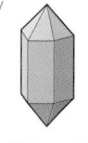

Trigonal/ Hexagonal

twinned ilmenite crystals

oligoclase
feldspar
groundmass

SG: 4.72	Cleavage: None	Fracture: Conchoidal to uneven

Group: OXIDES	Composition: Fe_2O_3	Hardness: 5–6

Hematite

The crystals of this mineral are tabular, or rhombohedral, and occasionally prismatic or pyramidal. Tabular crystals may form as rosettes, when they are called iron roses. Other habits are massive, compact, columnar, fibrous, reniform, botryoidal, stalactitic, foliated, and granular. When hematite forms in a reniform habit, it is known as kidney ore. Its color ranges from brownish, bright red, blood red, and brownish red to steel gray and iron black. The streak is brownish red. It is an opaque mineral with a metallic to dull luster.

FORMATION Occurs as a hydrothermal and replacement mineral. It also forms in igneous rocks as an accessory mineral.
TESTS This mineral may become magnetic when heated.

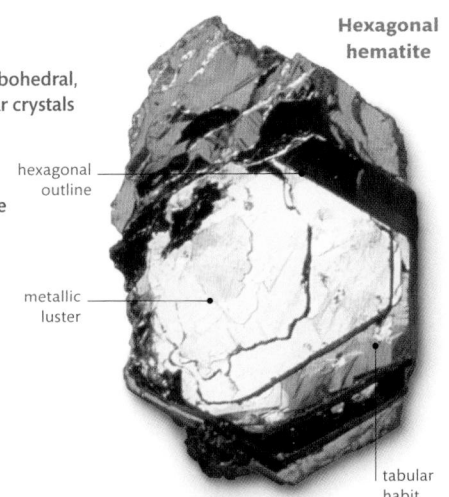

Hexagonal hematite

hexagonal outline

metallic luster

tabular habit

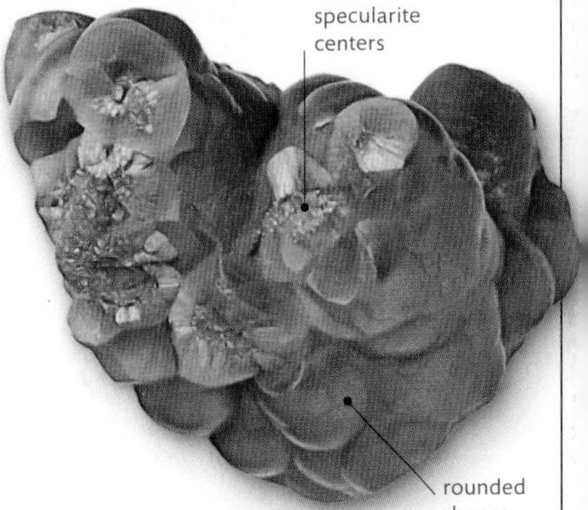

Specular hematite

specularite centers

Kidney ore

rounded shapes

mass of specular hematite crystals

specular hematite

bright metallic luster

kidney ore groundmass

weathered specimen showing massive habit

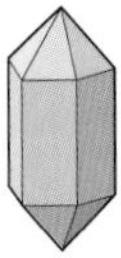

Trigonal/ Hexagonal

Massive hematite

SG: 5.26	Cleavage: None	Fracture: Uneven to subconchoidal

Group: OXIDES	Composition: $BeAl_2O_4$	Hardness: $8\frac{1}{2}$

Chrysoberyl

Chrysoberyl crystals are tabular or prismatic and commonly twinned. Other habits are granular and massive. The color varies from green or yellow to brownish or gray, and the streak is white. The gem variety, alexandrite, is green in daylight but is red in tungsten light. Chrysoberyl is a transparent to translucent mineral, and it has a vitreous luster.

FORMATION Forms in many rocks, including pegmatites, schists, gneisses, and marbles. Chrysoberyl also occurs in placer sands, which are alluvial deposits. Its occurrence here is largely due to its great hardness and resistance to weathering and erosion.
TESTS It is an insoluble mineral.

Orthorhombic

vitreous luster

striations on crystal faces

transparent to translucent crystal

SG: 3.75	Cleavage: Distinct	Fracture: Conchoidal to uneven

Group: OXIDES	Composition: SnO_2	Hardness: 6–7

Cassiterite

This mineral may form as stumpy or slender prismatic, or bipyramidal, crystals. Other habits are massive, granular, botryoidal, and reniform. Typically, it is brown to black, but it may also be yellowish or colorless. The streak is white, gray, or brownish. Cassiterite is transparent to nearly opaque. The luster is adamantine on crystal faces and greasy when fractured.

FORMATION Forms in high-temperature hydrothermal veins, where associated minerals include quartz, chalcopyrite, and tourmaline. It also occurs in some contact metamorphic rocks.
TESTS This mineral is insoluble in acids. Cassiterite is also infusible.

adamantine luster on crystal faces

twinned crystals

short, prismatic crystal

Tetragonal

SG: 6.99	Cleavage: Poor	Fracture: Subconchoidal to uneven

Group: OXIDES	Composition: Al_2O_3	Hardness: 9

Corundum

This mineral forms steep bipyramidal, prismatic, tabular, or rhombohedral crystals. It also occurs in massive and granular habits. Corundum can be many colors but always has a white streak. It is transparent to translucent, with a vitreous to adamantine luster.

FORMATION Forms in silica-poor igneous rocks and metamorphic rocks rich in aluminum.
TESTS It is insoluble.

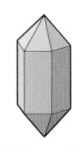

Trigonal/ Hexagonal

bipyramidal crystal

translucent

SG: 4.00–4.10	Cleavage: None	Fracture: Conchoidal to uneven

Group: OXIDES	Composition: Al_2O_3	Hardness: 9

Ruby

A variety of corundum, ruby forms as bipyramidal, prismatic, tabular, or rhombohedral crystals. It is red in color and has a white-colored streak. Ruby is translucent to transparent, with a vitreous or adamantine luster.

FORMATION Forms in igneous and metamorphic rocks. Because of its hardness and density, ruby also occurs in river gravels.
TESTS Insoluble in acids.

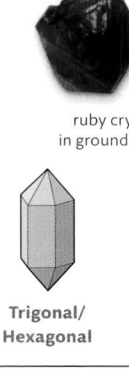

Trigonal/ Hexagonal

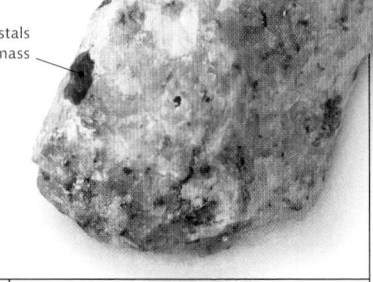

vitreous luster

ruby crystal

ruby crystals in groundmass

SG: 4.00–4.10	Cleavage: None	Fracture: Conchoidal to uneven

Group: OXIDES	Composition: Al_2O_3	Hardness: 9

Sapphire

The blue-colored variety of corundum, sapphire forms as bipyramidal, prismatic, tabular, or rhombohedral crystals. Other habits are massive and granular. The streak is white. Sapphire is transparent to translucent, with a vitreous or adamantine luster.

FORMATION Sapphire forms in certain igneous and metamorphic rocks. It also occurs in sedimentary alluvial deposits.
TESTS It is insoluble in acids and is infusible.

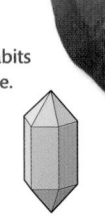

Trigonal/ Hexagonal

bipyramidal crystal

sapphire crystals in rock groundmass

SG: 4.00–4.10	Cleavage: None	Fracture: Conchoidal to uneven

Group: OXIDES	Composition: MnO_2	Hardness: 2–6½

Pyrolusite

Crystals are prismatic but very rare. The usual habits are massive, compact, columnar, or fibrous. Powdery coatings are common. It is black to dark gray in color and has a black or bluish-black streak. Pyrolusite is an opaque mineral, and it has a metallic to dull or earthy luster.

FORMATION Forms as a precipitate in lakes and bogs and also in nodules on the deep ocean bed. Pyrolusite is a secondary mineral in manganese veins.

TESTS Soluble in hydrochloric acid. It will leave sooty marks if touched.

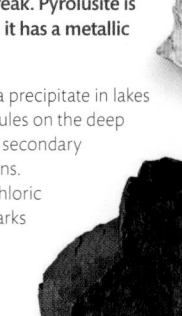

dendritic habit on a rock surface

Powdery pyrolusite

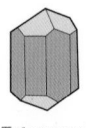

Tetragonal

uneven fracture

dull luster

Massive pyrolusite

SG: 5.06	Cleavage: Perfect	Fracture: Uneven

Group: OXIDES	Composition: $CaTiO_3$	Hardness: 5½

Perovskite

This mineral forms pseudocubic crystals with striations parallel to the edges. It also occurs as reniform masses. The color is yellow, amber, dark brown, or black, and there is a colorless to pale gray streak. Perovskite is a transparent to opaque mineral, and it has a metallic to adamantine luster.

FORMATION Forms in certain mafic and ultramafic igneous rocks, schists rich in talc and chlorite, and in some marbles. Perovskite is also an accessory mineral in some rocks. An accessory mineral is not an important rock former, and its presence does not influence the bulk chemistry or classification of the rock.

TESTS It is soluble only in hot, sulfuric acid. Perovskite is infusible.

pseudocubic crystal

Orthorhombic

striated crystal

SG: 4.01	Cleavage: Imperfect	Fracture: Subconchoidal to uneven

Group: OXIDES	Composition: TiO_2	Hardness: 6–6½

Rutile

Together with brookite and anatase, rutile forms a trimorphous series. The crystals are prismatic and are often striated. Rutile also forms as very slender acicular crystals in quartz (rutilated quartz). Twinning is common. It can be massive in habit. The color is reddish brown, red, yellow, or black, and there is a pale brown to yellowish streak. Rutile is a transparent to opaque mineral with submetallic to adamantine luster.

FORMATION Forms as an accessory mineral in many igneous rocks and also in metamorphic schists and gneisses. Slender needles sometimes form as inclusions ("cat's eye" and "star" asterism) in quartz, corundum, and other transparent host minerals.

TESTS This mineral is insoluble in acids.

acicular crystals in quartz

Rutilated quartz

uneven fracture

rock groundmass

Tetragonal　　**Massive rutile**

SG: 4.23	Cleavage: Distinct	Fracture: Conchoidal to uneven

Group: OXIDES	Composition: TiO_2	Hardness: 5½–6

Brookite

This mineral forms as tabular crystals, striated vertically, and also as prismatic crystals. The color is brown, reddish brown, or brownish black. The streak can be white, gray, or yellowish. It is a transparent to opaque mineral with an adamantine to submetallic luster.

FORMATION This mineral occurs in a number of geological situations. It forms in certain metamorphic rocks, especially high-grade schists and gneisses, in veins cutting through the rock. Brookite is often associated with quartz, rutile, and feldspars. It can also occur in sedimentary rocks as a detrital mineral, after being eroded from its original location and then being redeposited.

TESTS It is insoluble in acids and infusible.

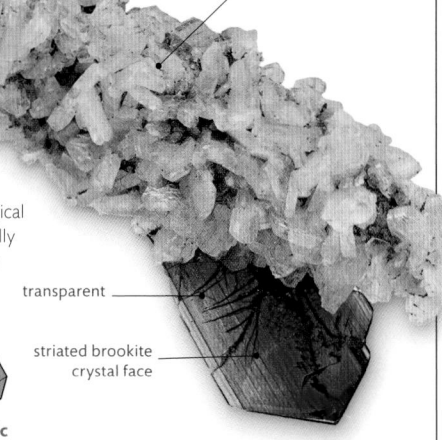

albite, an associated mineral

transparent

striated brookite crystal face

Orthorhombic

SG: 4.08–4.18	Cleavage: Poor	Fracture: Subconchoidal to uneven

Group: OXIDES	Composition: TiO$_2$	Hardness: 5½–6

Anatase

The pyramidal crystals formed by anatase are often striated. Crystals may also be tabular and highly modified. The color is brown, deep blue, or black, and the streak is colorless, white, or pale yellow. Anatase can be a transparent to nearly opaque mineral, and it has an adamantine to submetallic luster.

FORMATION This particular type of titanium dioxide forms in certain metamorphic rocks, especially schist and gneiss. It can occur in some igneous rocks, such as diorite and granite, where it is an accessory mineral. Anatase is also found in placer deposits, after it has been removed from its original location and then redeposited alluvially.

TESTS This mineral is insoluble in all acids.

Tetragonal

albite, an associated mineral

bipyramidal crystal

SG: 3.79–3.97	Cleavage: Perfect basal	Fracture: Subconchoidal

---

Group: OXIDES	Composition: UO$_2$	Hardness: 5–6

Uraninite

This mineral occurs as cubic, cubo-octahedral, octahedral, or dodecahedral crystals. More often, it forms in massive (when it is known as "pitchblende"), botryoidal, or granular habits. The color and streak can be black to brownish black or grayish black. Uraninite is an opaque mineral and has a submetallic, greasy, dull, or pitchlike luster.

FORMATION It forms in hydrothermal veins and also occurs in stratified sedimentary rocks, such as sandstone and conglomerate, and in some igneous rocks, including pegmatites and granites.

TESTS Uraninite is highly radioactive. It is infusible and is insoluble in hydrochloric acid, but it does dissolve slowly if put in nitric acid.

opaque

Cubic

dull luster

botryoidal habit

SG: 10.63–10.95	Cleavage: Indistinct	Fracture: Conchoidal to uneven

Group: OXIDES	Composition: SiO$_2$	Hardness: 7

Quartz

One of the most common minerals, quartz forms hexagonal prisms, terminated by rhombohedral, or pyramidal shapes. Quartz faces are often striated and the crystals twinned and distorted. It also occurs in massive, granular, concretionary, stalactitic, and cryptocrystalline habits. The coloring is amazingly variable, and quartz may be white, gray, red, purple, pink, yellow, green, brown, and black, as well as being colorless. It is the source of a wide variety of semiprecious gemstones—many of which are shown here. The streak is white. Quartz is a transparent to translucent mineral, and it has a vitreous luster on fresh surfaces.

FORMATION This mineral occurs commonly in igneous, metamorphic, and sedimentary rocks and can be frequently found in mineral veins with metal ores.
TESTS Quartz is insoluble unless placed in hydrofluoric acid.

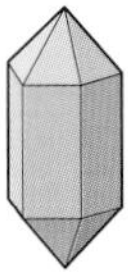

Trigonal/
Hexagonal

Amethyst

vitreous luster

pyramidal termination

milky quartz groundmass

vitreous luster

Smoky quartz

uneven fracture

Rose quartz

SG: 2.65–2.66	Cleavage: None	Fracture: Conchoidal to uneven

prismatic
crystal habit

pyramidal
termination

Rock crystal

Milky quartz

vitreous luster

hexagonal
crystal

uneven fracture
at base of crystal

vitreous luster

Citrine

Group: OXIDES	Composition: SiO$_2$	Hardness: 6½–7

Chalcedony

A microcrystalline variety of silicon dioxide, chalcedony usually occurs as mammillary or botryoidal masses. The color is highly variable and may be white, blue, red, green, brown, or black. Varieties of chalcedony include jasper, an opaque form; agate, a form with concentric banding of different colors; moss agate, with dark dendritic patterns; chrysoprase, a green variety; and onyx, in which the banding is parallel. Carnelian is red to reddish brown, and sard is light to dark brown. There is a white streak. Chalcedony is a transparent to translucent or opaque mineral, and it has a vitreous to waxy or dull luster.

FORMATION This mineral forms in cavities in rocks of different types, especially lavas. Most chalcedony develops at relatively low temperatures as a precipitate from silica-rich solutions. It can also be formed as a dehydration product of opal.

TESTS Its higher specific gravity can help distinguish chalcedony from opal.

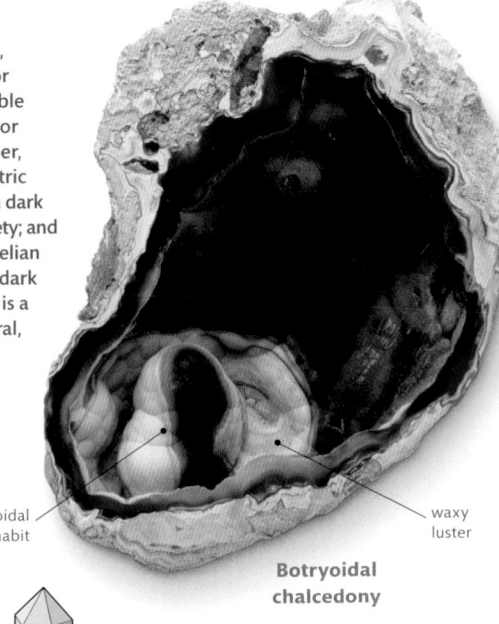

botryoidal habit

waxy luster

Botryoidal chalcedony

Trigonal/ Hexagonal

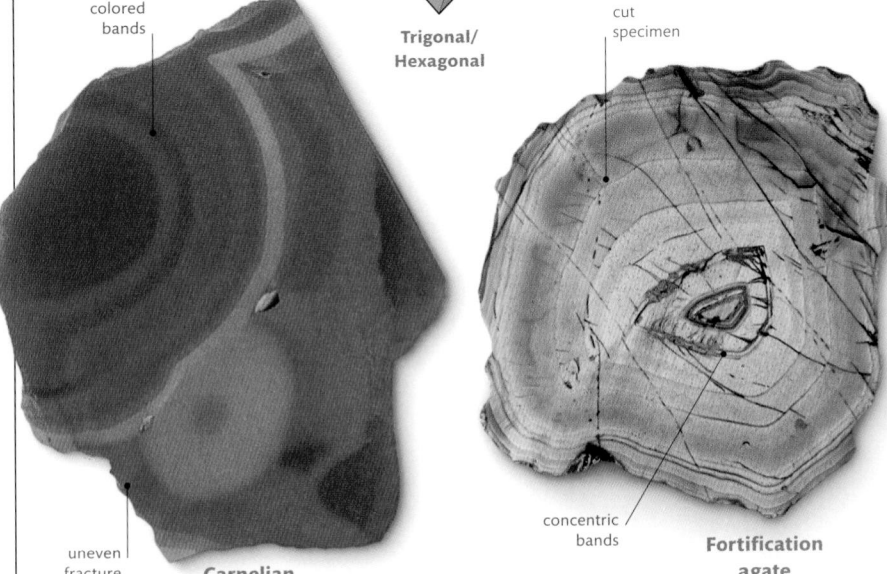

different-colored bands

uneven fracture

Carnelian

cut specimen

concentric bands

Fortification agate

SG: 2.60	Cleavage: None	Fracture: Conchoidal

waxy luster

Chrysoprase

mammillary habit

Jasper

bands of different colors

uneven fracture

vitreous luster

parallel bands

Onyx

Group: OXIDES	Composition: $Fe^{2+}Nb_2O_6$ to $Mn^{2+}Nb_2O_6$		Hardness: 6

Columbite series

Minerals in this series, from columbite-(Fe) to columbite-(Mn), have tabular or prismatic crystals, often twinned. Massive habit also occurs. The color is black to brownish black, and the streak is black or dark red. The minerals are transparent to opaque, with a vitreous to submetallic luster.

FORMATION Forms in granitic pegmatites.
TESTS These minerals are insoluble and nearly infusible.

opaque

Orthorhombic

SG: 5.20–6.65	Cleavage: Distinct	Fracture: Subconchoidal to uneven

---

Group: OXIDES	Composition: $YFe^{3+}Nb_2O_8$		Hardness: 5–6

Samarskite-(Y)

This mineral occurs as prismatic crystals, which have a rectangular cross-section, and in massive or compact habits. The color is black or brownish, and the streak is dark reddish brown to black. Samarskite is a translucent to opaque mineral, and it has a resinous, vitreous, or submetallic luster on fresh surfaces.

FORMATION Forms in granitic pegmatites.
TESTS It is soluble in hot acids and radioactive.

opaque

Monoclinic

SG: 5.00–5.69	Cleavage: Indistinct	Fracture: Conchoidal

Group: OXIDES	Composition: $Mn^{2+}Mn^{3+}_2O_4$		Hardness: 5½

Hausmannite

The pseudo-octahedral and pyramidal crystals are frequently twinned. This mineral also forms as granular masses. The color is brownish black, and the streak is reddish brown. Hausmannite is opaque and has a resinous, dull, or submetallic luster.

FORMATION Forms in rocks that have undergone contact metamorphism. It also occurs in hydrothermal veins.
TESTS It is soluble in concentrated hydrochloric acid.

twinned crystals

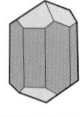
Tetragonal

SG: 4.83–4.85	Cleavage: Good	Fracture: Uneven

Group: OXIDES	Composition: Oxides and hydroxides	Hardness: 1–6½

Wad

Not strictly a mineral, wad is a mixture of several oxide and hydroxide minerals, especially of manganese. It usually contains hollandite, todorokite, and romanechite. It has an amorphous appearance and may be reniform, arborescent, encrusting, or massive in habit. Wad is often a dull black color, though it may be lead gray, bluish, or brownish black. The streak is dark brown or blackish. It is an opaque mineral with a dull or earthy luster.

FORMATION Occurs in sedimentary environments with manganese minerals.
TESTS When heated in a closed test tube, water is given off.

massive habit

rock groundmass

dull luster

SG: 2.80–4.40	Cleavage: None	Fracture: Uneven

Group: HYDROXIDES	Composition: $(Ba,H_2O)_2(Mn^{4+},Mn^{3+})_5O_{10}$	Hardness: 5–6

Romanechite

Formerly sometimes known as psilomelane, romanechite rarely occurs as crystals, but forms in massive, botryoidal, reniform, stalactitic, and earthy habits. It is black to dark gray, and the streak is black or brownish black and shining. It is opaque, with a submetallic or dull luster.

FORMATION Forms by the alteration of other minerals, especially manganese-rich silicates and carbonates. Romanechite is a common mineral and is found in concretions and where limestones have been replaced by other materials.
TESTS It is soluble in hydrochloric acid, giving off chlorine gas. It gives off water if heated in a closed test tube.

Massive romanechite

opaque

submetallic luster

Botryoidal romanechite

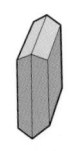

Monoclinic

SG: 3.30–4.70	Cleavage: None	Fracture: Uneven

Group: OXIDES	Composition: Pyrochlore $(Na,Ca,U)_2(Nb,Ta,Ti)_2O_6(OH,F)$	Hardness: 5–5½

Pyrochlore group

quartz groundmass

This group of minerals usually forms as octahedral crystals, which are sometimes twinned. Other habits are as grains and irregular masses. Its color is brown, reddish brown, or black. The streak is yellowish to brown. The group minerals are transparent to opaque and have a vitreous to resinous luster.

FORMATION Forms in pegmatites and carbonatites. Minerals of the pyrochlore group are also found as accessory minerals in nepheline syenites.

TESTS The minerals in this group are infusible. They are soluble in hydrochloric acid, but only with great difficulty. A number of elements, such as thorium and uranium, can replace calcium and sodium in the chemical structure when the mineral becomes radioactive.

Pyrochlore

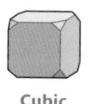

Cubic

twinned octahedra

uneven fracture on surfaces

Microlite

SG: 4.48–6.40	Cleavage: Distinct	Fracture: Subconchoidal to uneven

Group: OXIDES	Composition: $WO_3.H_2O$	Hardness: 2½

Tungstite

Crystals are microscopic and platy but are rarely visible to the eye. Tungstite more commonly forms in massive, earthy, or powdery habits. The color may be yellow or yellowish green, and the streak is yellow. It is a transparent to translucent mineral with an earthy or resinous luster.

FORMATION Forms in environments where primary tungsten minerals have been altered.

TESTS Tungstite is soluble in alkaline solutions, but it is insoluble in acids.

quartz groundmass

yellowish tungstite

Orthorhombic

SG: 5.50	Cleavage: Perfect	Fracture: Uneven

Group: OXIDES	Composition: $SiO_2.nH_2O$	Hardness: $5\frac{1}{2}$–$6\frac{1}{2}$

Opal

The structure of opal is amorphous. It forms in a wide variety of habits, including massive, botryoidal, reniform, stalactitic, globular, nodular, and concretionary. Precious opal is milky white or black, with a brilliant interplay of colors, commonly red, blue, and yellow. The colors often change as a result of the warming of water in the mineral. Precious opals warmed in the hand, for example, will be particularly brilliant. Fire opal is orange or reddish and may or may not have an interplay of colors. Common opal is gray, black, or green and has no interplay of colors. The streak is white. Opal is transparent to opaque. Its luster varies from vitreous to resinous, waxy, pearly, or dull, though vitreous is the most common luster.

iron nodule

nodule broken to reveal opal

Precious opal

FORMATION Forms at low temperatures from silica-rich water, especially around hot springs, but it can occur in almost any geological environment.

TESTS Opal often fluoresces in ultraviolet light and is insoluble in acids. When heated, it decomposes and may turn into quartz as the water molecules are removed. When opal is exposed to air for any length of time, the mineral structure becomes fragile because of the loss of water.

concentric bands representing the growth rings from a tree

red coloring typical of fire opal

vitreous luster on freshly broken surfaces

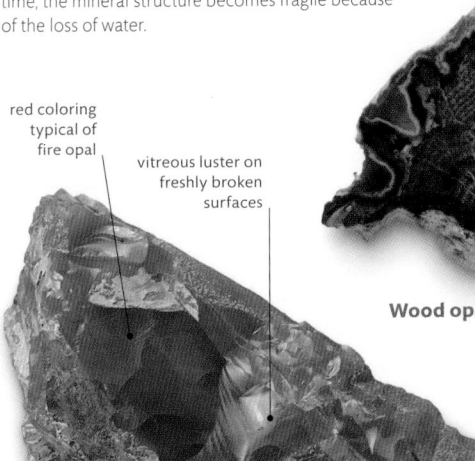

Wood opal

Fire opal

SG: 1.99–2.25	Cleavage: None	Fracture: Conchoidal to uneven

Group: HYDROXIDES	Composition: Mg(OH)₂	Hardness: 2½–3

Brucite

This mineral forms as broad, tabular crystals. It can be massive, foliated, fibrous (nemalite), and granular in habit. It is white, pale green, gray, bluish, and—when it contains manganese—yellow to brown in color. There is a white streak. Brucite is transparent to translucent. It has a waxy, vitreous, or pearly luster. (The fibrous varieties are silky.) Flexible, inelastic laminae are produced from the perfect cleavage when this mineral is carefully broken.

FORMATION Forms in metamorphosed limestones and in schists and serpentinites.
TESTS Brucite is soluble in hydrochloric acid, with no effervescence. It is also infusible.

Crystalline brucite

tabular crystal

fibrous habit

silky luster

Nemalite

Trigonal/ Hexagonal

SG: 2.39	Cleavage: Perfect	Fracture: Uneven

Group: HYDROXIDES	Composition: FeO(OH)	Hardness: 5–5½

Goethite

This mineral sometimes occurs as vertically striated, prismatic crystals but more frequently as massive, botryoidal, stalactitic, and earthy specimens. The color is blackish brown or reddish to yellowish brown. The streak is orange to brownish. Goethite is opaque. The luster is adamantine on crystal faces and otherwise dull.

striated goethite crystals

groundmass of quartz

FORMATION Goethite forms by the oxidation of iron-rich deposits.
TESTS Becomes magnetic when heated.

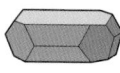

Orthorhombic

SG: 4.27–4.29	Cleavage: Perfect	Fracture: Uneven

Group: HYDROXIDES	Composition: FeO(OH).nH₂O	Hardness: 4–5½

"Limonite"

Limonite is now regarded as a form of goethite. It is an amorphous material and occurs in earthy masses, concretions, mammillary, and stalactitic forms. It is often found as a pseudomorph after pyrite and other iron minerals. The color is yellow, brownish yellow, brown, or blackish. There is a yellow-brown streak. It is opaque and has a dull, earthy luster.

FORMATION Forms in the oxidation zones of iron deposits. Limonite also occurs by precipitation in the seawater and freshwater and in bogs.
TESTS This material gives off water when heated in a closed test tube. Dissolves very slowly in acid.

earthy mass

dull luster

SG: 2.70–4.30	Cleavage: None	Fracture: Uneven

Group: HYDROXIDES	Composition: MnO(OH)	Hardness: 4

Manganite

This mineral forms as striated, prismatic crystals, which are often in bundles. Twinning is common. It also occurs in massive, fibrous, columnar, granular, concretionary, and stalactitic habits. It is dark gray to black. There is a reddish-brown to black streak. Manganite is an opaque mineral, and it has a submetallic luster.

FORMATION Forms in low-temperature hydrothermal veins and also in shallow marine deposits, lakes, and bogs. Some manganite is deposited from meteoric water circulating underground. It is often partially altered to pyrolusite by fluids circulating in and on the Earth's surface. Its own crystal form remains unchanged.
TESTS Soluble in hydrochloric acid, giving off chlorine.

Monoclinic

prismatic, striated crystals

opaque

submetallic luster

SG: 4.33	Cleavage: Perfect	Fracture: Uneven

Group: HYDROXIDES	Composition: Variable	Hardness: 1–3

Bauxite

A mixture of several minerals, bauxite's composition includes hydrated aluminum oxide, gibbsite, boehmite, diaspore, and iron oxides. Strictly speaking, bauxite should be classified as a rock, but it is sometimes grouped with minerals. The varied composition means that its properties are also variable. The habit is generally massive, concretionary, oolitic, or pisolitic. The color varies from white to yellowish or red and reddish-brown. Bauxite has a dull or earthy luster and is opaque.

FORMATION Forms by the weathering and decay of rocks that contain aluminum silicates. This is most likely to occur under tropical conditions, when heavy rains leach the silicates from the rock, leaving behind the aluminum minerals.
TESTS Bauxite smells of wet clay if breathed on. It is infusible and virtually insoluble.

pisolitic habit

rounded fragments in groundmass

SG: 2.30–2.70	Cleavage: None	Fracture: Uneven

Group: HYDROXIDES	Composition: AlO(OH)	Hardness: 6½–7

Diaspore

This mineral forms as platy, acicular, or tabular crystals, as well as in massive, foliated, scaly, or stalactitic habits. It is frequently disseminated and granular. The color may be white, colorless, grayish, yellowish, greenish, brown, purple, or pink. There is a white streak. Diaspore is a transparent to translucent mineral. The luster is vitreous but pearly on cleavages.

FORMATION Forms in altered igneous rocks and in marbles. It occurs with many minerals, including magnetite, spinel, dolomite, chlorite, and corundum. Diaspore is also found in clay deposits, when it occurs with bauxite and aluminum-rich clay minerals.
TESTS It is insoluble, and infusible.

platy habit

emery groundmass

Orthorhombic

SG: 3.20–3.50	Cleavage: Perfect	Fracture: Conchoidal

Group: HYDROXIDES	Composition: FeO(OH)		Hardness: 5

Lepidocrocite

submetallic luster

This mineral may form as flattened, platy crystals but more commonly occurs in massive or fibrous habits. The color is deep red to reddish-brown, and the streak is orange. Lepidocrocite is a transparent mineral with a submetallic luster.

FORMATION Forms with minerals such as goethite as a secondary mineral.
TESTS Lepidocrocite is strongly magnetic when heated. It dissolves slowly in hydrochloric acid but much more quickly in nitric acid.

Orthorhombic

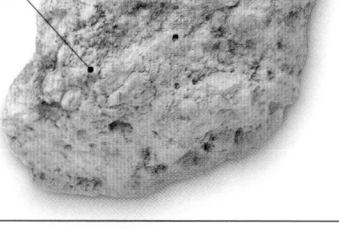

SG: 4.05–4.13	Cleavage: Perfect	Fracture: Uneven

Group: HYDROXIDES	Composition: $Al(OH)_3$		Hardness: $2\frac{1}{2}$–3

Gibbsite

massive habit

This mineral forms tabular, pseudohexagonal crystals. Gibbsite also occurs in a massive habit, as coatings, and as crusts. It is white, gray, greenish, pinkish, or reddish; the streak is white. Gibbsite is a transparent to translucent mineral, and it has a vitreous to pearly or earthy luster.

irregular surface

FORMATION Forms in hydrothermal veins and as an alteration product of aluminum minerals.
TESTS Gibbsite smells of wet clay when breathed on.

Monoclinic

SG: 2.40	Cleavage: Perfect	Fracture: Uneven

Group: HYDROXIDES	Composition: $Sb^{3+}Sb^{5+}_2O_6(OH)$		Hardness: $5\frac{1}{2}$–7

Stibiconite

pseudomorphic after stibnite

This mineral may be prismatic. The usual habits are massive, compact, or botryoidal, though stibiconite also forms as crusts. The color is white to pale yellowish; it may be orange, brown, gray, or black due to impurities. The streak is yellow-white. Stibiconite is transparent to translucent, with a pearly to earthy luster.

FORMATION Forms by the alteration of stibnite.
TESTS Gives off water when heated in a closed test tube.

Cubic

SG: 3.50–5.50	Cleavage: Not determined	Fracture: Uneven

CARBONATES, NITRATES, AND BORATES

CARBONATES ARE compounds in which one or more metallic or semimetallic elements combine with the carbonate $(CO_3)^{-2}$ radical. Calcite, the most common carbonate, forms when calcium combines with the carbonate radical. The substitution of barium for calcium produces witherite; when manganese substitutes, rhodochrosite is formed. Carbonates usually occur as well-developed rhombohedral crystals. They tend to dissolve readily in hydrochloric acid and are generally vividly colored.

Nitrates are compounds in which one or more metallic elements combine with the nitrate $(NO_2)^{-1}$ radical (for example, nitratine). Borates, also included in this section, are formed when metallic elements combine with the borate $(BO_3)^{-3}$ radical (for example, ulexite, colemanite).

Group: CARBONATES	Composition: $CaCO_3$	Hardness: $3\frac{1}{2}$–4

Aragonite

The prismatic and elongated crystals formed by aragonite are often twinned. If intergrown, such twins may produce pseudohexagonal forms. The habit can also be columnar, stalactitic, fibrous, radiating, and coral-like, when it is called *flos ferri*, meaning "flower of iron." Aragonite is white, colorless, gray, yellowish, green, blue, violet, reddish, or brown. There is a white streak. It is transparent to translucent and has a vitreous or resinous luster.

FORMATION Widespread, forming in metamorphic and sedimentary rocks, in caves in limestone areas, in mineral veins, and around hot springs.

TESTS It is soluble in cold, dilute hydrochloric acid, with effervescence, and is often fluorescent under ultraviolet light.

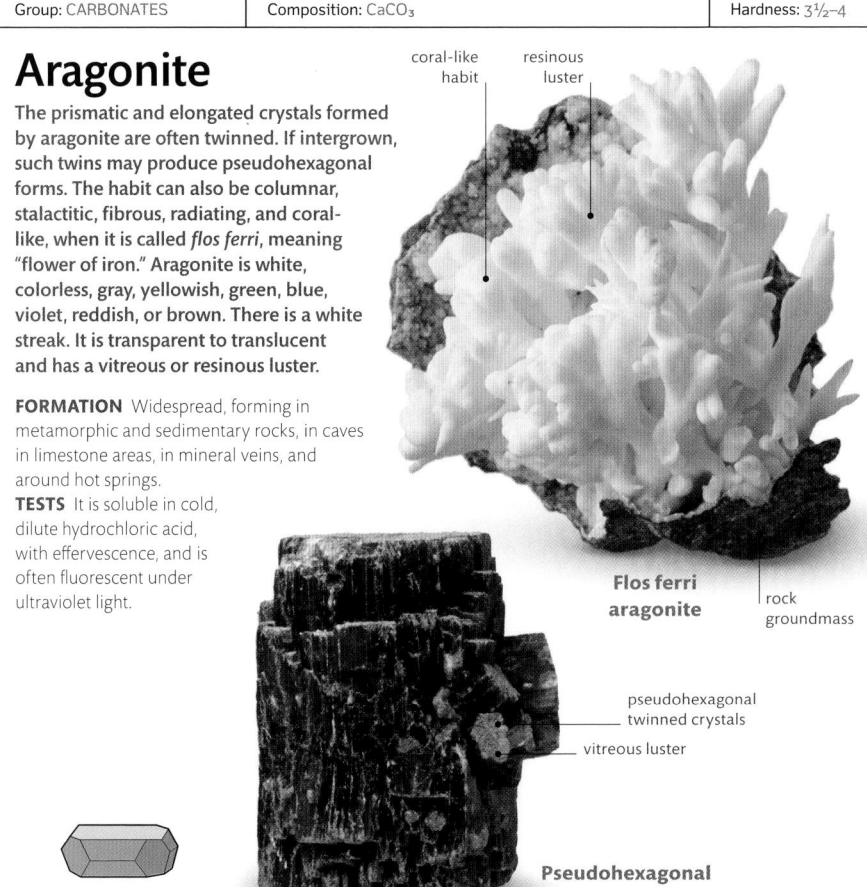

coral-like habit

resinous luster

Flos ferri aragonite

rock groundmass

pseudohexagonal twinned crystals

vitreous luster

Orthorhombic

Pseudohexagonal aragonite

SG: 2.95	Cleavage: Distinct	Fracture: Subconchoidal

Group: CARBONATES	Composition: CaCO$_3$		Hardness: 3

Calcite

Crystals are rhombohedral and scalenohedral, with combinations producing nail-head and dog-tooth forms. Iceland spar rhombs show double refraction. Twinning is common. Calcite can also form in massive, granular, fibrous, and stalactitic habits. It is white, colorless, gray, red, brown, green, and black. The streak is white. Calcite is transparent to translucent, with a vitreous to pearly or dull luster.

FORMATION Forms in many rocks. Calcite makes up the bulk of limestones and marbles.
TESTS It effervesces with cold, dilute hydrochloric acid.

Iceland spar

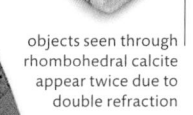

objects seen through rhombohedral calcite appear twice due to double refraction

rhombic cleavage planes visible on crystal surfaces

Scalenohedral calcite

galena, an associated mineral

Nail-head calcite

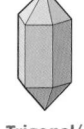

Trigonal/ Hexagonal

SG: 2.71	Cleavage: Perfect		Fracture: Subconchoidal

Group: CARBONATES	Composition: BaCa(CO$_3$)$_2$		Hardness: 4

Barytocalcite

This mineral occurs as striated, prismatic crystals and in a massive habit. It is white, yellowish, gray, or greenish with a white streak. Barytocalcite is transparent to translucent and has a vitreous or resinous luster.

FORMATION Forms in hydrothermal veins—faults or joints in the rock strata that have been invaded by hot, chemically active fluids. The veins may be derived from residual liquids, associated with granitic magmas, and brines trapped in buried marine sediments. Minerals are formed from the chemical elements carried in these fluids.
TESTS This mineral effervesces with hydrochloric acid.

prismatic barytocalcite crystal

rock groundmass

Monoclinic

SG: 3.66–3.71	Cleavage: Perfect		Fracture: Subconchoidal to uneven

Group: CARBONATES	Composition: MnCO$_3$	Hardness: 3½–4

Rhodochrosite

This mineral sometimes forms as rhombohedral, scalenohedral, prismatic, or tabular crystals. More often, rhodochrosite occurs in massive, granular, stalactitic, globular, nodular, or botryoidal habits. The color is typically pink to red, though it may also be brown, orange, or yellowish. The streak is white. Transparent to translucent, rhodochrosite has a vitreous to pearly luster.

FORMATION Forms in hydrothermal veins and in altered manganese deposits.
TESTS Rhodochrosite is soluble in warm hydrochloric acid, with effervescence.

rhombohedral crystal

Rhodochrosite crystals

nodular specimen, cut open to show concentric banding

Banded rhodochrosite

Trigonal/ Hexagonal

SG: 3.70	Cleavage: Perfect	Fracture: Uneven to conchoidal

Group: CARBONATES	Composition: CaMg(CO$_3$)$_2$	Hardness: 3½–4

Dolomite

The crystals are rhombohedral with curved faces, which become "saddle-shaped." Dolomite may also form in massive and granular habits. It is colorless, white, gray, pink, or brown; the streak is white. Ranging from transparent to translucent, it has a vitreous to pearly luster.

FORMATION Forms in hydrothermal veins and in magnesian limestones.
TESTS It dissolves slowly in cold, dilute hydrochloric acid. This is a good test for distinguishing it from calcite, which reacts vigorously, effervescing.

quartz groundmass

twinned dolomite crystals

curved crystal faces

Trigonal/ Hexagonal

SG: 2.85	Cleavage: Perfect	Fracture: Subconchoidal

Group: CARBONATES	Composition: Ca(Fe,Mg,Mn)(CO₃)₂	Hardness: 3½–4

Ankerite

This mineral, which is part of a group with dolomite, forms rhombohedral crystals. Other habits in which it occurs are massive and granular. Ankerite is white, gray, yellowish brown, or brown in color, and the streak is white. This is a translucent mineral with a vitreous to pearly luster.

FORMATION Ankerite forms in mineral veins, sometimes with gold and sulfides.
TESTS Soluble when placed in hydrochloric acid.

twinned, rhombohedral crystals

pearly luster

Trigonal/ Hexagonal

SG: 2.93–3.10	Cleavage: Perfect	Fracture: Hackly

Group: CARBONATES	Composition: ZnCO₃	Hardness: 4–4½

Smithsonite

This mineral forms rhombohedral crystals, often with curved faces, and sometimes scalenohedral crystals. Smithsonite may also occur in massive, botryoidal, reniform, granular, and stalactitic habits. It can be white, gray, yellow, green, blue, pink, purple, or brown. The streak is white. This is a translucent mineral, and it has a vitreous or pearly luster.

FORMATION Forms in parts of oxidized copper-zinc deposits, associated with malachite, azurite, pyromorphite, cerussite, and hemimorphite.
TESTS It is soluble in hydrochloric acid.

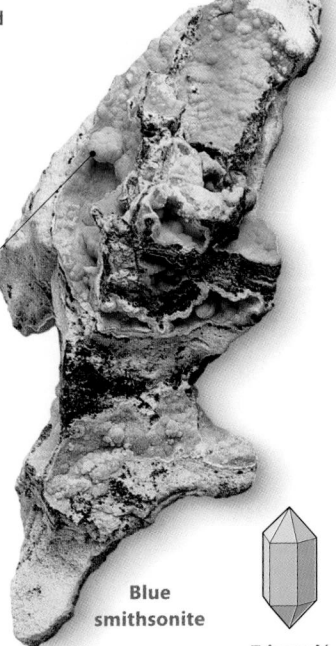

small, rounded mass

rock groundmass

botryoidal smithsonite

White smithsonite

Blue smithsonite

Trigonal/ Hexagonal

SG: 4.42–4.44	Cleavage: Perfect	Fracture: Subconchoidal to uneven

Group: CARBONATES	Composition: FeCO₃		Hardness: 4

Siderite

This mineral forms as rhombohedral, tabular, prismatic, and scalenohedral crystals, often with curved faces, and sometimes twinned. It also occurs in massive, granular, compact, botryoidal, and oolitic habits. Siderite is pale yellowish, gray, brown, greenish, reddish, or almost black in color. The streak is white. It is a translucent mineral, and it has a vitreous, pearly, or silky luster.

FORMATION Forms in hydrothermal veins, as well as in sedimentary strata.
TESTS Siderite becomes magnetic when heated, and it dissolves slowly in cold hydrochloric acid. When the acid is heated, the solution effervesces.

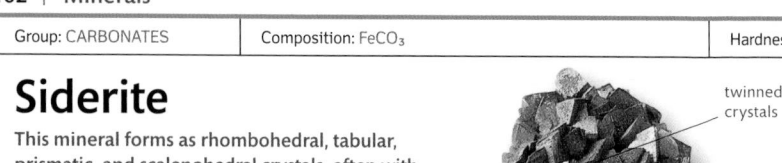

twinned crystals

Rhombohedral siderite

weathered limestone groundmass

botryoidal siderite

Botryoidal siderite

Trigonal/ Hexagonal

SG: 3.96	Cleavage: Perfect rhombohedral	Fracture: Uneven

Group: CARBONATES	Composition: MgCO₃		Hardness: 3½–4½

Magnesite

This mineral forms as rhombohedral crystals and, rarely, as prismatic, tabular, or scalenohedral crystals. It also occurs in massive, lamellar, fibrous, and granular habits. It may be colorless, white, gray, yellowish, or brown; the streak is white. It varies from transparent to translucent and has a vitreous or dull luster.

FORMATION Forms in hydrothermal veins, metamorphic rocks, and sediments.
TESTS Magnesite is soluble in warm hydrochloric acid, with effervescence.

phlogopite, an associated mineral

uneven fracture

serpentine, an associated mineral

perfect rhombohedral cleavage

magnesite cleavage mass

Trigonal/ Hexagonal

SG: 3.00–3.10	Cleavage: Perfect rhombohedral	Fracture: Conchoidal to uneven

Group: CARBONATES	Composition: $BaCO_3$	Hardness: $3–3\frac{1}{2}$

Witherite

The crystals form as twinned prismatic, often pseudohexagonal, dipyramids. Witherite also occurs in massive, granular, fibrous, and columnar habits. It may be colorless, white, gray, yellow, green, or brown, with a white streak. Transparent to translucent, it has a vitreous to resinous luster.

FORMATION Forms in hydrothermal veins with quartz, calcite, and barite.
TESTS Witherite is soluble in dilute hydrochloric acid, with effervescence. Barium in the structure raises specific gravity. Powdered witherite colors a flame apple green.

galena, an associated mineral

twinned witherite crystals

striations on crystal face

translucent witherite crystals

Orthorhombic

SG: 4.29	Cleavage: Distinct	Fracture: Uneven

Group: CARBONATES	Composition: $SrCO_3$	Hardness: $3\frac{1}{2}$

Strontianite

This mineral forms in prismatic, often acicular crystals. It also occurs in massive, granular, fibrous, and concretionary habits. It may be white, colorless, gray, yellowish, brownish, greenish, or reddish; the streak is consistently white. Strontianite is a transparent to translucent mineral and has a vitreous to resinous luster.

FORMATION Forms in hydrothermal veins and in hollows in limestone and marl. Strontianite also forms in sulfide-rich veins, associated with galena, sphalerite, and chalcopyrite; it is also associated with carbonates, such as calcite and dolomite, and with quartz.
TESTS This mineral is soluble in dilute hydrochloric acid, with effervescence. Strontianite colors a flame crimson if powdered before it is tested.

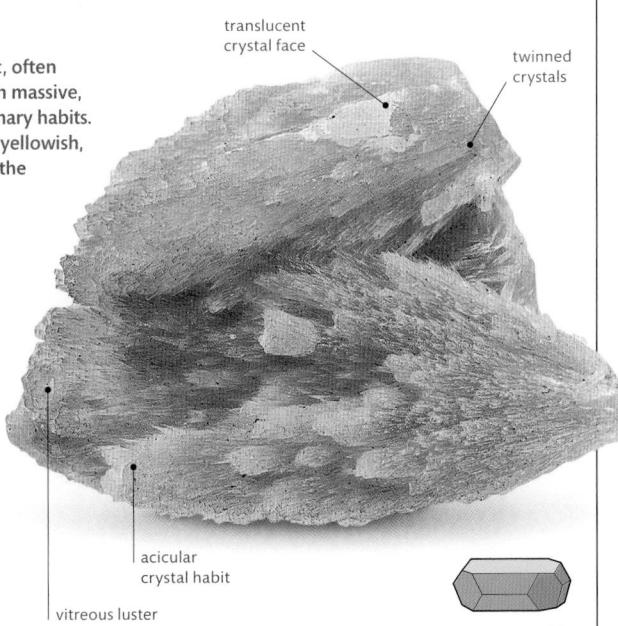

translucent crystal face

twinned crystals

acicular crystal habit

vitreous luster

Orthorhombic

SG: 3.78	Cleavage: Perfect prismatic	Fracture: Uneven

Group: CARBONATES	Composition: $PbCO_3$	Hardness: $3–3\frac{1}{2}$

Cerussite

Crystals are often tabular but can be acicular. Clusters of twinned crystals are common. Cerussite also occurs in massive, granular, compact, and stalactitic habits. It is often white or colorless but can be gray, greenish, or blue in color as a result of inclusions, such as lead. The streak is white. Cerussite is transparent to translucent, and it has an adamantine, vitreous, or resinous luster.

FORMATION Forms in the altered parts of mineral veins with lead, copper, and zinc.
TESTS Soluble in acids—in particular, dilute nitric acid, when it produces effervescence. Sometimes it fluoresces in ultraviolet light.

striations on crystal faces

prismatic cleavage

vitreous luster

twinned, tabular crystals

Orthorhombic

SG: 6.55	Cleavage: Distinct prismatic	Fracture: Conchoidal

Group: CARBONATES	Composition: $Mg_2CO_3(OH)_2.3H_2O$	Hardness: $2\frac{1}{2}$

Artinite

This mineral forms as sprays of acicular crystals. It can also occur as fibrous aggregates, which frequently radiate, and as spherical masses. The color and streak are white. It is a transparent mineral. The crystals have a vitreous luster, and the fibrous aggregates are silky.

FORMATION Artinite is found in ultramafic igneous rocks that have been oxidized by a process called serpentinization, which is similar to metamorphism and which is brought about by fluids permeating the rocks.
TESTS Artinite dissolves readily in dilute cold acids, with effervescence. It does not fuse, but gives off water and carbon dioxide when it is heated in a flame.

small radiating artinite crystals

silky luster on aggregates

serpentine, an associated mineral

Monoclinic

SG: 2.02	Cleavage: Perfect	Fracture: Uneven

Group: CARBONATES	Composition: $Cu_2CO_3(OH)_2$	Hardness: 3½–4

Malachite

When they occur, crystals are acicular or prismatic and often twinned. More usual habits are stalactitic, botryoidal masses with a fibrous, banded structure and crusts. Malachite is a rich green and has a pale green streak. It is translucent to opaque, and it has a vitreous to adamantine luster on crystal faces; fibrous habits have a silky luster.

FORMATION Forms in the altered and oxidized regions of copper deposits, often with secondary minerals, including azurite.
TESTS It is soluble in dilute hydrochloric acid, with effervescence.

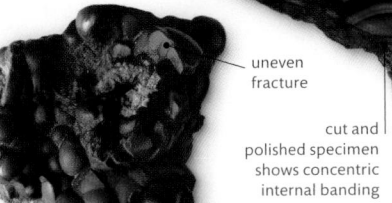

uneven fracture

cut and polished specimen shows concentric internal banding

Banded malachite

Botryoidal malachite

Monoclinic

SG: 4.05	Cleavage: Perfect	Fracture: Subconchoidal to uneven

Group: CARBONATES	Composition: $Cu_3(CO_3)_2(OH)_2$	Hardness: 3½–4

Azurite

This mineral forms as tabular and short, prismatic crystals, which may be twinned. It also occurs in massive, nodular, stalactitic, and earthy habits. It is usually a rich, deep azure-blue. The streak is a paler blue. Azurite varies from transparent to opaque, and it has a vitreous or dull luster.

FORMATION Forms in the oxidized regions of copper deposits.
TESTS It is soluble in hydrochloric acid, with effervescence. It fuses easily and turns black when heated.

twinned azurite crystals

vitreous luster

limonite groundmass

patches of green malachite around margins

short, tabular azurite crystals

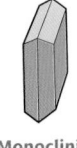

Monoclinic

SG: 3.77	Cleavage: Perfect	Fracture: Conchoidal

Group: CARBONATES	Composition: $(Zn,Cu)_5(CO_3)_2(OH)_6$	Hardness: 1–2

Aurichalcite

This mineral forms as acicular or slender, lath-shaped crystals. It also occurs as tufted aggregates and encrustations and is occasionally granular, columnar, or lamellar in habit. The color is pale green, greenish blue, or sky blue, and the streak is pale blue-green. It is a transparent mineral, and it has a silky or pearly luster.

FORMATION Forms in the altered and oxidized parts of copper and zinc veins with copper minerals, such as azurite and malachite.

TESTS Aurichalcite is soluble in dilute hydrochloric acid, with effervescence. It colors a flame green as a result of its copper content, but it does not fuse.

silky luster

small, tufted aurichalcite aggregates

Orthorhombic

limonite groundmass

radiating masses of acicular aurichalcite crystals

SG: 3.96	Cleavage: Perfect	Fracture: Uneven

Group: CARBONATES	Composition: $Pb_4(SO_4)(CO_3)_2(OH)_2$	Hardness: 2½–3

Leadhillite

Crystals are pseudohexagonal, tabular, or prismatic; twinned crystals are common. Leadhillite can also occur in massive or granular habits. It is white, colorless, gray, yellowish, pale green, or pale blue. The streak is white. Leadhillite is transparent to translucent. The luster is resinous to adamantine.

FORMATION Leadhillite forms in the oxidized parts of lead-bearing veins. It occurs with minerals such as galena, cerussite, anglesite, and linarite.

TESTS Leadhillite may sometimes fluoresce orange.

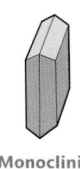

Monoclinic

perfect cleavage

twinned, tabular crystals

oxidized groundmass

SG: 6.55	Cleavage: Perfect basal	Fracture: Conchoidal

Group: CARBONATES	Composition: $Zn_5(CO_3)_2(OH)_6$	Hardness: 2–2½

Hydrozincite

This mineral rarely forms as crystals; when they occur, crystals are small, flattened or elongated, and lath-shaped, often tapering to a sharp point. More commonly, habits are massive, compact, botryoidal, encrusting, and stalactitic. The color is usually white or pale gray but may be yellow, pink, or brown. Hydrozincite has a white streak. It is a translucent mineral, with a pearly to silky or sometimes a dull luster.

FORMATION Forms in the altered parts of zinc-bearing veins.
TESTS It is soluble in hydrochloric acid. When heated, it changes into a yellowish mass of zincite. It sometimes fluoresces blue under ultraviolet light.

pearly luster

encrusting habit

botryoidal habit

Monoclinic

SG: 3.50–4.00	Cleavage: Perfect	Fracture: Uneven

Group: CARBONATES	Composition: $Na_3H(CO_3)_2.2H_2O$	Hardness: 2½

Trona

This mineral forms as prismatic or tabular crystals. It can also occur in massive, fibrous, and columnar habits. The color is grayish white, pale yellow, or pale brown. The streak is white. Trona is a transparent to translucent mineral. It has a glistening, vitreous luster.

FORMATION Occurs in evaporite deposits with borax, glauberite, and other salts and with evaporite minerals, such as halite, gypsum, sylvite, and dolomite. Trona also occurs as an efflorescence on the soil surface in arid regions.
TESTS Trona is soluble in hydrochloric acid, with effervescence. It gives off water when it is heated in a closed test tube.

massive habit

layered structure

vitreous luster

Monoclinic

SG: 2.14	Cleavage: Perfect	Fracture: Uneven

Group: NITRATES	Composition: NaNO₃		Hardness: 1½–2

Nitratine

Crystals, which rarely occur, are rhombohedral in form and often twinned. Nitratine more commonly forms in massive or granular habits and as crusts. White or colorless, it is frequently discolored by impurities, when it becomes gray, yellow, or brown. The streak is white. It is a transparent mineral with a vitreous luster.

FORMATION Occurs in arid areas as an efflorescent deposit on the surface, associated with gypsum. Nitratine often covers large areas of land. In the deserts of northern Chile, vast deposits occur over a region about 450 miles (724 kilometers) long and from 10 to 50 miles (16 to 80 kilometers) wide.

TESTS Nitratine is easily soluble in water. It will dissolve in surface waters when in crusts on the ground. If placed in a flame, it fuses very easily and colors the flame bright yellow. This mineral is deliquescent, which means it takes in atmospheric moisture.

sandy coating indicates arid nature of origin

massive habit

crust of granular crystals

Trigonal/ Hexagonal

SG: 2.27	Cleavage: Perfect	Fracture: Conchoidal

Group: BORATES	Composition: Na₂B₄O₅(OH)₄.8H₂O		Hardness: 2–2½

Borax

This mineral forms short, prismatic crystals, which are rarely twinned. It also occurs in a massive habit and as crusts. Borax is white, colorless, gray, greenish, or bluish. The streak is white. This is a translucent to opaque mineral that has a vitreous or earthy luster.

FORMATION Borax forms around hot springs and in evaporite deposits.

TESTS Borax is soluble in water. When placed in a flame, it fuses very easily and colors the flame yellow. After a period of time, it will start to lose water and will always turn white. A bittersweet taste is characteristic of borax.

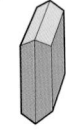

Monoclinic

vitreous luster

opaque crystal face

prismatic crystal

SG: 1.70	Cleavage: Perfect	Fracture: Conchoidal

Group: BORATES	Composition: $CaB_3O_4(OH)_3.H_2O$	Hardness: $4\frac{1}{2}$

Colemanite

Crystals are short and prismatic. Colemanite also occurs in massive and granular habits and as rounded aggregates. The mineral may be colorless, white, yellow, or gray; the streak is white. Colemanite ranges from transparent to translucent. The luster is vitreous.

FORMATION This mineral forms in evaporite deposits.
TESTS Colemanite is soluble in hydrochloric acid. It fuses easily, breaks up, and colors a flame green.

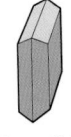
Monoclinic

prismatic crystal

translucent crystal

SG: 2.42	Cleavage: Perfect	Fracture: Uneven to conchoidal

Group: BORATES	Composition: $NaCaB_5O_6(OH)_6.5H_2O$	Hardness: $2\frac{1}{2}$

Ulexite

Crystals are acicular, often in rounded aggregates. The habit may also be fibrous or as tufted masses. Ulexite is white or colorless, and the streak is white. This mineral is transparent to translucent and has a vitreous or silky luster.

FORMATION In evaporite basins.
TESTS Ulexite is insoluble in cold water but soluble in hot water. It fuses easily and swells and also colors a flame yellow.

mass of thin, fibrous crystals

silky luster

Triclinic

SG: 1.95	Cleavage: Perfect	Fracture: Uneven

Group: BORATES	Composition: $Na_2B_4O_6(OH)_2.3H_2O$	Hardness: $2\frac{1}{2}$

Kernite

Crystals are short and prismatic but rare. The habit is usually as cleaved masses with a fibrous structure. Kernite is colorless when fresh; otherwise, it is white. The streak is white. This is a transparent to translucent mineral, and it has a vitreous or silky luster.

FORMATION Kernite forms in evaporite deposits and in mineral veins.
TESTS Soluble in cold water.

vitreous luster

cleaved mass

Monoclinic

SG: 1.91	Cleavage: Perfect	Fracture: Splintery

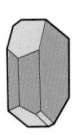

SULFATES, CHROMATES, MOLYBDATES, AND TUNGSTATES

SULFATES ARE compounds in which one or more metallic elements combine with the sulfate $(SO_4)^{-2}$ radical. Gypsum, the most abundant sulfate, occurs in evaporite deposits. Barite typically occurs in hydrothermal veins. Most sulfates are soft, light in color, and tend to have low densities. Chromates are compounds in which metallic elements combine with the chromate $(CrO_4)^{-2}$ radical. Chromates are small in number, rare, and brightly colored (such as crocoite). Molybdates and tungstates form when metallic elements combine with molybdate $(MoO_4)^{-2}$ and tungstate $(WO_4)^{-2}$ radicals. These are often dense, brittle, and vividly colored (such as wulfenite, lead molybdate, scheelite, and calcium tungstate).

Group: SULFATES	Composition: $CaSO_4.2H_2O$	Hardness: 2

Gypsum

Crystals are tabular and diamond-shaped. Twinning is common. Gypsum also occurs in massive, granular (alabaster), and fibrous (satin spar) habits. Rosette-shaped masses are called desert roses, and radiating forms are termed daisy gypsum. It varies from colorless to white, gray, greenish, yellowish, brownish, and reddish. The streak is white. It is transparent (selenite) to opaque, with a vitreous luster (pearly on cleavages); fibrous forms may be silky, while massive forms are often dull.

FORMATION Forms as an evaporite around hot springs and in clay beds.
TESTS Soluble in acids.

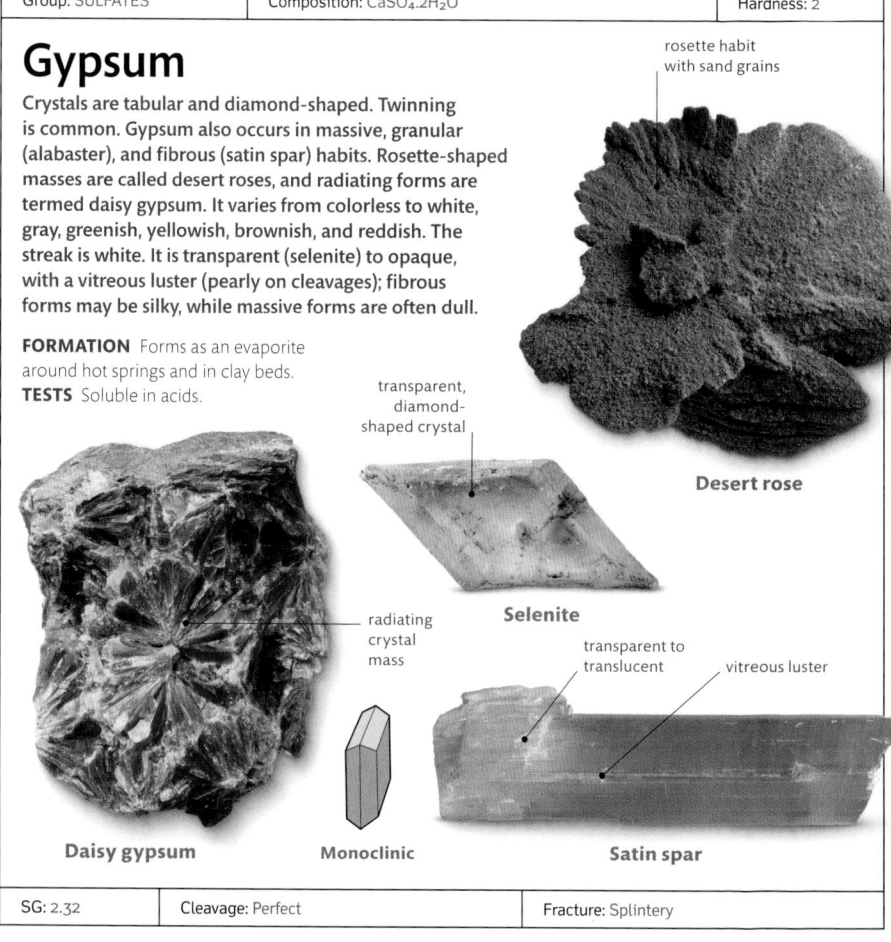

rosette habit with sand grains

transparent, diamond-shaped crystal

Desert rose

Selenite

radiating crystal mass

transparent to translucent

vitreous luster

Daisy gypsum

Monoclinic

Satin spar

SG: 2.32	Cleavage: Perfect	Fracture: Splintery

Group: SULFATES	Composition: SrSO$_4$	Hardness: 3–3½

Celestine

The crystals form as tabular or prismatic specimens. Other habits are massive, fibrous, granular, or nodular. Celestine is colorless, white, gray, blue, green, yellowish, orange, reddish, or brown. The streak is white. It is transparent to translucent and has a vitreous luster (pearly on cleavages).

FORMATION Forms in hydrothermal veins with minerals such as calcite and quartz, as well as in many sedimentary rocks, like limestones. Also found in some evaporite deposits and some basic igneous rocks.

TESTS Sometimes fluoresces under ultraviolet light. It is insoluble in acids but slightly soluble in water. When heated, this mineral fuses easily, giving a milk-white globule and coloring the flame crimson.

prismatic celestine crystals
sulfur groundmass

Orthorhombic

SG: 3.96–3.98	Cleavage: Perfect	Fracture: Uneven

Group: SULFATES	Composition: CaSO$_4$	Hardness: 3–3½

Anhydrite

This mineral occurs as tabular or prismatic crystals but usually forms in massive, granular, and fibrous habits. Anhydrite ranges from white, gray, or bluish, to pinkish, reddish, and brownish. A colorless form also occurs. There is a white streak. It is a transparent to translucent mineral, and it has a vitreous, pearly, or greasy luster.

FORMATION It is commonly found as an evaporite with other evaporites, such as dolomite, gypsum, halite, sylvite, and calcite—often in salt domes. Very rarely, it occurs as a hydrothermal vein mineral with quartz and calcite.

TESTS When heated, it fuses easily and colors the flame brick red.

massive habit
cleavage planes

Orthorhombic

SG: 2.98	Cleavage: Perfect	Fracture: Uneven to splintery

Group: SULFATES	Composition: BaSO$_4$	Hardness: 3

Barite

This mineral forms tabular and prismatic crystals, which can be very large. It also occurs as small, sand-bearing, rose-shaped concretions called desert roses. Other habits are granular, lamellar, fibrous, cockscomb, earthy, or columnar. Barite can be colorless, white, gray, yellowish, brown, reddish, bluish, or greenish. The streak is white. Barite is a transparent to opaque mineral with a vitreous, resinous, or pearly luster.

FORMATION Forms in hydrothermal veins with a number of other minerals, including quartz, calcite, fluorite, galena, pyrite, dolomite, chalcopyrite, and sphalerite. Barite also occurs in clay nodules, in veins in sedimentary strata, and around hot springs.

TESTS This mineral fuses with difficulty, coloring the flame yellowish green. It is insoluble in acids, and some varieties are fluorescent. Its high specific gravity is a useful aid to identification.

transparent, colorless, prismatic crystal

vitreous luster

Crystalline barite

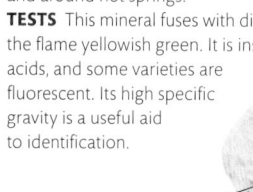
cockscomb mass

Cockscomb barite

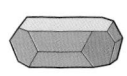
Orthorhombic

SG: 4.50	Cleavage: Perfect	Fracture: Uneven

Group: SULFATES	Composition: PbSO$_4$	Hardness: 2½–3

Anglesite

Crystals are tabular and prismatic. Other habits are massive, granular, nodular, and stalactitic. Anglesite can be colorless, white, gray, yellowish, pale green, or pale blue. The streak is colorless. This is a transparent to opaque mineral. It has a vitreous, adamantine, or resinous luster.

FORMATION Forms in the oxidized parts of lead veins.

TESTS Often shows yellow fluorescence under ultraviolet light.

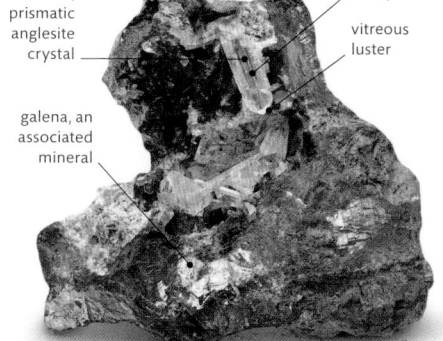
striated, prismatic anglesite crystal

transparent

vitreous luster

galena, an associated mineral

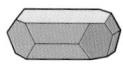
Orthorhombic

SG: 6.37–6.39	Cleavage: Good	Fracture: Conchoidal

Group: SULFATES	Composition: $CuSO_4.5H_2O$	Hardness: $2\frac{1}{2}$

Chalcanthite

Short, prismatic, and thick, tabular crystals are formed by chalcanthite. Other habits exhibited are stalactitic, fibrous, massive, granular, compact, and encrusting. The color is sky blue to dark blue, greenish blue, or greenish, and the streak is white. This is a transparent to translucent mineral. It has a vitreous to resinous luster.

FORMATION Chalcanthite forms in oxidized parts of copper sulfide veins. This oxidation is usually brought about by waters circulating from above, which have their origin in rain (meteoritic). Hydrothermal fluids originating from deep underground and rising under pressure can also alter mineral veins. When water seeps through mine tunnels and shafts, chalcanthite crystallizes as crusts and stalactites on roofs and supports. It is found most frequently in areas of the world that have an arid climate.
TESTS Chalcanthite is soluble in water. It gives off water when heated in a closed test tube.

kaolinite, an associated mineral

rock groundmass

Triclinic

SG: 2.29	Cleavage: Imperfect	Fracture: Conchoidal

Group: SULFATES	Composition: $MgSO_4.7H_2O$	Hardness: $2–2\frac{1}{2}$

Epsomite

Crystals rarely occur. Epsomite is usually massive, as acicular crusts, or stalactitic. It is white, pinkish, colorless, or greenish, and the streak is white. This is a transparent to translucent mineral. It has a vitreous to silky or dull luster.

FORMATION Forms on walls in mines, in limestone caverns, and on rock faces. Epsomite is also found in arid regions of the world, where it occurs in the oxidized parts of pyrite deposits.
TESTS This mineral is very soluble in water. It has a bitter, salty taste. Epsomite effloresces in dry air and gives off water when it is heated in a test tube.

silky luster

Orthorhombic

SG: 1.68	Cleavage: Perfect	Fracture: Conchoidal

Group: SULFATES	Composition: $KAl_3(SO_4)_2(OH)_6$	Hardness: $3\frac{1}{2}$–4

Alunite

This mineral forms rhombohedral, often pseudocubic crystals but usually occurs in massive, granular, and compact habits. It may also be fibrous. The color is usually white but may be grayish, reddish, yellowish, or brown with discoloration. The streak is white. Alunite is transparent to nearly opaque, with a vitreous or pearly luster.

FORMATION In volcanic vents and as a vein mineral.
TESTS It gives off water when heated in a closed test tube.

compact habit

Trigonal/ Hexagonal

SG: 2.6–2.9	Cleavage: Distinct basal	Fracture: Conchoidal

Group: SULFATES	Composition: $KFe^{3+}_3(SO_4)_2(OH)_6$	Hardness: $2\frac{1}{2}$–$3\frac{1}{2}$

Jarosite

Very small, tabular or pseudocubic crystals are formed by jarosite. Other habits are massive, granular, fibrous, or earthy. The color varies from yellowish brown to brown. The streak is pale yellow. This mineral is translucent. Jarosite may have a vitreous or resinous luster on clean surfaces.

FORMATION Forms in fissures and layers within iron-rich deposits. Jarosite occurs as a result of secondary alteration of iron-rich minerals. This is brought about by the circulation of water and other fluids through the upper parts of the earth's crust.
TESTS Jarosite's distinctive pseudocubic crystals are a useful aid to identification.

goethite, an associated mineral

vitreous luster

Trigonal/ Hexagonal

SG: 2.90–3.26	Cleavage: Distinct	Fracture: Uneven

| Group: SULFATES | Composition: Na₂Ca(SO₄)₂ | Hardness: 2½–3 |

Glauberite

This mineral forms tabular, prismatic, or dipyramidal crystals. It may be colorless, gray, or yellowish, with a white streak. Glauberite is a transparent to translucent mineral. It has a vitreous luster, which changes to pearly on cleavage surfaces.

FORMATION Glauberite forms in evaporite deposits. These deposits are formed when areas of saline water, salt lakes, or marine lagoons cut off from the main part of an ocean dry out.

TESTS This mineral is partially soluble in water and soluble in hydrochloric acid.

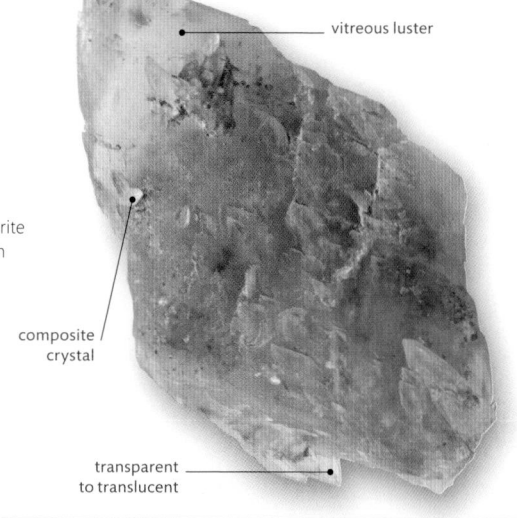
vitreous luster
composite crystal
transparent to translucent

Monoclinic

| SG: 2.75–2.85 | Cleavage: Perfect | Fracture: Conchoidal |

| Group: SULFATES | Composition: Na₂SO₄ | Hardness: 2½–3 |

Thenardite

Crystals are tabular, dipyramidal, or prismatic and commonly twinned. Thenardite also forms as crusts. It may be colorless, grayish white, yellowish, brownish, or reddish. Thenardite is a transparent to translucent mineral. It has a vitreous or resinous luster.

FORMATION Forms in the deposits of salt lakes, as well as occurring on the soil surface in arid areas. When it occurs in salt lakes, thenardite may be associated with other evaporites, such as gypsum, halite, sylvite, and glauberite. Thenardite may also be found on the surface of recently erupted and cooled lava flows. It can occur around fumaroles, where it forms as a crustlike deposit.

TESTS This mineral is highly soluble when placed in cold water. In common with several other evaporites, such as halite and sylvite, thenardite has a salty taste.

group of pyramidal crystals
resinous luster
transparent to translucent

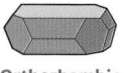

Orthorhombic

| SG: 2.66 | Cleavage: Perfect | Fracture: Uneven |

Group: SULFATES	Composition: $K_2MgCa_2(SO_4)_4.2H_2O$	Hardness: $2\frac{1}{2}-3\frac{1}{2}$

Polyhalite

This mineral rarely forms crystals; when they occur, crystals are small, highly modified, elongated, or tabular. Usually, the habit is as fibrous or foliated masses. Polyhalite is frequently flesh pink to brick red as a result of iron oxide inclusions. When pure, it is colorless, white, or gray. It has a white streak. This is a transparent to translucent mineral; the luster is resinous or silky.

FORMATION Forms in evaporite sequences of rocks with minerals such as halite, gypsum, sylvite, carnallite, and anhydrite. Forms rarely from volcanic activity.

TESTS Tastes salty, but more bitter than halite.

transparent to translucent

fibrous habit

Triclinic

SG: 2.78	Cleavage: Perfect	Fracture: Uneven

Group: SULFATES	Composition: $PbCu(SO_4)(OH)_2$	Hardness: $2\frac{1}{2}$

Linarite

The thin, tabular or prismatic crystals formed by linarite are often randomly orientated in aggregates. Twinned crystals are common. As well as in these habits, linarite forms in crusts. Its color is deep blue, and it has a pale blue streak. This is a translucent to transparent mineral. Its luster is vitreous to subadamantine.

FORMATION Forms in the oxidized parts of lead and copper veins that have been altered by circulating fluids, mainly water, where it is associated with many other secondary minerals, such as brochantite, anglesite, and chalcanthite.

TESTS Linarite produces a white coating and no effervescence when placed in dilute hydrochloric acid. However, it is soluble in dilute nitric acid. When placed in a flame, it fuses. With continued heating it crackles, turning black.

prismatic linarite crystals

Monoclinic

rock groundmass

SG: 5.35	Cleavage: Perfect	Fracture: Conchoidal

| Group: SULFATES | Composition: $Fe^{+2}Fe_4^{+3}(SO_4)_6(OH)_2.2OH_2O$ | Hardness: $2\frac{1}{2}$–3 |

Copiapite

The usual habits of this mineral are as tabular crystals, crusts, and scaly aggregates, or masses. Copiapite is yellow, golden-yellow, or orange-yellow, though it may be greenish yellow to olive-green. It is transparent to translucent and has a pearly luster.

FORMATION Forms when sulfides, such as iron pyrite, are oxidized.
TESTS Soluble in water, producing a yellowish color. It fuses at quite low temperatures.

scaly aggregates of crystals

Triclinic

| SG: 2.08–2.17 | Cleavage: Perfect | Fracture: Uneven |

| Group: SULFATES | Composition: $Cu_4Al_2(SO_4)(OH)_{12}.2H_2O$ | Hardness: 1–3 |

Cyanotrichite

This mineral forms minute, acicular crystals in tufted aggregates. Other habits are as coatings or fibrous veinlets. It is pale to dark blue and has a pale blue streak. Cyanotrichite is a translucent mineral and has a silky luster.

FORMATION Forms in the oxidized zone of ore veins, especially those of copper.
TESTS Soluble in acids. Fuses in a flame.

radiating acicular crystals

rock groundmass

Orthorhombic

| SG: 2.76 | Cleavage: None | Fracture: Uneven |

| Group: SULFATES | Composition: $Cu_4SO_4(OH)_6$ | Hardness: $3\frac{1}{2}$–4 |

Brochantite

The usual habits are as stout prismatic, acicular, or tabular crystals, aggregates, and drusy crusts. Twinning is common. It is emerald green to blackish green; the streak is pale green. Brochantite is transparent to translucent. Its luster is vitreous.

FORMATION Forms in oxidation zone of copper deposits.
TESTS This mineral is soluble in hydrochloric and nitric acids.

azurite, an associated mineral

mass of acicular brochantite crystals

Monoclinic

| SG: 3.97 | Cleavage: Perfect | Fracture: Conchoidal to uneven |

Group: CHROMATES	Composition: PbCrO₄	Hardness: 2½–3

Crocoite

Slender, prismatic crystals are formed by crocoite, usually in aggregates. This mineral also occurs in a massive habit. The color is orange-red, often bright, and sometimes orange, red, or yellow. The streak is orange-yellow. Crocoite is a translucent mineral. It has an adamantine to vitreous luster.

FORMATION Forms in the altered and oxidized parts of veins and deposits containing chromium and lead. Crocoite is a secondary mineral resulting from the alteration of other lead minerals by hydrothermal fluids. It occurs with a variety of other minerals, including wulfenite, cerussite, pyromorphite, and vanadinite.
TESTS Crocoite fuses fairly easily in a flame and is soluble in strong acids. The first extraction of chromium was carried out from this mineral.

prismatic crystal

some striations on crystal faace

Monoclinic

SG: 5.97–6.02	Cleavage: Distinct prismatic	Fracture: Conchoidal to uneven

Group: MOLYBDATES	Composition: PbMoO₄	Hardness: 2½–3

Wulfenite

This mineral forms square-shaped, tabular crystals and also prismatic crystals. Other habits are massive and granular. Wulfenite is typically colored orange or yellow but may be brown, gray, or greenish brown. The colors often appear brilliant. The streak is white. This is a transparent to translucent mineral. It has a resinous to adamantine luster.

FORMATION Forms in the parts of ore veins that have been altered by circulating fluids, mainly water. Wulfenite can occur with a great variety of other minerals, including cerussite, limonite, vanadinite, galena, pyromorphite, and malachite, as well as mimetite.
TESTS Wulfenite fuses easily. It is soluble in hydrochloric acid when heated, but it dissolves more slowly in cold acid.

square, tabular wulfenite crystal

vitreous luster

dark groundmass

Tetragonal

SG: 6.50–7.50	Cleavage: Distinct pyramidal	Fracture: Subconchoidal

Group: TUNGSTATES	Composition: (Fe,Mn)WO$_4$	Hardness: 4–4½

Wolframite

An intermediate member in the ferberite-hübnerite series of minerals. The prismatic or tabular crystals formed by wolframite are often twinned. The mineral also occurs in a massive habit. It is brownish black in color, with a reddish brown to brownish black streak. This is a translucent to opaque mineral, with a submetallic luster.

FORMATION Forms in quartz veins of granitic pegmatites, often associated with minerals such as cassiterite and arsenopyrite.
TESTS Wolframite fuses slowly. The brownish color is due to the presence of ferberite, while hübnerite contributes to its reddish-brown coloring.

tabular crystal with striated face

prismatic crystal

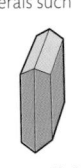

Monoclinic

SG: 7.10–7.50	Cleavage: Perfect	Fracture: Uneven

Group: TUNGSTATES	Composition: CaWO$_4$	Hardness: 4½–5

Scheelite

Pseudo-octahedral or dipyramidal crystals are formed by scheelite. The crystals are commonly twinned. Other habits are massive, granular, or columnar. Scheelite is white, colorless, gray, pale yellow, orange-yellow, brownish green, reddish, or purple. The streak is white. It is a transparent to translucent mineral, with a vitreous to adamantine luster.

FORMATION Forms in hydrothermal veins, in contact metamorphic rocks, and in pegmatites. It also occurs in placer deposits and is frequently found with wolframite. It is an important ore of tungsten.
TESTS This mineral gives a bright, bluish-white fluorescence under shortwave ultraviolet light. It is also soluble in acids, as well as fusible, but only with difficulty.

bipyramidal scheelite crystals

magnetite groundmass

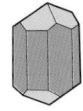

Tetragonal

SG: 6.10	Cleavage: Distinct	Fracture: Subconchoidal to uneven

PHOSPHATES, ARSENATES, AND VANADATES

PHOSPHATES, arsenates, and vanadates are all compounds in which metallic elements combine with phosphate $(PO_4)^{-8}$; arsenate $(ASO_4)^{-8}$, $(ASO_3)^{-1}$; or vanadate $(VO_4)^{-3}$, $(VO_3)^{-1}$ radicals. Although several hundred phosphate, arsenate, and vanadate species are recognized, they are not abundant. Some phosphates, such as arsenic, are primary; however, most members of the overall group form from the oxidation of primary sulfides. Their properties are variable, but generally they tend to be soft, brittle, colorful, and well crystallized. Phosphates include the radioactive minerals torbernite and autunite; lead-rich pyromorphite; bright blue lazulite; and turquoise, which gives its name to a shade of blue. The hardness of phosphates is particularly variable, ranging from 1½ in vivianite to 5–6 in turquoise.

Many of the arsenates are highly sought after by collectors, particularly the well-crystallized and brightly colored species, such as adamite, erythrite, mimetite, and bayldonite. Arsenates tend to have a specific gravity of 3.00–5.00—apart from mimetite which, because it contains lead, has a specific gravity of 7.10–7.30. These minerals are usually found to be of low hardness. Vanadinite is probably the best known and most common of the vanadates and occurs as beautiful red or orange hexagonal crystals.

Group: PHOSPHATES	Composition: LiAl(PO₄)F	Hardness: 5½–6

Amblygonite

This mineral forms short, prismatic crystals, which often have rough faces and are frequently twinned. Amblygonite also occurs in cleavable masses. It is white to grayish white and may also be pinkish, colorless, yellowish, greenish, or bluish. The streak is white. Amblygonite is a transparent to translucent mineral, and it has a vitreous to greasy luster.

FORMATION It forms in coarse-grained granitic igneous rocks, including pegmatites.
TESTS This is the fluorine-rich end-member of the amblygonite-montebrasite series of minerals. It fuses easily, coloring a flame red due to the presence of lithium. It is soluble in acids, but only with difficulty.

transparent to translucent

cleaved mass

Triclinic

SG: 3.04–3.11	Cleavage: Perfect	Fracture: Uneven

Group: PHOSPHATES	Composition: MgAl$_2$(PO$_4$)$_2$(OH)$_2$	Hardness: 5½–6

Lazulite

Pseudodipyramidal crystals are usually formed by lazulite, but tabular crystals also form. The crystals can be quite large and are frequently twinned. Other habits in which this mineral commonly forms are massive, granular, and compact. Its color is blue but ranges from a rich azure to light blue or bluish green. The streak is white. Lazulite is a translucent to opaque mineral, with a vitreous to dull luster.

FORMATION Lazulite forms in a variety of environments, including quartz veins, granitic pegmatites, and metamorphic rocks, such as metaquartzite. Pegmatic lazulite typically occurs with andalusite and rutile. Metamorphic associates include quartz, garnet, kyanite, muscovite, pyrophyllite, sillimanite, and corundum.
TESTS This mineral gives off water when heated in a closed test tube.

pyramidal lazulite crystal

twinned lazulite crystals

vitreous luster on crystal face

quartz groundmass

Monoclinic

SG: 3.12–3.24	Cleavage: Indistinct to good prismatic	Fracture: Uneven to splintery

Group: PHOSPHATES	Composition: Pb$_5$(PO$_4$)$_3$Cl	Hardness: 3½–4

Pyromorphite

This mineral usually forms short, hexagonal prisms, which are often barrel-shaped. It also occurs in globular, reniform, granular, earthy, botryoidal, and fibrous habits. It can be green, orange, gray, brown, or yellow in color. The streak is white. Pyromorphite is a transparent to translucent mineral. It has a resinous to adamantine luster.

FORMATION Forms in the oxidation zone of lead veins as a secondary mineral.
TESTS Pyromorphite is soluble in certain acids.

limonite groundmass

aggregates of prismatic, hexagonal pyromorphite crystals

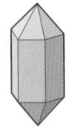

Trigonal/ Hexagonal

SG: 7.04	Cleavage: Very poor prismatic	Fracture: Uneven to subconchoidal

Group: PHOSPHATES	Composition: Fe$_3$(PO$_4$)$_2$.8H$_2$O		Hardness: 1½–2

Vivianite

vitreous luster

elongated, prismatic crystals in clusters

dark coloring caused by exposure to light

Elongated, prismatic, or tabular crystals are usually formed. It also occurs in massive, bladed, or fibrous habits. It is colorless when fresh. The mineral's streak is colorless to bluish white. It is transparent to translucent, and it has a vitreous or pearly luster.

FORMATION Forms in the oxidation zone of iron and manganese-rich deposits.
TESTS Soluble in hydrochloric acid and fuses easily.

Monoclinic

SG: 2.67–2.69	Cleavage: Perfect	Fracture: Uneven

Group: PHOSPHATES	Composition: Cu(UO$_2$)$_2$(PO$_4$)$_2$.12H$_2$O		Hardness: 2–2½

Torbernite

tabular torbernite crystals

iron-rich groundmass

vitreous luster

This mineral forms as tabular crystals. Other habits are as scaly or lamellar aggregates. It is green in color, and the streak is pale green. Torbernite is a transparent to translucent mineral, and it has a vitreous to pearly luster.

FORMATION A secondary uranium mineral derived from the alteration of uraninite.
TESTS It is radioactive. It is also chemically unstable and often becomes metatorbernite.

Tetragonal

SG: 3.22	Cleavage: Perfect basal	Fracture: Uneven

Group: PHOSPHATES	Composition: Ca(UO$_2$)$_2$(PO$_4$)$_2$.10–12H$_2$O		Hardness: 2–2½

Autunite

vitreous luster

translucent

tabular, twinned crystal aggregate

perfect basal cleavage

This mineral forms as tabular crystals, which are sometimes twinned. It also occurs as crusts, aggregates, and grains. The color is yellow to green. The streak is yellow. It is transparent to translucent. The luster is vitreous to pearly.

FORMATION Forms by the alteration of primary uranium minerals.
TESTS Autunite is a radioactive mineral.

Tetragonal

SG: 3.05–3.20	Cleavage: Perfect basal	Fracture: Uneven

Group: PHOSPHATES	Composition: YPO$_4$	Hardness: 4–5

Xenotime-(Y)

This mineral forms as prismatic and pyramidal crystals. It may also occur as equant crystals. Rough crystals occur in aggregates, and rosette-shaped crystal groups sometimes form. Twinned crystals are rare. The color is yellowish brown to reddish brown or gray, pale yellow, greenish, or reddish. The streak is pale brown or can be yellowish brown. It is translucent to opaque, and it has a vitreous to resinous luster.

FORMATION Forms in pegmatites and also in many other acid igneous rocks, but in very small quantities. In addition, xenotime-(Y) forms in metamorphic rocks and in alpine veins. It has been found in sediments as a detrital mineral.
TESTS It is very similar to zircon, but zircon is much harder.

Tetragonal

pyramidal crystal

aggregate of rough crystals

SG: 4.40–5.10	Cleavage: Perfect prismatic	Fracture: Uneven

Group: PHOSPHATES	Composition: (Ce,La,Nd,Th)PO$_4$	Hardness: 5–5½

Monazite

prismatic crystal

This forms a series of monazite-(Ce), monazite-(La), and monazite-(Nd). The crystals are tabular or prismatic crystals and are usually small and twinned. Crystal faces are often rough or striated. The habit can also be as granular masses. Monazite is brown, reddish brown, yellowish brown, pink, yellow, greenish, or nearly white in color. The streak is white. This is a transparent to translucent mineral, and it has a resinous, waxy, or vitreous luster.

FORMATION Forms in pegmatites, in metamorphic rocks, and in veins. It is common in placer deposits, including river and beach sands. Very large monazite crystals weighing several pounds have been found in pegmatites.
TESTS Monazite is a mildly radioactive mineral.

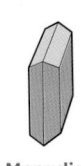

Monoclinic

uneven fracture

vitreous luster

SG: 4.60–5.50	Cleavage: Distinct	Fracture: Conchoidal to uneven

Group: PHOSPHATES	Composition: $Cu(Al,Fe^{3+})_6(PO_4)_4(OH)_8 \cdot 4H_2O$	Hardness: 5–6

Turquoise

This mineral rarely forms crystals, but when these occur, they are small, short, prismatic specimens. The more common habits are massive, granular, cryptocrystalline, stalactitic, and concretionary; it also forms as crusts and veinlets. Turquoise is bright blue to pale blue, greenish blue, green, and gray. It has a white or pale green streak. The crystals are transparent and have a vitreous luster; massive forms are opaque, with a waxy or dull luster.

FORMATION Forms in igneous and sedimentary, aluminum-rich rocks that have been very altered, often by surface water.
TESTS Turquoise is soluble in hydrochloric acid that has been heated.

crust of turquoise

rock groundmass

Triclinic

SG: 2.60–2.80	Cleavage: Perfect	Fracture: Subconchoidal to uneven

Group: PHOSPHATES	Composition: $Al_3(PO_4)_2(OH,F)_3 \cdot 5H_2O$	Hardness: $3\frac{1}{2}$–4

Wavellite

This mineral occurs occasionally as minute, prismatic crystals. It also forms as acicular, radiating aggregates, which are often spherical. Additionally, it forms crusts. The color is white to greenish white and green, as well as yellowish green to yellow and yellowish brown. There is a white streak. Wavellite is a transparent to translucent mineral and has a vitreous, resinous, or pearly luster.

FORMATION Forms on rock fracture and joint surfaces as a secondary mineral.
TESTS This mineral dissolves in most acids and is infusible. It gives off water when heated in a closed test tube.

radiating acicular wavellite crystals

rock groundmass

Orthorhombic

SG: 2.36	Cleavage: Perfect	Fracture: Subconchoidal to uneven

Group: PHOSPHATES	Composition: $Al(PO_4).2H_2O$	Hardness: $3\frac{1}{2}–4\frac{1}{2}$

Variscite

Pseudo-octahedral crystals are rare. Commonly, it occurs in massive and concretionary habits and as crusts or veins. The color is green, and the streak is white. Variscite is transparent to translucent. It has a vitreous to waxy or dull luster.

FORMATION Forms where water rich in phosphates has altered aluminum-rich rocks.
TESTS Soluble only if heated before being placed in acid. It is infusible.

Orthorhombic

alteration rind
concretionary variscite

SG: 2.57–2.61	Cleavage: Perfect	Fracture: Conchoidal or uneven to splintery

Group: PHOSPHATES	Composition: $Ca_5(PO_4)_3(F,Cl,OH)$	Hardness: 5

Apatite

This is a closely related mineral group that forms as prismatic or tabular crystals and in massive, compact, and granular habits. Apatite is usually green in color but may be white, colorless, yellow, bluish, reddish, brown, gray, or purple. It has a white streak. Apatite is transparent to translucent, with a vitreous or subresinous luster.

FORMATION Forms in igneous rocks and in metamorphosed limestones.
TESTS Soluble in hydrochloric acid.

Trigonal/ Hexagonal

calcite groundmass
prismatic apatite crystals

SG: 3.10–3.20	Cleavage: Poor	Fracture: Conchoidal to uneven

Group: PHOSPHATES	Composition: $CaBe(PO_4)(F,OH)$	Hardness: $5–5\frac{1}{2}$

Herderite

This mineral occurs as prismatic or tabular crystals, which are often pseudo-orthorhombic. It also forms in fibrous aggregates. Herderite is colorless, pale yellow, or greenish white. It is transparent to translucent and has a vitreous luster.

FORMATION Herderite forms in granitic pegmatites.
TESTS This mineral is soluble in most acids. Some specimens fluoresce under ultraviolet light.

Monoclinic

vitreous luster
prismatic crystal

SG: 3.02	Cleavage: Poor	Fracture: Subconchoidal

Group: ARSENATES	Composition: $Zn_2AsO_4(OH)$	Hardness: $3\frac{1}{2}$

Adamite

Forms as elongated, tabular, or equant crystals, which may be twinned. It can also occur in a habit of spheroidal masses. It is usually bright yellow-green in color. The streak is white. Adamite is a transparent to translucent mineral. It has a vitreous luster.

FORMATION Forms in the oxidized parts of ore veins. Adamite is associated with many other minerals, such as calcite, limonite, and malachite, as well as azurite, smithsonite, and hemimorphite.
TESTS This mineral is soluble in dilute acids. Adamite is also sometimes fluorescent in ultraviolet light and is fusible when tested with a flame.

spheroidal adamite masses

limonite groundmass

Spheroidal adamite

crust of limonite

uneven fracture

twinned, tabular adamite crystals

Crystalline adamite

Orthorhombic

SG: 4.32–4.48	Cleavage: Good		Fracture: Subconchoidal to uneven

---

Group: ARSENATES	Composition: $Ni_3(AsO_4)_2\cdot8H_2O$	Hardness: $1\frac{1}{2}$–$2\frac{1}{2}$

Annabergite

This mineral forms prismatic, striated crystals. Other habits are as crusts and earthy or powdery masses. Annabergite is white, gray, pale green, or yellow-green. The streak is paler than the color. It is a transparent to translucent mineral, and it has a vitreous or pearly luster.

FORMATION Forms in the altered parts of nickel veins.
TESTS Gives off water when heated in a closed test tube.

crusty coating of annabergite on rock surface

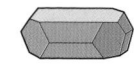

Monoclinic

pearly luster

SG: 3.07	Cleavage: Perfect		Fracture: Uneven

Group: ARSENATES	Composition: $Cu_3(AsO_4)(OH)_3$	Hardness: $2\frac{1}{2}$–3

Clinoclase

The crystals form as elongated or tabular shapes and may have a rhombohedral appearance, in which case they are described as pseudorhombohedral. Crystals occur either isolated or as rosettes. This mineral is dark greenish blue to greenish black in color and has a bluish-green streak. Clinoclase is transparent to translucent. It has a vitreous luster on crystal faces, which becomes pearly on the cleavage surfaces.

FORMATION Forms as a secondary mineral in the oxidation zone of copper sulfide deposits both on and beneath the earth's surface. Clinoclase is frequently associated with olivenite, a member of the same mineral group.

TESTS Clinoclase is soluble in acids and produces a garlic smell when heated.

broken clinoclase rosette with internal, radiating structure

uneven fracture

olivenite, an associated mineral

vitreous luster

Monoclinic

SG: 4.38	Cleavage: Perfect	Fracture: Uneven

Group: ARSENATES	Composition: $Co_3(AsO_4)_2 \cdot 8H_2O$	Hardness: $1\frac{1}{2}$–$2\frac{1}{2}$

Erythrite

The prismatic to acicular crystals formed by this mineral are often striated or in bladed aggregates. Erythrite also occurs in a habit of earthy masses. In color, it is deep purple to pale pink. The streak is just a shade paler than the color. This mineral ranges from transparent to translucent, and it has an adamantine to vitreous or pearly luster.

FORMATION Forms in the parts of cobalt veins that have been altered by circulating fluids and where oxidation has occurred.

TESTS Soluble in hydrochloric acid.

bladed aggregates of crystals in striated acicular habit

vitreous luster

Monoclinic

SG: 3.06	Cleavage: Perfect	Fracture: Uneven

Group: ARSENATES	Composition: $Pb_5(AsO_4)_3Cl$	Hardness: $3\frac{1}{2}$–4

Mimetite

This mineral forms acicular to slender prismatic crystals; sometimes, these crystals can be barrel-shaped, in which case they are called campylite crystals. Other habits include botryoidal, reniform, and granular. Mimetite ranges in color from yellow, orange, and brown to white, colorless, and greenish. It has a white streak. This is a transparent to translucent mineral, and it has a vitreous to resinous luster.

FORMATION Forms in the oxidation zone of lead deposits that have been altered by circulating hydrothermal fluids. It is often found with pyromorphite, vanadinite, galena, anglesite, hemimorphite, and arsenopyrite.

TESTS Soluble in hydrochloric acid. It will fuse easily if put in a flame, when a very strong smell that is reminiscent of garlic is produced.

prismatic crystal

translucent

Prismatic mimetite

barrel-shaped campylite crystals

romanechite and associated groundmass

Campylite

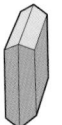

Monoclinic

SG: 7.24	Cleavage: None	Fracture: Subconchoidal to uneven

Group: ARSENATES	Composition: $Cu_2(AsO_4)(OH)$	Hardness: 3

Olivenite

Prismatic, acicular, or tabular crystals are formed by olivenite. Other habits are as globular or reniform masses. The color is olive-green, brown, yellowish, gray, or white. Olivenite has an olive-green streak. Its name derives from this color connection. It is a translucent to opaque mineral, and the luster is vitreous to silky.

FORMATION Forms in the oxidation zone of copper sulfide deposits. Olivenite occurs with the minerals malachite, azurite, calcite, goethite, and dioptase, as well as scorodite.

TESTS It is soluble in acids, and produces a garlic smell when heated.

globular masses of acicular olivenite crystals

quartz groundmass

Orthorhombic

SG: 4.46	Cleavage: Indistinct	Fracture: Uneven to conchoidal

Group: ARSENATES	Composition: $FeAsO_4 \cdot 2H_2O$	Hardness: $3\frac{1}{2}$–4

Scorodite

The crystals formed by scorodite are pyramidal, prismatic, and tabular. Scorodite also occurs in massive and earthy habits. It is pale green, grayish green, bluish green, blue, brownish, colorless, yellowish, or violet. The streak is white. This is a transparent to translucent mineral. Its luster is vitreous to resinous or dull.

FORMATION Forms in the oxidation zone of arsenic deposits.

TESTS This mineral is soluble in hydrochloric and nitric acids. When heated, a smell that is reminiscent of garlic is produced. If heated in a closed test tube, water is given off.

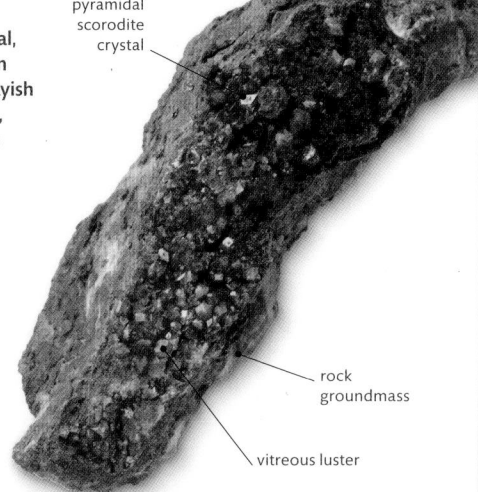

pyramidal scorodite crystal

rock groundmass

vitreous luster

Orthorhombic

SG: 3.27	Cleavage: Imperfect	Fracture: Subconchoidal

Group: ARSENATES	Composition: $(Pb,Cu)_3(AsO_4)_2(OH)_2$	Hardness: $4\frac{1}{2}$

Bayldonite

Usually forms in a massive habit but also in granular and powdery habits. The latter habits may occur on rock surfaces, and it is difficult to detect any crystal form unless a high magnification is used. This mineral also occurs as crusts and rounded concretions, which may have a fibrous, threadlike, internal structure. The color is often bright grass green but can be yellowish or dark green. No streak has been determined. Light hardly passes through crystalline specimens, so bayldonite is described as subtranslucent. The luster is resinous, and the surface is almost sticky in appearance.

FORMATION This mineral forms in the oxidation zone of copper-bearing deposits. Balydonite is associated with many minerals, including olivenite, azurite, malachite, and mimetite.

TESTS Balydonite will give off water when it is heated in a closed test tube.

crust of bayldonite on quartz groundmass

Monoclinic

resinous luster

SG: 5.24–5.65	Cleavage: None	Fracture: Uneven

Group: VANADATES	Composition: $K_2(UO_2)_2V_2O_8.3H_2O$	Hardness: 2

Carnotite

Crystals are very small and platy. Carnotite also forms as powdery, microcrystalline masses or crusts. It is bright yellow or greenish yellow. The streak is yellow. It is semiopaque. The crystals have a pearly luster, but the masses are dull.

FORMATION Forms as a secondary mineral, deposited from ground waters passing through uranium deposits.
TESTS Carnotite is radioactive and dissolves in acids.

rock groundmass

crust of carnotite

Monoclinic

SG: 4.70	Cleavage: Perfect basal	Fracture: Uneven

Group: VANADATES	Composition: $Ca(UO_2)_2V_2O_8.5-8H_2O$	Hardness: 1½–2

Tyuyamunite

This mineral forms as very small scales and laths. Other habits are massive, compact, and microcrystalline. The color is greenish yellow to yellow, and the streak is yellow. Tyuyamunite is translucent to opaque and has a waxy, pearly, adamantine, or dull luster.

FORMATION Tyuyamunite forms as a secondary alteration product of primary uranium minerals.
TESTS It is a radioactive mineral.

scaly habit

tyuyamunite coating on rock surface

dull luster

Orthorhombic

SG: 3.57–4.35	Cleavage: Perfect basal	Fracture: Uneven

Group: VANADATES	Composition: $Cu_3V_2O_7(OH)_2.2H_2O$	Hardness: 3½

Volborthite

This mineral forms as encrusting scales, often with triangular or hexagonal outlines. Lamellar twinning is common. It also occurs as rosettelike or honeycomb aggregates. The color is green, yellow, or brown, and the streak is undetermined. It is translucent, with a vitreous to pearly luster.

FORMATION An alteration product of other vanadium minerals.
TESTS It is soluble in acids.

crusty coating of volborthite

rock groundmass

Monoclinic

SG: 3.50–3.80	Cleavage: Perfect basal	Fracture: Uneven

Group: VANADATES	Composition: $Pb_5(VO_4)_3Cl$	Hardness: $2\frac{1}{2}$–3

Vanadinite

The prismatic crystals formed by vanadinite are sometimes hollow. The color ranges from bright red and orange-red to brownish red, brown, or yellow. The streak may be white or yellowish. Vanadinite is a transparent to translucent mineral, and it has a resinous to subadamantine luster.

FORMATION Forms in the oxidation zone of lead deposits.
TESTS Vanadinite gives a number of characteristic results when tested with acids or heat. It fuses easily in a flame and is soluble in nitric acid. If the resulting liquid is left to evaporate, a red residue will remain, distinguishing it from other related minerals that will leave a white deposit.

subadamantine luster

prismatic vanadinite crystals

rock groundmass

Trigonal/ Hexagonal

SG: 6.88	Cleavage: None	Fracture: Conchoidal to uneven

Group: VANADATES	Composition: $PbZn(VO_4)(OH)$	Hardness: 3–$3\frac{1}{2}$

Descloizite

This mineral forms as pyramidal, tabular, or prismatic crystals. The crystals often have rough or uneven faces. It also occurs as crusts, plumose aggregates, and botryoidal masses. The color is orange-red to reddish brown or blackish brown, and the streak is yellowish orange to reddish brown. Descloizite is a transparent to translucent mineral, and it has a vitreous to greasy luster.

FORMATION Forms as a secondary mineral in the parts of ore veins and deposits that have been altered by oxidation.
TESTS It is soluble in hydrochloric and nitric acids. Descloizite also fuses easily in a flame.

plumose mass of crystals

translucent

vitreous to greasy luster

Orthorhombic

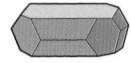

SG: 6.20	Cleavage: None	Fracture: Uneven to conchoidal

SILICATES

SILICATES ARE compounds in which metallic elements combine with either single or linked Si-O tetrahedra $(SiO_4)^{-4}$. Structurally, silicates are divided into six classes: Neosilicates have isolated $(SiO_4)^{-4}$ tetrahedra linked by a nonsilicon cation; sorosilicates feature two tetrahedra joined and sharing one common oxygen ion; cyclosilicates have tetrahedra joined into rings; inosilicates have tetrahedra joined into either single or double chains; phyllosilicates have sheetlike structures formed by the sharing of three oxygen ions by each adjacent tetrahedron; and tectosilicates are "framework" silicates in which every silicon atom shares all four of its oxygen ions with neighboring silicon atoms.

Silicates are the largest and most abundant class of minerals, while primary silicates are the main constituents of igneous and metamorphic rocks. Silicates tend to be hard, transparent to translucent, and of average density.

Group: SILICATES	Composition:	Hardness:

Olivine

This series of minerals forms as thick, tabular crystals, frequently with wedge-shaped terminations. Other habits are massive, compact, and granular. The color is green, greenish yellow, yellowish brown, brown, and white, and the streak is colorless. These are transparent to translucent minerals, and they have a vitreous luster. The gem variety of forsteritic olivine is called peridot.

FORMATION An end-member of the olivine series of minerals, forsterite forms in basic and ultrabasic igneous rocks and is also found in marbles. It is rich in magnesium. Fayalite, the other end-member, is rich in iron and forms in acid igneous rocks that have cooled rapidly.

TESTS Olivine is soluble in hydrochloric acid, with gelatinization.

transparent

striated crystal

Peridot

tabular forsterite crystals

vitreous luster

altered limestone groundmass

Forsterite

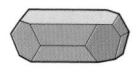

Orthorhombic

SG: 3.27–4.32	Cleavage: Imperfect	Fracture: Conchoidal

Group: SILICATES	Composition: $Mg_3Al_2(SiO_4)_3$	Hardness: $7\frac{1}{2}$

Pyrope garnet

The crystals are dodecahedral or trapezohedral. Pyrope usually occurs as rounded grains. The color ranges from pinkish or purplish red to crimson and nearly black. The streak is white in color. The mineral is transparent to translucent, and it has a vitreous luster.

FORMATION Pyrope forms in a variety of ultrabasic igneous rocks, including peridotite. It also occurs in associated serpentinites.
TESTS Fuses fairly easily and is virtually insoluble in acids.

Cubic

rounded grains

conchoidal fracture

SG: 3.58	Cleavage: None	Fracture: Conchoidal

Group: SILICATES	Composition: $Ca_3Al_2(SiO_4)_3$	Hardness: $6\frac{1}{2}$–7

Grossular garnet

This mineral forms as dodecahedral or trapezohedral crystals. Other habits are massive, compact, or granular. The color varies greatly and may be green, yellowish green, yellow, brown, red, orange, reddish brown, white, pink, gray, or black. It has a white streak. Grossular is transparent to nearly opaque and has a vitreous or resinous luster.

FORMATION Forms in a variety of metamorphic rocks, though it most commonly occurs in marble.
TESTS Insoluble in acids.

Cubic

striated crystal

twinning

SG: 3.59	Cleavage: None	Fracture: Uneven to conchoidal

Group: SILICATES	Composition: $Fe^{2+}_3Al_2(SiO_4)_3$	Hardness: 7–$7\frac{1}{2}$

Almandine garnet

The crystals are dodecahedral, rhombdodecahedral, or trapezohedral. Almandine also forms in massive, granular, and compact habits. Its color may be deep red to reddish brown and brownish black. There is a white streak. It is transparent to translucent, with a vitreous or resinous luster.

FORMATION This mineral forms in regionally metamorphosed rocks, such as schist.
TESTS It is insoluble in acids. It fuses fairly easily.

Cubic

rhombdodecahedral almandine crystals

mica schist groundmass

SG: 4.32	Cleavage: None	Fracture: Uneven to conchoidal

Group: SILICATES	Composition: $(Mg,Fe^{2+})_7(SiO_4)_3(F,OH)_2$	Hardness: 6

Humite

Small, stubby crystals with a varied, often highly modified habit are formed by this mineral. The color is white, yellow, dark orange, or brown. Humite is transparent to translucent, and it has a vitreous luster on fresh crystal surfaces.

FORMATION Forms in contact metamorphosed limestones and in some mineral veins. It occurs with numerous minerals, including calcite, graphite, spinel, diopside, idocrase, garnet, and other types of minerals typical of metamorphosed limestones. The humite group consists of humite, clinohumite, norbergite, and chondrodite.

TESTS No further tests are required to identify it.

yellowish-brown humite crystals

sanidine, an associated mineral

mica

rock groundmass

Orthorhombic

SG: 3.20–3.32	Cleavage: Poor	Fracture: Uneven

Group: SILICATES	Composition: $(Mg,Fe^{2+})_5(SiO_4)_2(F,OH)_2$	Hardness: 6–6½

Chondrodite

This mineral is a member of the humite group. It forms as varied, usually highly modified crystals, in which lamellar twinning is common. The habit may also be massive. The color is yellow, red, or brown. Chondrodite is a transparent to translucent mineral, and it has a vitreous luster.

FORMATION Forms in limestones that have been altered by contact metamorphism. It sometimes occurs in the rare, calcite-rich group of igneous rocks called carbonatites.

TESTS It is soluble in hot hydrochloric acid and produces a precipitate that takes on a gelatinous appearance as the solution cools down. It is also infusible.

twinned chondrodite crystals

rock groundmass

crystals with magnetite, an associated mineral

Monoclinic

SG: 3.16–3.26	Cleavage: Poor	Fracture: Uneven

Group: SILICATES	Composition: $Al_2SiO_4(F,OH)_2$	Hardness: 8

Topaz

This mineral occurs as well-formed prismatic crystals, which can be of great size and may weigh over 220 lb (100 kg). Topaz can also form in massive, granular, and columnar habits. The color of this mineral is very variable: it may be white, colorless, gray, yellow, orange, brown, bluish, greenish, purple, or pink. The streak is colorless. Topaz is transparent to translucent and has a vitreous luster.

FORMATION Forms most commonly in pegmatites. Topaz can also form in veins and cavities in granitic rocks. Topaz occurs with a variety of minerals, including quartz.
TESTS Insoluble in acids; infusible when flame heated.

prismatic topaz crystal

pegmatite groundmass

Orthorhombic

SG: 3.40–3.60	Cleavage: Perfect	Fracture: Subconchoidal to uneven

Group: SILICATES	Composition: Zn_2SiO_4	Hardness: 5½

Willemite

Hexagonal prismatic crystals, which are frequently terminated by rhombohedra, are formed by this mineral. It may also occur in massive, fibrous, compact, and granular habits. Willemite may be white, colorless, gray, green, yellow, brown, or reddish. The streak is colorless. Willemite is transparent to translucent, and it has a vitreous or resinous luster.

FORMATION Forms in the oxidized zone of zinc ore deposits, in veins, by secondary alteration, and in metamorphosed limestone rocks.
TESTS It can be very phosphorescent. It is soluble in hydrochloric acid. Also exhibits bright-green fluorescence under ultraviolet light.

vitreous to resinous luster

franklinite, an associated mineral

prismatic willemite crystals

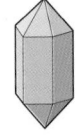
Trigonal/ Hexagonal

SG: 3.89–4.19	Cleavage: Distinct	Fracture: Uneven

Group: SILICATES	Composition: $Fe^{2+}_2Al_9Si_4O_{23}(OH)$	Hardness: $7-7\frac{1}{2}$

Staurolite

This mineral forms short, prismatic crystals, which are often in the form of cruciform twins. The color is dark brown, reddish brown, yellowish brown, or brownish black. The streak is colorless to grayish. Staurolite is translucent to nearly opaque and has a vitreous to resinous luster.

FORMATION Forms deep in the earth's crust in regionally metamorphosed rocks, such as gneisses and mica schists, that have been formed by extremes of temperature and pressure. It is associated with metamorphic minerals such as kyanite, muscovite, garnet, and quartz.

TESTS Some varieties have manganese traces, in which case they will fuse.

twinned staurolite crystals

prismatic staurolite crystal

mica schist groundmass

uneven to subconchoidal fracture

vitreous luster

Monoclinic

SG: 3.74–3.83	Cleavage: Distinct	Fracture: Uneven to subconchoidal

Group: SILICATES	Composition: $(Fe^{2+},Mg,Mn^{2+})Al_2(SiO_4)O(OH)_2$	Hardness: $6\frac{1}{2}$

Chloritoid

Crystals are rare. When they occur, they are tabular or pseudohexagonal and commonly twinned. Chloritoid usually forms in foliated or massive habits or as scales or plates. It is dark gray or greenish to greenish black in color. No streak has been determined. This is a translucent mineral. It has a pearly luster on cleavage surfaces.

FORMATION Forms in rocks, such as schist and phyllite, which have been regionally metamorphosed. Chloritoid also forms in pegmatites. Associated minerals are muscovite, chlorite, garnet, staurolite (above), as well as kyanite.

TESTS Chloritoid is soluble in concentrated sulfuric acid but not in hydrochloric acid. It fuses, but only with some difficulty.

foliated chloritoid

dark gray chloritoid crystals in pegmatite groundmass

pearly luster on cleavage surfaces

Monoclinic

SG: 3.40–3.80	Cleavage: Perfect	Fracture: Uneven

Group: SILICATES	Composition: $ZrSiO_4$	Hardness: $7\frac{1}{2}$

Zircon

This mineral forms as prismatic crystals with bipyramidal terminations and also as radiating fibrous aggregates. Twinned crystals are common. Other habits include irregular grains. Zircon is colorless, red, brown, yellow, green, or gray. Zircon is a transparent to opaque mineral and has a vitreous, adamantine, or greasy luster.

FORMATION Forms in igneous rocks, such as syenite, and in certain metamorphic rocks. Zircon also occurs in many detrital sedimentary rocks, where it is a product of weathering and erosion of primary, zircon-bearing rocks.
TESTS Zircon is often a radioactive mineral, because it can contain small amounts of uranium and thorium.

zircon crystals set in syenite groundmass

vitreous luster

prismatic zircon

Tetragonal

SG: 4.60–4.70	Cleavage: Imperfect	Fracture: Uneven to conchoidal

Group: SILICATES	Composition: $Al_2(SiO_4)O$	Hardness: $6\frac{1}{2}$–$7\frac{1}{2}$

Andalusite

This mineral forms prismatic crystals, with an almost square cross-section. (Chiastolite is a variety of andalusite with a cruciform cross-section.) Andalusite also occurs in massive, fibrous, or columnar habits. The color is pink, reddish, brownish, whitish, grayish, or greenish, and the streak is colorless. This is a transparent to nearly opaque mineral. Its luster is vitreous.

FORMATION Forms in granites and pegmatites and in many metamorphosed rocks. It occurs with kyanite, cordierite, sillimanite, and corundum.
TESTS This mineral is insoluble in any fluids and infusible when heated with a flame.

prismatic andalusite crystal

distinct cleavage

uneven fracture

Orthorhombic

SG: 3.13–3.21	Cleavage: Distinct prismatic	Fracture: Uneven to subconchoidal

Group: SILICATES	Composition: $Al_2(SiO_4)O$	Hardness: $6\frac{1}{2}$–$7\frac{1}{2}$

Sillimanite

Long prismatic crystals with an almost square cross-section are formed by this mineral. It can occur in fibrous masses. Sillimanite may be white, colorless, gray, yellowish, brownish, greenish, or bluish. The streak is colorless. It is a transparent to translucent mineral, and it has a vitreous to silky luster.

FORMATION Sillimanite forms in metamorphic rocks and also in some igneous rocks.
TESTS This mineral is infusible and is insoluble in acids.

vitreous luster

elongated prismatic sillimanite crystals

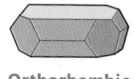

Orthorhombic

SG: 3.23–3.27	Cleavage: Perfect	Fracture: Uneven

Group: SILICATES	Composition: $Al_2(SiO_4)O$	Hardness: $5\frac{1}{2}$–7

Kyanite

Trimorphous with sillimanite and andalusite, kyanite forms elongated, flattened, and bladed crystals that are often twisted or bent. It also occurs in massive and fibrous habits. The color is blue, white, gray, green, yellow, pink, or almost black and often varies in a single crystal. There is a colorless streak. It is a transparent to translucent mineral, and it has a vitreous luster, which becomes pearly on cleavage surfaces.

FORMATION Kyanite forms in many metamorphic rocks, especially schists and gneisses. Its presence in schists allows geologists to estimate the temperature and pressure conditions in which they formed.
TESTS Its hardness is 6–7 across cleavage planes but only 4–5 along cleavage planes.

elongated kyanite crystals

vitreous luster

staurolite, an associated mineral

rock groundmass

Triclinic

SG: 3.53–3.67	Cleavage: Perfect	Fracture: Uneven

Group: SILICATES	Composition: $CaTi(SiO_4)O$	Hardness: 5–5½

Titanite

The crystals formed by titanite are wedge-shaped or prismatic and commonly twinned. This mineral also occurs in massive, lamellar, and compact habits. The color may be brown, yellow, green, gray, red, or black and often varies within a single crystal. A colorless form also occurs. The streak is white. It is a transparent to nearly opaque mineral, and it has an adamantine to resinous luster.

FORMATION Titanite occurs in many igneous rocks as an accessory mineral.
TESTS It is soluble in sulfuric acid.

twinned crystals

adamantine luster

wedge-shaped crystals

Monoclinic

SG: 3.48–3.60	Cleavage: Distinct	Fracture: Conchoidal

Group: SILICATES	Composition: $(Al,Fe^{3+})_7(SiO_4)_3(BO_3)O_3$	Hardness: 7–8

Dumortierite

On the rare occasions that dumortierite forms crystals, they are prismatic. The usual habits are massive, fibrous, radiating, and columnar. The color may be blue, violet, pink, or brown, and the streak is white. Dumortierite is a transparent to translucent mineral, and it has a vitreous to dull luster.

FORMATION This mineral forms in coarse-grained, acid igneous rocks, including pegmatites. Rocks rich in aluminum often contain dumortierite, especially when they have been altered by contact metamorphism. The exceptionally coarse-grained pegmatites are formed by very slow cooling of magmatic fluids in a chemically rich environment at some depth in the earth's crust.
TESTS It does not dissolve in any acids, and it is infusible if placed in a flame.

prismatic dumortierite crystals

quartz, an associated mineral

rock groundmass

Orthorhombic

SG: 3.21–3.41	Cleavage: Good	Fracture: Uneven

Group: SILICATES	Composition: BeAlSiO₄(OH)	Hardness: 7½

Euclase

This mineral forms as prismatic crystals. It may be colorless, whitish, pale green, blue, or pale blue. The streak is white. Euclase is transparent to translucent, and it has a vitreous luster on crystal surfaces.

FORMATION Forms in granite pegmatites. It can also occur in alluvial placer sediments.

TESTS This mineral is insoluble in acids and fuses with some difficulty.

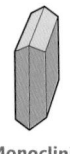
Monoclinic

prismatic crystal

perfect cleavage

SG: 2.99–3.10	Cleavage: Perfect	Fracture: Conchoidal

Group: SILICATES	Composition: K₂Ca₄Al₂Be₄Si₂₄O₆₀.H₂O	Hardness: 6

Milarite

This mineral forms as prismatic crystals. It is colorless, brownish, pale green, or yellowish green, with a white streak. This is a transparent to translucent mineral that has a vitreous luster.

FORMATION Milarite forms in alpine veins and pegmatites.

TESTS Gives off water when heated in a closed test tube.

Trigonal/ Hexagonal

rock groundmass

prismatic milarite crystal

SG: 2.46–2.61	Cleavage: None	Fracture: Conchoidal to uneven

Group: SILICATES	Composition: Na₁₅Ca₆Fe₃Zr₃Si(Si₂₅O₇₃)(O,OH,H₂O)₃(Cl,OH)₂	Hardness: 5–6

Eudialyte

Crystals are tabular, rhombohedral, or prismatic. Eudialyte is yellowish brown to brownish red, red, or pink in color, and the streak is white to pale pink. This is a translucent mineral that has a vitreous to dull luster.

FORMATION Forms in coarse-grained acid and intermediate igneous rocks.

TESTS This mineral is easily dissolved in acids.

Trigonal/ Hexagonal

uneven fracture

arfvedsonite, an associated mineral

SG: 2.74–3.10	Cleavage: Perfect	Fracture: Uneven

Group: SILICATES	Composition: $CaBSiO_4(OH)$	Hardness: 5–5½

Datolite

This mineral forms as short, prismatic crystals and also as granular or compact masses. It is colorless, white, pale yellow, pale green, or tinted pink, reddish, or brown by impurities. The streak is white. Datolite is a transparent to opaque mineral with a vitreous luster.

FORMATION This mineral forms in veins and cavities in basaltic igneous rocks. It occurs with calcite, quartz, and some zeolite minerals.

TESTS Datolite is soluble in acids and turns a flame green.

short, prismatic crystals

vitreous luster

Monoclinic

SG: 2.96–3.00	Cleavage: None	Fracture: Uneven to conchoidal

Group: SILICATES	Composition: $Y_2Fe^{2+}Be_2Si_2O_{10}$	Hardness: 6½–7

Gadolinite-(Y)

Crystals are prismatic but rarely form. Gadolinite-(Y) usually occurs in massive and compact habits. The color varies considerably from black to greenish black, brown, and sometimes light green, with a greenish-gray streak. It is an opaque mineral with a vitreous to greasy luster.

FORMATION Forms in coarse-grained intermediate igneous rocks. Gadolinite-(Y) can also occur in acid igneous rocks and in pegmatites formed by the slow cooling of intruded magma. This mineral is found with other minerals, including allanite and fluorite, and has been discovered in schists and other regionally metamorphosed rocks.

TESTS Gadolinite-(Y) is a radioactive mineral that dissolves in acids, leaving a gelatinous precipitate. Although gadolinite-(Y) is not fusible when heated, it will, however, become flaky and turn brown in color.

Monoclinic

vitreous luster

SG: 4.36–4.77	Cleavage: None	Fracture: Conchoidal

Group: SILICATES	Composition: $Ca_2(Al,Fe)_3(SiO_4)_3(OH)$	Hardness: 6

Epidote

Occurring as prismatic crystals, which are often striated, epidote also forms thick, tabular, and acicular crystals. Other habits are massive, granular, and fibrous. The color is yellowish green to green, brownish green to greenish black, or black. There is a colorless streak. Epidote is a transparent to nearly opaque mineral, and it has a vitreous luster.

FORMATION Forms in metamorphic and igneous rocks.
TESTS It is insoluble and fuses fairly easily.

vitreous luster

striated prismatic crystal

Monoclinic

SG: 3.38–3.49	Cleavage: Perfect	Fracture: Uneven

Group: SILICATES	Composition: $Ca_2Al_3[Si_2O_7][SiO_4]O(OH)$	Hardness: 6–7

Zoisite

This mineral occurs as prismatic crystals, which often have deep vertical striations. It also forms in massive, compact, and columnar habits. The color may be white, gray, green, greenish brown, pink (thulite), colorless, blue, or purple (tanzanite). There is a white streak. It is a transparent to translucent mineral. The luster is vitreous.

FORMATION Zoisite forms in many rocks, including granites and metamorphosed sediments.
TESTS Insoluble in acids.

Thulite

massive habit

pegmatite groundmass

prismatic zoisite crystals

deep striations on crystal faces

Zoisite

Orthorhombic

SG: 3.15–3.36	Cleavage: Perfect	Fracture: Uneven to conchoidal

Group: SILICATES	Composition: $Ca_2Al_3[Si_2O_7][SiO_4]O(OH)$	Hardness: 7

Clinozoisite

Crystals are prismatic and often deeply striated. The mineral also forms as acicular crystals and in massive, granular, or fibrous habits. It may be gray, yellow, pale green, pink, or colorless. The streak is grayish. Clinozoisite is a transparent to translucent mineral and has a vitreous luster.

FORMATION Forms in contact metamorphosed limestones and regionally metamorphosed rocks.
TESTS Insoluble in acids.

Monoclinic

SG: 3.30–3.40	Cleavage: Perfect	Fracture: Uneven

Group: SILICATES	Composition: $Ca_2Al(AlSiO_7)$	Hardness: 5–6

Gehlenite

A member of the melilite group, gehlenite occurs as short, prismatic crystals and also in massive and granular habits. Gehlenite can be grayish green, brown, yellow, or colorless. The streak is white or grayish. It is transparent to translucent, with a vitreous to resinous luster.

FORMATION Gehlenite forms in basaltic lavas and contact metamorphosed limestones.
TESTS Soluble in strong acids.

calcite, an associated mineral

short, prismatic gehlenite crystals

Tetragonal

SG: 3.04	Cleavage: Distinct	Fracture: Uneven to conchoidal

Group: SILICATES	Composition: $Ca_2MgSi_2O_7$	Hardness: 5–6

Akermanite

This mineral forms prismatic crystals, which may be twinned. It can occur in massive and granular habits. Akermanite varies from colorless to grayish, brown, and green. The streak is white. It is transparent to translucent, with a vitreous to resinous luster.

FORMATION Forms in thermally metamorphosed impure limestones.
TESTS It is soluble in strong acids, with gelatinization.

prismatic crystal

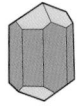

Tetragonal

SG: 2.94	Cleavage: Distinct	Fracture: Uneven to conchoidal

Group: SILICATES	Composition: $Zn_4Si_2O_7(OH)_2 \cdot H_2O$	Hardness: $4\frac{1}{2}$–5

Hemimorphite

This mineral forms as thin, tabular crystals with vertical striations. The crystals have different terminations at each end, which are termed hemimorphic. Hemimorphite also occurs in massive, compact, granular, botryoidal, stalactitic, fibrous, and encrusting habits. The color is white, colorless, blue, greenish, gray, yellowish, or brown, and the streak is white. It is transparent to translucent, with a vitreous or silky luster.

FORMATION Forms where zinc veins have been altered by oxidation. It commonly occurs in mineral veins along with many other minerals, including smithsonite, galena, calcite, anglesite, sphalerite, cerussite, and aurichalcite.

TESTS Hemimorphite gives off water when heated in a closed tube. It is soluble in acids with gelatinization and fuses only with great difficulty.

Botryoidal hemimorphite

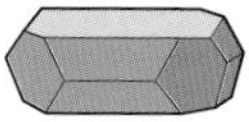

crust of strikingly colored, rounded masses

rock groundmass

Orthorhombic

clusters of crystals

botryoidal masses

Green hemimorphite

translucent crystals

vitreous luster

Crystalline hemimorphite

SG: 3.47	Cleavage: Perfect	Fracture: Uneven to conchoidal

Group: SILICATES	Composition: $(Ca,Na)_{19}(Al,Mg,Fe)_{13}(SiO_4)_{10}(Si_2O_7)_4(OH,F,O)_{10}$	Hardness: $6\frac{1}{2}$

Vesuvianite

Also known as idocrase, this mineral forms short, prismatic and pyramidal crystals. It can also occur in massive, granular, columnar, and compact habits. Idocrase is green, brown, white, yellow, red, or purple. A blue variety is called cyprine, and californite is green. The streak is white. This transparent to translucent mineral has a vitreous to resinous luster. A semiprecious gemstone when transparent, vesuvianite was discovered at Mount Vesuvius in Italy.

FORMATION Vesuvianite forms in impure limestones that have been altered by contact metamorphism. It also occurs in some igneous rocks, including nepheline syenite. It is found with many minerals, including diopside, epidote, garnets, calcite, phlogopite, and wollastonite.
TESTS This mineral is virtually insoluble in acids.

prismatic crystal

vitreous luster on crystal faces

Vesuvianite

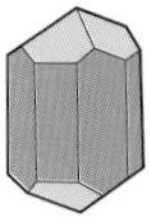

Tetragonal

massive habit

columnar crystal

Cyprine

thulite, an associated mineral

Californite

SG: 3.32–3.43	Cleavage: Indistinct	Fracture: Uneven to conchoidal

Group: SILICATES	Composition: $Be_3Al_2Si_6O_{18}$	Hardness: $7\frac{1}{2}$–8

Beryl

This mineral occurs as prismatic crystals, which are sometimes terminated with small pyramids. The crystals are often striated parallel to their length and may be of vast size; specimens up to 18 feet (5.5 m) long have been recorded. Beryl also forms in massive, compact, and columnar habits. The color varies greatly and gives rise to named varieties. It may be colorless, white, green (emerald), yellow (heliodor), pink (morganite), red, and blue (aquamarine). The streak is white. Beryl is transparent to translucent, with a vitreous luster.

FORMATION Forms in pegmatites and granites and in some regionally metamorphosed rocks.
TESTS It fuses with difficulty, rounding the edges of small fragments.

transparent

prismatic crystal

Beryl

rock groundmass

rock groundmass

vitreous luster

perfect prismatic crystal

Aquamarine

Emerald

Trigonal/ Hexagonal

transparent to translucent

translucent

Heliodor

Morganite

vitreous luster

SG: 2.63–2.92	Cleavage: Indistinct	Fracture: Uneven to conchoidal

Group: SILICATES	Composition: $Na(Mg,Fe,Li,Mn,Al)_3Al_6(BO_3)_3Si_6.O_{18}(OH,F)_4$	Hardness: 7

Tourmaline

The prismatic crystals formed by this group are often vertically striated and may be rounded triangular in cross-section. Tourmaline also forms in massive and compact habits. Seven distinct minerals make up the tourmaline group: elbaite (multihued), schorl (black), buergerite and dravite (brown), rubellite (pink), chromdravite (green), and uvite (black, brown, yellow-green). Crystals are often pink at one end and green at the other and may be of considerable size. There is a colorless streak. Tourmaline is transparent to opaque and has a vitreous luster.

FORMATION Forms in granites and pegmatites, as well as in some metamorphic rocks. Tourmaline may be found with a wide range of minerals, including beryl, zircon, quartz, and feldspar.

TESTS This group is insoluble in acids. The darker minerals tend to fuse with more difficulty than the red and green varieties.

vertically striated crystal

Rubellite

quartz, an associated mineral

schorl crystal

Schorl

vitreous luster

prismatic crystal

Elbaite

Trigonal/
Hexagonal

feldspar groundmass

transparent two-colored crystal

vitreous luster

Tourmaline

SG: 2.90–3.10	Cleavage: Very indistinct	Fracture: Uneven to conchoidal

Group: SILICATES	Composition: $CaFe^{3+}Fe^{2+}_2(Si_2O_7)O(OH)$	Hardness: 5½–6

Ilvaite

The crystals of this mineral are thick and prismatic, and diamond-shaped in cross-section. The crystal faces may be striated vertically. Ilvaite also occurs in massive, columnar, and compact habits. It is a very dark-colored mineral, often black to grayish brown or brownish black in color. The streak is black, often with greenish or brownish tints. This is an opaque mineral with a dull, submetallic luster, which sometimes appears glossy.

FORMATION Forms in rocks that have been intruded by magma or come into contact with lava, and as a result have been altered by contact metamorphism. It also occurs, less commonly, in the igneous rock syenite.

TESTS When placed in hydrochloric acid, ilvaite is soluble, with gelatinization. It fuses easily in a flame.

submetallic luster

diamond-shaped crystal cross-sections

vertical striations

prismatic crystals

Orthorhombic

SG: 3.99–4.05	Cleavage: Distinct	Fracture: Uneven

Group: SILICATES	Composition: $CuSiO_3.H_2O$	Hardness: 5

Dioptase

This mineral forms prismatic crystals, often with rhombohedral terminations. It may also occur as crystalline aggregates or in a massive habit. The color is a striking emerald to deep bluish green, and the streak is pale greenish blue. Dioptase is transparent to translucent. It has a vitreous luster.

FORMATION Occurs where copper veins have been altered by oxidation and in hollows and cavities in the surrounding rocks. Dioptase is usually associated with limonite, chrysocolla, and cerussite, as well as wulfenite.

TESTS Soluble in hydrochloric acid, nitric acid, and ammonia. Infusible.

prismatic crystals

rhombohedral terminations

aggregate of crystals

Trigonal/ Hexagonal

SG: 3.28–3.35	Cleavage: Perfect	Fracture: Uneven to conchoidal

Group: SILICATES	Composition: $(Mg,Fe)_2Al_3(AlSi_5O_{18})$	Hardness: 7–7½

Cordierite

Crystals are short and prismatic, and twinning is common. Other habits are massive and granular. This mineral is blue, but can be greenish, yellowish, gray, or brown, and is often strongly pleochroic. The streak is colorless. Cordierite is transparent to translucent, with a vitreous luster.

FORMATION Cordierite forms in igneous and contact metamorphic rocks.
TESTS Fusible on thin edges in a flame.

rock groundmass

prismatic cordierite crystal

Orthorhombic

SG: 2.60–2.66	Cleavage: Distinct	Fracture: Conchoidal

Group: SILICATES	Composition: $Ca_2(Fe^{+2},Mn^{+2})Al_2BSi_4O_{15}(OH)$	Hardness: 6½–7

Axinite

Crystals are tabular and wedge-shaped. Other habits are massive and lamellar. Axinite is reddish brown, yellow, colorless, blue, violet, or gray and has a colorless streak. It is transparent to translucent and has a vitreous luster.

FORMATION Forms in calcareous rocks altered by contact metamorphism.
TESTS Axinite fuses easily.

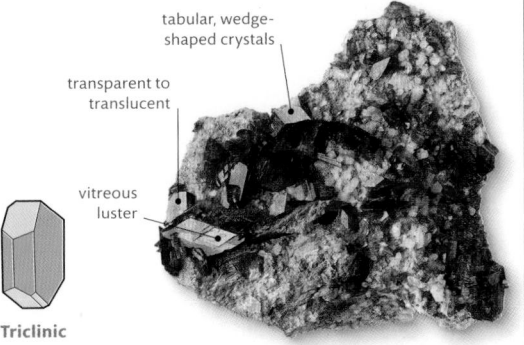

tabular, wedge-shaped crystals

transparent to translucent

vitreous luster

Triclinic

SG: 3.25–3.28	Cleavage: Good	Fracture: Uneven to conchoidal

Group: SILICATES	Composition: $BaTiSi_3O_9$	Hardness: 6–6½

Benitoite

The crystals are pyramidal or tabular. Benitoite is blue, purple, pink, white, or colorless and often multicolored. The streak is colorless. Benitoite is a transparent to translucent mineral with a vitreous luster.

FORMATION Forms in serpentinites and also in schists.
TESTS It fluoresces blue under shortwave ultraviolet light.

rock groundmass

Trigonal/ Hexagonal

pyramidal benitoite crystals

natrolite, an associated mineral

SG: 3.65	Cleavage: Indistinct	Fracture: Conchoidal to uneven

Group: SILICATES	Composition: MgSiO₃		Hardness: 5–6

Enstatite

small prismatic crystals

A member of the pyroxene group, enstatite forms rarely as prismatic crystals, usually in massive, fibrous, or lamellar habits. It may be colorless, green, brown, or yellowish and has a white or gray streak. Enstatite is a transparent to nearly opaque mineral with a vitreous or pearly luster.

FORMATION Commonly forms in mafic and ultramafic igneous rocks, such as gabbro, dolerite, norite, and peridotite.
TESTS Insoluble and almost infusible.

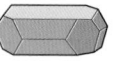

Orthorhombic

SG: 3.20–3.90	Cleavage: Good		Fracture: Uneven

Group: SILICATES	Composition: (Mg,Fe)SiO₃		Hardness: 5½–6

Hypersthene

Hypersthene is a pyroxene usually found in massive or lamellar habits, rarely as prismatic crystals. The color is brownish green, grayish, or black. The streak is brownish gray. It is a translucent to opaque mineral and has a vitreous or silky luster.

FORMATION Hypersthene forms in both ultramafic and mafic igneous rocks.
TESTS It is fusible and may display schillerization.

Orthorhombic

SG: 3.4–3.8	Cleavage: Good		Fracture: Uneven

Group: SILICATES	Composition: CaMgSi₂O₆		Hardness: 5½–6½

Diopside

A pyroxene, diopside forms short, prismatic crystals, which are often twinned. Other habits are massive, lamellar, granular, and columnar. It is colorless, white, gray, green, greenish black, yellowish brown, or reddish brown and has a white streak. It is transparent to nearly opaque, with a vitreous or dull luster.

FORMATION Diopside forms in many metamorphic rocks and in mafic igneous rocks.
TESTS It is insoluble in acids.

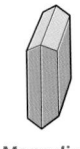

Monoclinic

SG: 3.22–3.38	Cleavage: Good		Fracture: Uneven to conchoidal

Group: SILICATES	Composition: $CaFe^{2+}Si_2O_6$	Hardness: $5\frac{1}{2}$–$6\frac{1}{2}$

Hedenbergite

mass of bladed crystals

Crystals are short and prismatic and commonly twinned. More usual habits are massive, bladed, or lamellar. The color varies from brownish green, grayish green, or dark green to grayish black or black. There is a white or gray streak. Hedenbergite is transparent to nearly opaque, with a vitreous or dull luster.

FORMATION In marbles and a variety of igneous rocks.
TESTS This pyroxene is insoluble and fuses fairly easily.

Monoclinic

SG: 3.56	Cleavage: Good	Fracture: Uneven to conchoidal

Group: SILICATES	Composition: $(Ca,Mg,Fe)_2Si_2O_6$	Hardness: $5\frac{1}{2}$–6

Augite

prismatic augite crystal

vitreous luster

A pyroxene, augite occurs as short, prismatic crystals, which are often twinned. It also forms in massive, compact, and granular habits. The color is brown, greenish, or black. There is a grayish-green or brownish streak. Augite is translucent to nearly opaque, with a vitreous to dull luster.

FORMATION Forms in many mafic and ultramafic igneous rocks and in high-grade metamorphic rocks.
TESTS Usually insoluble in acids.

Monoclinic

rock groundmass

SG: 3.19–3.56	Cleavage: Good	Fracture: Uneven to conchoidal

Group: SILICATES	Composition: $NaFe^{3+}Si_2O_6$	Hardness: 6

Aegirine

striated prismatic aegirine crystal

A member of the pyroxene group, aegirine forms long, vertically striated, prismatic crystals, which are often twinned. It also occurs as fibrous aggregates. The color is dark green, greenish black, black, or reddish brown. There is a pale yellowish-gray streak. Aegirine is transparent to opaque, with a vitreous luster.

FORMATION Forms in intermediate igneous rocks and in metamorphic rocks.
TESTS Fuses easily.

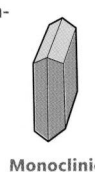

Monoclinic

SG: 3.50–3.60	Cleavage: Good	Fracture: Uneven

Group: SILICATES	Composition: $LiAlSi_2O_6$	Hardness: 6½–7

Spodumene

This mineral forms as prismatic crystals, which are often flattened, twinned, and vertically striated. They may be of great size. Spodumene also occurs as cleavable masses. The color varies greatly. It may be colorless, white, gray, yellowish, greenish, emerald green (hiddenite), pink, or lilac (kunzite). The streak is white. Spodumene is transparent to translucent. This pyroxene has a vitreous or dull luster.

FORMATION Forms in granitic pegmatites. It is found with other pegmatite minerals, including feldspar, muscovite, biotite and lepidolite, quartz, columbite, beryl, tourmaline, and topaz. Spodumene is often partially or totally altered to clay or mica.

TESTS Spodumene is an insoluble mineral. It fuses, coloring the flame red due to the presence of lithium.

Kunzite

prismatic habit

vitreous luster

striations

pegmatite groundmass

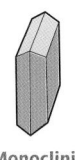

Monoclinic

Spodumene

SG: 3.10–3.20	Cleavage: Perfect	Fracture: Uneven

Group: SILICATES	Composition: $Na(Al,Fe^{3+})Si_2O_6$	Hardness: 6

Jadeite

It is rare for jadeite to form crystals. When it does, the crystals are small, prismatic, and elongated. They are usually striated and often twinned. It mostly occurs in massive or granular habits. The color is typically green but can be white; gray; lilac; and, when stained by iron oxides, brown or yellow. The streak is white. Jadeite is an important ornamental gem and is translucent, with a vitreous to pearly luster.

FORMATION Forms in serpentinized ultramafic igneous rocks and in some schists. It has also been found as small veins and lens-shaped inclusions in chert and greywacke.

TESTS Jadeite is insoluble.

massive habit

Monoclinic

SG: 3.25–3.35	Cleavage: Good	Fracture: Splintery

Group: SILICATES	Composition: $Ca_2(Mg,Fe)_4Al(Si_7Al)O_{22}(OH,F)_2$	Hardness: 6

Hornblende group

These amphiboles form prismatic crystals, often hexagonal in cross-section, and frequently twinned. They also occur in massive, compact, granular, columnar, bladed, and fibrous habits. They are green, greenish brown, or black. The streak is white or gray. These minerals are translucent to opaque. The luster is vitreous. There is an angle of 60° or 120° between cleavage planes.

FORMATION In igneous rocks and also found in the metamorphic rock amphibolite.
TESTS Insoluble. Fuses with difficulty.

Monoclinic

prismatic crystal

SG: 3.14–3.41	Cleavage: Perfect	Fracture: Uneven

Group: SILICATES	Composition: $(Mg,Fe)_7Si_8O_{22}(OH)_2$	Hardness: 5½–6

Anthophyllite

Anthophyllite forms prismatic crystals, but these are rare. It occurs in massive, fibrous, or lamellar habits. The color is white to gray, greenish, brownish green, and brown. There is a white or gray streak. This mineral is transparent to translucent. It has a vitreous luster.

FORMATION Forms in crystalline schists and gneisses.
TESTS Insoluble, but fuses with difficulty.

Orthorhombic

radiating crystals

SG: 2.85–3.57	Cleavage: Perfect	Fracture: Conchoidal

Group: SILICATES	Composition: $(Fe,Mg)_7Si_8O_{22}(OH)_2$	Hardness: 5–6

Grunerite

An end member of the cummingtonite-grunerite amphibole series, grunerite forms as fibrous or lamellar crystals, which are often in radiating aggregates. They are very commonly twinned. Grunerite is gray, dark green, or brown. It is translucent to nearly opaque and has a silky luster.

FORMATION In rocks that have undergone contact metamorphism.
TESTS Grunerite is insoluble.

Monoclinic

opaque

SG: 3.44–3.60	Cleavage: Good	Fracture: Uneven

Group: SILICATES	Composition: $Na_2(Mg,Fe)_3Al_2Si_8O_{22}(OH)_2$	Hardness: 5–6

Glaucophane

A member of the amphibole group, glaucophane forms as slender, prismatic crystals. Other habits are massive, fibrous, and granular. It is gray, lavender-blue, or bluish black. The streak is a grayish blue. Glaucophane is a translucent mineral and has a vitreous to pearly luster.

FORMATION Forms in metamorphic rocks, chiefly those subjected to low-temperature and high-pressure conditions.
TESTS It is insoluble in acids and fuses to a green-colored glass.

pearly luster

Monoclinic

SG: 3.08–3.15	Cleavage: Good	Fracture: Uneven to conchoidal

Group: SILICATES	Composition: $Na_2(Fe^{+2},Mg)_4Fe^{+3}Si_8O_{22}(OH)_2$	Hardness: 5–5½

Riebeckite

Long, prismatic crystals with parallel striations occur in this mineral. It may also be massive, fibrous, and asbestiform (crocidolite). The color is dark blue to black. The streak is pale gray to bluish gray. Riebeckite is translucent, and it has a vitreous or silky luster.

FORMATION Forms in many igneous rocks, and in schists.
TESTS Fuses fairly easily.

striated prismatic crystal

vitreous luster

Monoclinic

SG: 3.32–3.38	Cleavage: Perfect	Fracture: Uneven

Group: SILICATES	Composition: $Ca_2(Mg,Fe)_2Si_8O_{22}(OH)_2$	Hardness: 5–6

Actinolite

The crystals form as long, bladed specimens, commonly twinned. Actinolite may be in lamellar and columnar aggregates, often radiating, and in massive, fibrous, or granular habits. The color is light to blackish green. The streak is white. Actinolite is transparent to translucent and has a vitreous luster. A compact variety is called nephrite, a form of jade.

FORMATION Forms in schists and amphibolites, commonly from the metamorphism of mafic igneous rocks.
TESTS Insoluble in hydrochloric acid.

prismatic crystal

talc groundmass

Monoclinic

SG: 3.03–3.24	Cleavage: Good	Fracture: Splintery

Group: SILICATES	Composition: $Ca_2(Mg,Fe)_5Si_8O_{22}(OH)_2$	Hardness: 5–6

Tremolite

This mineral occurs as long, bladed crystals, which are often twinned. It also forms as columnar, fibrous, or plumose aggregates, often radiating, and in massive or granular habits. It is colorless, white, gray, green, pink, or brown. The streak is white. Tremolite is transparent to translucent; it has a vitreous to silky luster. It forms a series with actinolite.

radiating aggregate

FORMATION Found in contact metamorphosed dolomites and in serpentinites.
TESTS Insoluble in acids.

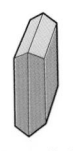
Monoclinic

SG: 2.99–3.03	Cleavage: Perfect	Fracture: Splintery

Group: SILICATES	Composition: $(Ca,Na)(Mg,Fe,Al,Ti)(Si,Al)_2O_6$	Hardness: 5½–6

Arfvedsonite

This mineral occurs as prismatic and tabular crystals, frequently in aggregates. It is often twinned. The color is bluish black to black. The streak is dark bluish gray. Arfvedsonite is almost opaque and has a vitreous luster.

FORMATION Forms in igneous rocks, especially syenite. Also found in some regionally metamorphosed rocks, including schists.
TESTS Insoluble in acids. Fuses easily, producing a magnetic black glass.

Monoclinic

rock groundmass

SG: 3.30–3.50	Cleavage: Perfect	Fracture: Uneven

Group: SILICATES	Composition: $Na_2Ca(Mg,Fe)_5Si_8O_{22}(OH)_2$	Hardness: 5–6

Richterite

The crystals formed by this mineral are long and prismatic. The color is brown, yellow, brownish red, or pale to dark green. There is a white streak. Richterite is transparent, and it has a vitreous luster on fresh surfaces.

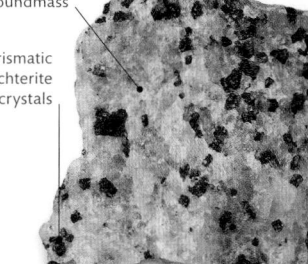
quartz groundmass

prismatic richterite crystals

FORMATION Forms in extrusive alkali-rich igneous rocks and in contact metamorphosed limestones.
TESTS This mineral is almost insoluble when placed in acids but fuses when heated in a flame.

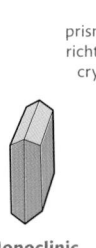
Monoclinic

SG: 3.10	Cleavage: Perfect	Fracture: Uneven

Group: SILICATES	Composition: $Mn^{2+}SiO_3$	Hardness: $5\frac{1}{2}$–$6\frac{1}{2}$

Rhodonite

This mineral occurs as tabular crystals, often with rounded edges, and also in massive, compact, and granular habits. The color is pink to rose red and can be brownish red. It often has black veins of manganese-rich alteration products. The streak is white. It is a transparent to translucent mineral. Rhodonite has a vitreous luster on crystal faces, which becomes pearly on cleavage surfaces.

FORMATION This mineral forms in metamorphic rocks rich in manganese and metasomatically altered sediments. These rocks include skarns and marbles, especially those that were originally impure limestones.

TESTS Rhodonite fuses fairly easily. This process produces a glassy substance that may be colored.

transparent to translucent

massive habit

uneven fracture

vitreous luster

Triclinic

SG: 3.57–3.76	Cleavage: Perfect	Fracture: Conchoidal to uneven

Group: SILICATES	Composition: $NaCa_2Si_3O_8(OH)$	Hardness: $4\frac{1}{2}$–5

Pectolite

This mineral occurs as aggregates of acicular (needlelike) crystals, which usually form globular masses. It may also form as tabular crystals. Pectolite is white, grayish, or colorless. The streak is white. This mineral is transparent to translucent, with a vitreous or silky luster.

FORMATION Pectolite forms in cavities in basaltic lava, often with zeolite minerals, such as heulandite-Na, phillipsite-K, analcime, chabazite, and natrolite. These cavities are usually vesicles where gas bubbles existed in the lava. When the vesicles are infilled, they are referred to as amygdales, and the rock texture is called amygdaloidal.

TESTS This mineral gelatinizes with hydrochloric acid. If heated in a closed test tube, water is given off.

Triclinic

radiating aggregate of acicular crystals

silky luster

SG: 2.84–2.90	Cleavage: Perfect	Fracture: Uneven

Group: SILICATES	Composition: $CaSiO_3$	Hardness: $4\frac{1}{2}$–5

Wollastonite

Crystals are tabular and frequently twinned. Wollastonite also forms in massive, fibrous, granular, and compact habits. The color is white to grayish and sometimes very pale green or colorless. There is a white streak. This is a transparent to translucent mineral, and it has a vitreous to pearly luster on fresh faces.

FORMATION Forms by the metamorphism of impure limestones. When this occurs, wollastonite may be associated with brucite and epidote. These minerals often produce the brightly colored veins in marble. Wollastonite is also found in some igneous rocks and in regionally metamorphosed slates, phyllites, and schists.

TESTS It is soluble in acids, producing a separation of the silica in its composition. This mineral also fuses fairly easily.

uneven fracture

twinned crystals

Triclinic

SG: 2.86–3.09	Cleavage: Perfect	Fracture: Uneven

Group: SILICATES	Composition: $Na_2KLiFe^{2+}_2Ti_2Si_8O_{24}$	Hardness: 5–6

Neptunite

This mineral occurs as prismatic crystals with a square cross-section. The color is black, though there may be some deep reddish-brown internal reflections. The streak is reddish brown in color. Neptunite is an almost opaque mineral and has a vitreous luster.

FORMATION Forms as an accessory mineral in intermediate, plutonic, igneous rocks, such as nepheline syenite, and in pegmatites of similar, broad chemical composition. It also occurs in serpentinites, where it is associated with the minerals benitoite and natrolite.

TESTS When placed in hydrochloric acid, neptunite is insoluble. In a flame, it is infusible.

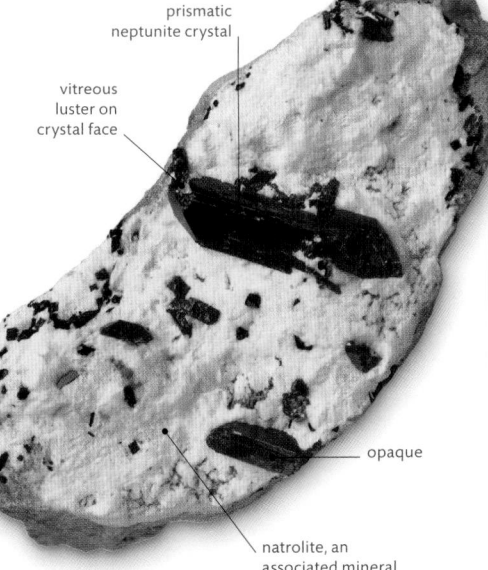

prismatic neptunite crystal

vitreous luster on crystal face

opaque

natrolite, an associated mineral

Monoclinic

SG: 3.19–3.23	Cleavage: Perfect	Fracture: Conchoidal

Group: SILICATES	Composition: $Mg_3Si_2O_5(OH)_4$	Hardness: $3\frac{1}{2}$–4

Antigorite

Crystals are minute and flaky or lath-shaped. Antigorite also occurs in massive, fibrous, or foliated habits. It is white, yellow, green, or brown. The streak is greenish white. This mineral is transparent to opaque, with a resinous or silky luster.

FORMATION Antigorite forms in serpentinites, derived from ultramafic, igneous rocks.
TESTS Fuses with difficulty.

fibrous habit

Monoclinic

SG: 2.50–2.60	Cleavage: Perfect	Fracture: Conchoidal or splintery

---

Group: SILICATES	Composition: $Mg_3Si_2O_5(OH)_4$	Hardness: $2\frac{1}{2}$

Chrysotile

This mineral has a fibrous habit, separating into flexible fibers. It is a variety of asbestos. The color is white, gray, green, yellow, or brown. It is translucent to opaque, with a silky luster.

FORMATION Forms in serpentinites by the alteration of ultramafic rocks.
TESTS Infusible, but soluble in strong acids.

mass of thin fibers

silky luster

Monoclinic

SG: 2.53–2.61	Cleavage: None	Fracture: Uneven

Group: SILICATES	Composition: $Mg_3Si_4O_{10}(OH)_2$	Hardness: 1

Talc

Crystals are rare. It usually occurs in massive, compact, foliated, and fibrous habits. The color is pale to dark green, gray, brownish, or white. There is a white streak. Talc is translucent, with a resinous to pearly or greasy luster.

FORMATION Forms by the alteration of ultramafic igneous rocks and dolomites.
TESTS Insoluble and infusible, it is easily scratched and feels greasy.

Triclinic

massive habit

SG: 2.58–2.83	Cleavage: Perfect	Fracture: Uneven

Group: SILICATES	Composition: $(Cu,Al)_2H_2Si_2O_5(OH)_4 \cdot nH_2O$	Hardness: 2½–3½

Chrysocolla

This mineral forms as acicular, microscopic crystals in radiating groups or close-packed aggregates. It also occurs in massive, earthy, cryptocrystalline, and botryoidal habits. The color is green, blue, and blue-green. Chrysocolla can also be brown to black when impurities are present. The streak is pale green. This mineral is translucent to nearly opaque, and it has a vitreous to earthy luster.

FORMATION Chrysocolla forms in the altered parts of copper deposits. It occurs with azurite, malachite, and cuprite. It is also an important mineral for ore prospectors, as its presence may suggest that copper deposits are nearby.
TESTS It decomposes in hydrochloric acid.

opaque

massive
habit

Orthorhombic

SG: 1.93–2.40	Cleavage: None	Fracture: Uneven to conchoidal

Group: SILICATES	Composition: Be_2SiO_4	Hardness: 7½–8

Phenakite

This mineral forms as prismatic or rhombohedral crystals, which are often twinned. It also occurs in granular habit and as radiating, fibrous spherulites. It may be colorless, white, yellow, pink, or brown, with a white streak. Phenakite is a transparent mineral and has a vitreous luster.

FORMATION Forms in hydrothermal veins and in granitic igneous rocks, including pegmatites and greisens (altered granites). It can also occur in some schists. In this occurrence, phenakite is associated with beryl, chrysoberyl, topaz, quartz, and apatite.
TESTS Phenakite is insoluble in acids and infusible.

rhombohedral
crystal

**Trigonal/
Hexagonal**

twinned
crystals

SG: 2.96–3.00	Cleavage: Distinct	Fracture: Conchoidal

Group: SILICATES	Composition: KAl$_2$(Si$_3$Al)O$_{10}$(OH)$_2$		Hardness: 2½

Muscovite

Tabular, pseudohexagonal crystals are formed by muscovite, and twinning is common. Other habits are lamellar and cryptocrystalline. Muscovite also forms as scaly and compact masses and disseminated flakes. It varies from colorless to white or gray and may be tinged with yellow, green, brown, red, or violet. The streak is white. It is a transparent to translucent mineral with a vitreous to pearly luster.

FORMATION Forms in igneous rocks, especially those of felsic composition like granite, and in metamorphic rocks such as schist and gneiss. There is a particular schist, called mica schist, which can be extremely rich in muscovite.
TESTS This mineral is insoluble in acids.

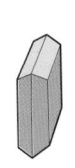

Monoclinic

pearly luster

tabular pseudo-hexagonal crystal

vitreous luster

SG: 2.77–2.88	Cleavage: Perfect	Fracture: Uneven

Group: SILICATES	Composition: KLi$_2$Al(Si$_4$O$_{10}$)(F,OH)$_2$		Hardness: 2½–3½

Lepidolite

This mineral occurs as tabular, pseudohexagonal crystals and as scaly aggregates and cleavable masses. The color is lilac, pink, grayish, and white, though it can be colorless. The streak is white. Lepidolite is a transparent to translucent mineral with a resinous to pearly luster.

FORMATION Forms in felsic igneous rocks, such as granite and pegmatite. This mineral is often associated with tourmaline, amblygonite, and spodumene.
TESTS It fuses easily, coloring a flame red, and is insoluble in acids.

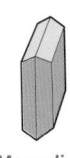

Monoclinic

tabular lepidolite crystal

pegmatitic groundmass

vitreous luster

SG: 2.80–2.90	Cleavage: Perfect	Fracture: Uneven

Group: SILICATES	Composition: $K(Mg,Fe^{+2})_3(Al,Fe^{+3})Si_3O_{10}(OH,F)_2$	Hardness: $2\frac{1}{2}$–3

Biotite

The name biotite is now a general term for any dark-colored, iron-rich mica. It occurs as tabular or short prismatic pseudohexagonal crystals and as disseminated flakes. The color is black, dark brown, or dark green, and the streak is white. Biotite is transparent to translucent, with a vitreous luster.

FORMATION Forms in both igneous and metamorphic rocks.
TESTS Biotite is soluble in hot, concentrated sulfuric acid.

tabular crystal

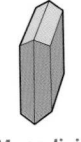
Monoclinic

SG: 2.70–3.40	Cleavage: Perfect basal	Fracture: Uneven

Group: SILICATES	Composition: $KMg_3(AlSi_3O_{10})(OH)_2$	Hardness: 2–3

Phlogopite

This mineral forms as prismatic and pseudohexagonal crystals, which are often tapered and sometimes twinned. It also occurs as plates and scales. Phlogopite can be brownish, yellowish, or greenish. There is a white streak. The mineral is transparent to translucent, with a vitreous to pearly luster.

FORMATION In ultramafic igneous and metamorphic rocks.
TESTS This mineral is soluble in concentrated sulfuric acid.

prismatic phlogopite crystal

rock groundmass

Monoclinic

SG: 2.78–2.85	Cleavage: Perfect	Fracture: Uneven

Group: SILICATES	Composition: $(K,Na)(Fe^{3+},Al,Mg)_2(Si,Al)_4O_{10}(OH)_2$	Hardness: 2

Glauconite

Glauconite occurs as minute crystals, but usually as rounded, granular aggregates. It is dull green, bluish green, or yellowish green. Glauconite is a translucent to opaque mineral with a dull or earthy luster.

FORMATION This mineral forms in marine sedimentary strata.
TESTS Glauconite dissolves easily in hydrochloric acid.

aggregate of small, indistinct grains

dull luster

Monoclinic

SG: 2.40–2.95	Cleavage: Perfect	Fracture: Uneven

Group: SILICATES	Composition: (Mg,Fe,Al)$_3$(Al,Si)$_4$O$_{10}$(OH)$_2$.4H$_2$O	Hardness: 1½–2

Vermiculite

Vermiculite forms platy, tabular crystals with a pseudohexagonal outline in the monoclinic system. The color varies from greenish to golden yellow or brown. The streak is pale yellow. Vermiculite is a translucent mineral with a vitreous luster.

FORMATION Forms by the alteration of biotite and phlogopite.
TESTS When heated, it can expand into a twisted, wormlike shape.

Monoclinic

pseudohexagonal outline

flat tabular habit

SG: 2.30	Cleavage: Perfect	Fracture: Uneven

Group: SILICATES	Composition: Mg$_5$Al(AlSi$_3$O$_{10}$)(OH)$_8$	Hardness: 2–2½

Clinochlore

Crystals are tabular, with a hexagonal cross-section. Clinochlore also occurs in massive, foliated, scaly, granular, or earthy habits. It may be white to yellowish or colorless, as well as green. The streak is colorless to greenish white. This mineral is transparent to opaque, with a pearly luster.

FORMATION Forms in many metamorphic rocks, especially schists.
TESTS Soluble in strong acids.

pearly luster

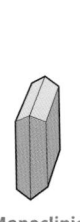

Monoclinic

SG: 2.60–3.02	Cleavage: Perfect	Fracture: Uneven

Group: SILICATES	Composition: (Fe^{2+},Mg,Al,Fe^{3+})$_6$(Si,Al)$_4$O$_{10}$(OH,O)$_8$	Hardness: 3

Chamosite

Occurring in compact, massive habits, chamosite may also be oolitic. The color ranges from greenish to black. There is a white or pale green streak. Chamosite is a translucent mineral with a vitreous or earthy luster.

FORMATION This mineral forms in various sedimentary rocks, such as ironstones and clays, where it occurs with siderite (iron carbonate).
TESTS Gives off water when heated.

earthy luster

massive habit

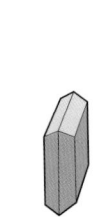

Monoclinic

SG: 3.12	Cleavage: Not determined	Fracture: Uneven

Group: SILICATES	Composition: $Al_2Si_2O_5(OH)_4$	Hardness: 2–2½

Kaolinite

This group of minerals—which includes kaolinite, nacrite, and halloysite—forms very small pseudohexagonal platelets or scales. It may also occur in massive, compact habits and in earthy or clayey masses. Kaolinite varies from white and colorless to yellowish, brownish, reddish, or bluish. There is a white streak. The kaolinite group is transparent to translucent, with a pearly to dull or earthy luster.

FORMATION Forms by the alteration of feldspars and other aluminum-rich silicate minerals. This can be brought about by weathering, especially in humid regions, or, on a much larger scale, by hydrothermal fluids rising from depth through rocks. When this occurs, granite is reduced to an unconsolidated mass of quartz and mica sand with white, kaolinite clay.

TESTS These minerals are plastic when moist and lose water when heated in a closed tube. Special optical tests are needed to tell kaolinite minerals apart.

dull luster

powdery habit

Kaolinite

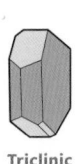

Triclinic

nacrite crystal aggregate

Nacrite

massive habit

Halloysite

SG: 2.63	Cleavage: Perfect basal	Fracture: Uneven

Group: SILICATES	Composition: $Ca_2Al_2Si_3O_{10}(OH)_2$	Hardness: $6–6\frac{1}{2}$

Prehnite

This mineral can form prismatic, tabular, or pyramidal crystals but usually occurs in botryoidal, reniform, stalactitic, granular, or compact habits. It is usually green in color but may be white, colorless, yellow, or gray. It has a colorless streak. Prehnite is transparent to translucent, with a vitreous to pearly luster.

FORMATION Forms in hollows in basaltic lavas.
TESTS This mineral gives off water when it is heated.

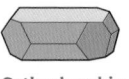

Orthorhombic

massive calcite

prehnite crystals

SG: 2.80–2.95	Cleavage: Distinct	Fracture: Uneven

Group: SILICATES	Composition: $(Ni,Mg)_3(Si_2O_5)(OH)_4$	Hardness: $2–2\frac{1}{2}$

Nepouite

The crystals formed by nepouite are usually lamellar. It can occur as microcrystalline crusts and in a massive habit. The brilliant green color is characteristic, though it may also be white. The streak is light green. It is a transparent to opaque mineral, and the luster can be greasy, waxy, or earthy.

FORMATION Forms when nickel sulfides are altered by fluids in igneous rocks.
TESTS It is infusible.

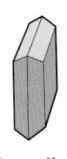

Monoclinic

massive habit

waxy luster

SG: 3.24	Cleavage: None	Fracture: Splintery

Group: SILICATES	Composition: $Mg_4Si_6O_{15}(OH)_2.6H_2O$	Hardness: 2

Sepiolite

This mineral occurs in massive, fibrous, compact, earthy, and nodular (meerschaum) habits. The color may be white, reddish, yellowish, grayish, or bluish green. The streak is whitish. Sepiolite is an opaque mineral, and it has a dull luster.

FORMATION Forms by the alteration of minerals in serpentinite.
TESTS Sepiolite often occurs as dry, porous masses that can float on water.

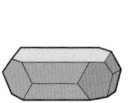

Orthorhombic

dull luster

massive habit

SG: 2.00–2.20	Cleavage: None	Fracture: Uneven

Group: SILICATES	Composition: $KCa_4Si_8O_{20}(F,OH).8H_2O$	Hardness: $4\frac{1}{2}$–5

Fluorapophyllite-(K)

Crystals formed by fluorapophyllite-(K) are pseudocubic, pyramidal, tabular, or prismatic. This mineral also forms in massive, lamellar, or granular habits. Fluorapophyllite-(K) may be white, colorless, yellow, pink, or green. There is a white streak. This mineral is transparent to translucent and has a vitreous to pearly luster on fresh surfaces.

FORMATION Fluorapophyllite-(K) forms in hydrothermal veins and in vesicular cavities formed in basaltic lavas when they were rich in gas. Minerals associated with fluorapophyllite-(K) include zeolites, gyrolite, calcite, quartz, stilbite-Ca, analcime, prehnite, and scolecite.

TESTS It colors a flame violet. It is soluble when placed in hydrochloric acid. It also gives off water if heated in a closed test tube.

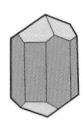

Tetragonal

vitreous luster

pseudocubic crystals

transparent to translucent

SG: 2.33–2.37	Cleavage: Perfect	Fracture: Uneven

Group: SILICATES	Composition: $NaCa_{16}Si_{23}AlO_{60}(OH)_8.14H_2O$	Hardness: $2\frac{1}{2}$

Gyrolite

This mineral occurs as radiating lamellar crystals, spherules, or concretions. Gyrolite may be white or colorless. It is transparent to translucent, and it has a vitreous luster.

FORMATION Forms by the alteration of calcium silicate minerals. As a secondary mineral, gyrolite is associated with fluorapophyllite-(K) and occurs in hollows and cavities in rocks, especially basalts. Gyrolite spherules up to 2 in (5 cm), and clusters up to 12 in (30 cm) have been found.

TESTS This mineral gives off water when heated in a closed test tube.

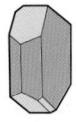

Triclinic

basalt groundmass

perfect cleavage

radiating lamellar gyrolite crystals

SG: 2.45–2.51	Cleavage: Perfect	Fracture: Uneven

Group: SILICATES	Composition: $Al_2Si_4O_{10}(OH)_2$	Hardness: 1–2

Pyrophyllite

This mineral forms as tabular, elongated crystals, which are often distorted. It usually occurs as foliated, fibrous, radiating, and lamellar masses. It is white, gray, bluish, yellowish, greenish, and greenish brown, with a white streak. It is transparent to translucent. The luster is pearly on fresh crystal surfaces, but this can become dull.

FORMATION Forms in crystalline schists with talc, andalusite, sillimanite, and lazulite. It is also found in hydrothermal veins with minerals such as mica and quartz.

TESTS Pyrophyllite has a greasy feel, similar to talc. It flakes when heated and is insoluble in most liquids.

radiating mass of pyrophyllite crystals

quartz, an associated mineral

Triclinic

SG: 2.65–2.90	Cleavage: Perfect	Fracture: Uneven

Group: SILICATES	Composition: $K_2NaFe2^+7Ti_2Si_8O_{28}(OH)_4F$	Hardness: 3

Astrophyllite

This mineral forms bladed crystals, often in stellate groups. The color is bronze yellow to golden yellow, and the streak is pale greenish brown. Astrophyllite is translucent in thin laminae, and the luster is submetallic to pearly.

FORMATION This mineral forms in cavities in igneous rocks, especially in syenite, which is a coarse-grained rock of intermediate composition. It also occurs in other plutonic rocks. Astrophyllite is associated with minerals such as quartz, feldspar, zircon, riebeckite, titanite, mica, and acmite.

TESTS When placed in acids, it is found to be slightly soluble. In a flame, astrophyllite fuses to a dark, glassy substance that is slightly magnetic. When astrophyllite cleaves, thin laminae are produced, which break very easily.

submetallic luster

perfect cleavage into thin, brittle laminae

radiating stellate groups of crystals

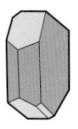
Triclinic

SG: 3.20–3.40	Cleavage: Perfect	Fracture: Uneven

Group: SILICATES	Composition: (Na,K) AlSi$_3$O$_8$	Hardness: 6–6½

Anorthoclase

Belonging to the alkali feldspar series, this mineral forms as short, prismatic or tabular crystals, with common twinning. It may occur as massive, lamellar, granular, or cryptocrystalline specimens. It is yellowish, colorless, reddish, white, gray, or greenish. It has a white streak and is transparent to translucent, with a vitreous luster.

FORMATION Forms mainly in volcanic igneous rocks.
TESTS It is insoluble in acids.

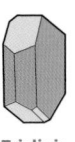

Triclinic

vitreous luster

a single prismatic crystal

SG: 2.56–2.62	Cleavage: Perfect	Fracture: Uneven

Group: SILICATES	Composition: KAlSi$_3$O$_8$	Hardness: 6–6½

Microcline

This mineral is an alkali feldspar and forms tabular or—more frequently—short, prismatic crystals, which are very commonly twinned. It also occurs in a massive habit. The color may be gray, white, yellowish, reddish, or pink. There is also a green-colored form of microcline, which is usually known as amazonstone. The streak is white. This is a transparent to translucent mineral, with a luster that is vitreous or is pearly on cleavage surfaces.

FORMATION Commonly forms in igneous rocks, especially granites, pegmatites, and syenites. It also occurs in certain metamorphic rocks, particularly schists. In addition, microcline can be found in hydrothermal veins and areas of contact metamorphism. It is often associated with quartz and albite when it forms in pegmatites.
TESTS It is insoluble in acids except hydrofluoric acid, which should be used with care. It is infusible in a flame.

short, prismatic microcline crystals

rock groundmass

Microcline

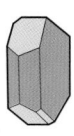

Triclinic

Amazonstone

typical green color

SG: 2.54–2.57	Cleavage: Perfect	Fracture: Uneven

Group: SILICATES	Composition: $KAlSi_3O_8$	Hardness: 6

Sanidine

In the alkali feldspar group, this mineral occurs as prismatic or tabular crystals, which are often twinned. Sanidine is whitish, gray, or colorless. There is a white streak. It is a translucent mineral with a vitreous luster on crystal faces.

FORMATION Forms in a variety of volcanic rocks, including trachyte and rhyolite. Sanidine can also be found in several varieties of contact metamorphosed rocks.

TESTS Sanidine is insoluble in most acids but will dissolve completely when placed in hydrofluoric acid. However, great care should be taken when using this acid.

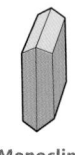

Monoclinic

prismatic sanidine crystal

trachyte lava groundmass

SG: 2.56–2.62	Cleavage: Perfect	Fracture: Conchoidal to uneven

Group: SILICATES	Composition: $NaAlSi_3O_8$	Hardness: 6–6½

Albite

The lower-temperature, sodium-rich end member of the plagioclase feldspar series, albite forms tabular, often platy crystals, which are very commonly twinned. It may also be massive, granular, or lamellar in habit. The laminae are frequently curved. Albite is usually white or colorless, but it may be bluish, gray, greenish, or reddish. There is a white streak. It is transparent to translucent, with a vitreous to pearly luster.

FORMATION This mineral occurs as an essential component of many igneous rocks, including granite, pegmatite, rhyolite, andesite, and syenite. Albite is also found in some metamorphic rocks, such as schists and gneisses, and in sedimentary rocks. Additionally, it may form in hydrothermal veins. In some situations, it is produced by the alteration of other feldspars by albitization.

TESTS It fuses with difficulty, coloring the flame yellow.

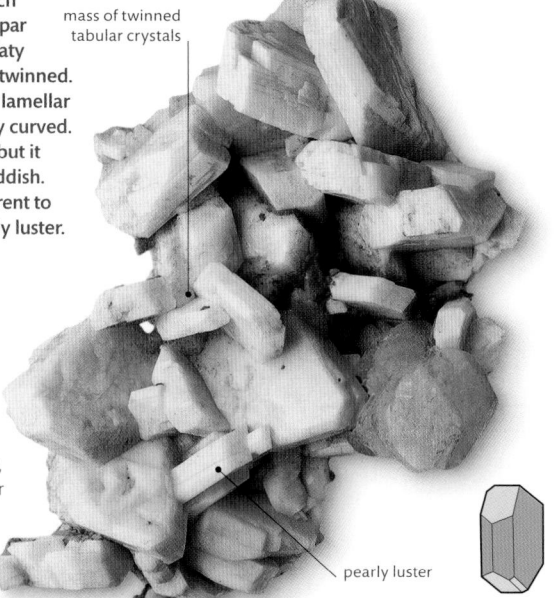

mass of twinned tabular crystals

pearly luster

Triclinic

SG: 2.60–2.65	Cleavage: Perfect	Fracture: Uneven to conchoidal

Group: SILICATES	Composition: $(Na,Ca)Al_{1-2}Si_{3-2}O_8$	Hardness: 6–6½

Labradorite

A member of the plagioclase feldspar series, labradorite rarely forms crystals; when these do occur, they are tabular and often twinned. Other habits are massive, granular, or compact. Labradorite is blue, gray, green, white, or colorless and frequently exhibits a rich play of colors on cleavage surfaces. The streak is white. It is a translucent mineral with a vitreous luster.

FORMATION This mineral is an important constituent of certain igneous and metamorphic rocks. These include basalt, gabbro, diorite, andesite, norite, and amphibolite. Labradorite is common in intermediate and mafic rocks but rare in granitic rocks.

TESTS The schillerization, or play of colors on broken surfaces, is very characteristic of labradorite. When powdered, it is soluble in acids.

schillerization

vitreous luster

uneven fracture

Triclinic

SG: 2.69–2.72	Cleavage: Perfect	Fracture: Uneven to conchoidal

Group: SILICATES	Composition: $CaAl_2Si_2O_8$	Hardness: 6–6½

Anorthite

The higher-temperature end member of the plagioclase feldspar series, anorthite forms short prismatic crystals, which are often twinned. Other habits are lamellar or massive. Anorthite is gray, white, pink, or colorless, and it has a white streak. It is a transparent to translucent mineral with a vitreous luster.

FORMATION Found in many igneous rocks, especially those of mafic composition, formed at high temperatures. These rocks include basalt, gabbro, dolerite, and peridotite. This calcium-rich plagioclase feldspar grades into sodium-rich albite, which is formed in lower-temperature rocks. Anorthite also occurs in some metamorphic rocks.

TESTS It is soluble in hydrochloric acid.

anorthite with associated augite

Triclinic

vitreous luster

SG: 2.74–2.76	Cleavage: Perfect	Fracture: Conchoidal to uneven

Group: SILICATES	Composition: (Na,Ca)Al$_{1-2}$Si$_{3-2}$O$_8$	Hardness: 6–6½

Andesine

A member of the plagioclase feldspar series, andesine sometimes forms as tabular crystals, which are frequently twinned. Usually it occurs in massive, compact, or granular habits. This mineral is gray, white, or colorless, and the streak is white. Andesine is transparent to translucent, with a vitreous luster on fresh crystal faces.

FORMATION Commonly forms in intermediate igneous rocks and in many metamorphic rocks. These include andesite lava and amphibolite. This member of the plagioclase feldspar series is almost intermediate between calcium-rich anorthite and sodium-rich albite.

TESTS Sodium colors a flame yellow, whereas calcium will turn it brick red. Both these colors will appear, according to temperature.

tabular andesine crystals set into igneous rock groundmass

uneven fracture

vitreous luster

Triclinic

SG: 2.66–2.68	Cleavage: Perfect	Fracture: Uneven to conchoidal

Group: SILICATES	Composition: (Na,Ca)Al$_{1-2}$Si$_{3-2}$O$_8$	Hardness: 6–6½

Oligoclase

A member of the plagioclase feldspar series, oligoclase forms as tabular crystals, which are commonly twinned. More common habits are massive, granular, or compact. It can be gray, white, greenish, yellowish, brown, reddish, or colorless, and there is a white streak. Oligoclase is transparent to translucent and has a vitreous luster.

FORMATION This mineral forms in many igneous and metamorphic rocks. The igneous rocks are plutonic and volcanic and include felsic granite and pegmatite, intermediate syenite, trachyte and andesite, and mafic basalt. In metamorphic situations, oligoclase is formed in high-grade, regionally metamorphosed gneiss and schist.

TESTS This mineral may show brilliant reflections from inclusions.

vitreous luster on crystal faces

doubly terminated oligoclase crystal on quartz

Triclinic

SG: 2.63–2.66	Cleavage: Perfect	Fracture: Uneven to conchoidal

Group: SILICATES	Composition: $KAlSi_3O_8$	Hardness: 6

Orthoclase

An important rock-forming mineral, orthoclase feldspar forms as prismatic or tabular crystals, which are often twinned. Other habits are massive, lamellar, and granular. It is white, reddish, colorless, yellow, gray, or green and has a white streak. Orthoclase is a transparent to translucent mineral, with a vitreous to pearly luster.

FORMATION Forms in many igneous and metamorphic rocks. The igneous rocks include granite, pegmatite, rhyolite, trachyte, and syenite; metamorphic examples include gneisses and schists. This mineral can also occur in some sedimentary rocks.
TESTS Orthoclase is insoluble in acids and is almost infusible.

Monoclinic

quartz, an
associated mineral

prismatic
orthoclase crystal

SG: 2.55–2.63	Cleavage: Perfect	Fracture: Uneven to conchoidal

Group: SILICATES	Composition: $(Na,Ca)Al_{1-2}Si_{3-2}O_8$	Hardness: 6–6½

Bytownite

A member of the plagioclase feldspar series, bytownite forms as tabular crystals, which are commonly twinned. More frequently, it occurs in massive, compact, and granular habits. It is white, gray, brownish, or colorless and has a white streak. It is transparent to translucent, and there is a vitreous luster.

FORMATION Forms as an essential component of many igneous rocks, such as dolerite, basalt, gabbro, norite, and anorthosite. It is also found in some metamorphic rocks, including gneiss and schist, formed by regional metamorphism.
TESTS In common with other members of the plagioclase feldspar series, bytownite shows multiple twinning. This helps distinguish it from orthoclase, which has simple twinning.

vitreous luster

perfect cleavage

uneven
fracture

Triclinic

SG: 2.72–2.74	Cleavage: Perfect	Fracture: Uneven to conchoidal

Group: SILICATES	Composition: $Na_3Ca(Si_3Al_3)O_{12}(SO_4)$	Hardness: 5½–6

Hauyne

The dodecahedral or octahedral crystals formed by hauyne are frequently twinned. It also occurs as rounded grains. The color ranges from blue to white, green, yellow, or red. The streak is bluish or white. Hauyne is a transparent to translucent mineral, and it has a vitreous or greasy luster.

FORMATION Hauyne forms in silica-poor lavas.
TESTS Soluble in acids with gelatinization.

Cubic

hauyne blue crystals

feldspar groundmass

SG: 2.44–2.50	Cleavage: Indistinct	Fracture: Uneven to conchoidal

---

Group: SILICATES	Composition: $Na_3Ca(Si_3Al_3)O_{12}S$	Hardness: 5–5½

Lazurite

Crystals are dodecahedral, octahedral, or cubic, but rare. The usual habits are massive or compact. The color is a deep blue, azure blue, violet blue, or greenish blue, and there is a bright blue streak. Lazurite is a translucent mineral, and it has a dull luster.

FORMATION Forms in limestones that have been metamorphosed by heat.
TESTS It is soluble in hydrochloric acid, giving off a "bad eggs" smell.

cubic habit on calcite groundmass

dull luster

Cubic

SG: 2.38–2.45	Cleavage: Imperfect	Fracture: Uneven

Group: SILICATES	Composition: $Na_8Al_6Si_6O_{24}Cl_2$	Hardness: 5½–6

Sodalite

This mineral occurs as dodecahedral crystals, commonly twinned. It can also form in massive or granular habits, with a concentric internal structure. Sodalite ranges from light to dark blue, though it can be white, colorless, yellowish, greenish, or reddish. The streak is colorless. It is a transparent to translucent mineral, with a vitreous to greasy luster.

FORMATION Forms in certain igneous rocks, including syenites.
TESTS Soluble in hydrochloric and nitric acids, with gelatinization.

massive habit

Cubic

SG: 2.27–2.33	Cleavage: Poor	Fracture: Uneven to conchoidal

Group: SILICATES	Composition: $KAlSi_2O_6$	Hardness: 5½–6

Leucite

This mineral forms as trapezohedral crystals, which may have striated faces. Twinning is common. It can also occur in massive or granular habits and as disseminated grains. Leucite can be white, gray, or colorless, and there is a colorless streak. It is a transparent to translucent mineral, with a vitreous luster.

FORMATION Forms in lavas of mafic composition, especially those rich in potassium, including basalts and phonolites. This mineral also alters very readily, and so is rarely found in lava of great geological age.

TESTS It is soluble in hydrochloric acid. If heated above 1,157°F (625°C), leucite's crystal structure changes from tetragonal to cubic symmetry.

Tetragonal

vitreous luster

trapezohedral leucite crystal

groundmass of tuff

SG: 2.45–2.50	Cleavage: Very poor	Fracture: Conchoidal

Group: SILICATES	Composition: $Na_3K(Al_4Si_4O_{16})$	Hardness: 5½–6

Nepheline

This mineral commonly forms as prismatic hexagonal crystals, which are frequently twinned. It may also occur as compact, massive, or granular specimens. Nepheline varies from white, colorless, and gray to yellowish, dark green, and brownish red. There is a white streak. It is a transparent to translucent mineral, and it has a vitreous to greasy luster.

FORMATION Forms in many silica-poor alkaline igneous rocks, particularly those of intermediate composition. It is found in syenites (nepheline syenite) and pegmatites and occasionally in schists and gneisses.

TESTS It gelatinizes when placed in hydrochloric acid. Nepheline also colors a flame yellow, indicating the presence of sodium in its chemical structure.

Trigonal/ Hexagonal

cavity with filling of hexagonal nepheline prisms

vitreous luster

rock groundmass

transparent to translucent

SG: 2.55–2.66	Cleavage: Indistinct	Fracture: Conchoidal

Group: SILICATES	Composition: $Na_8(Al_6Si_6O_{24})(SO_4).H_2O$	Hardness: $5\frac{1}{2}$

Nosean

This mineral forms as dodecahedral crystals but is usually massive or granular in habit. It varies greatly, ranging from gray, bluish, and brown to colorless and white. Nosean has a colorless streak. It is a transparent to translucent mineral, and it has a vitreous luster on fresh surfaces.

FORMATION Forms in silica-poor lavas. These include the intermediate rock phonolite, in which this sodalite-group mineral often occurs as larger crystals set into the rock groundmass, producing a porphyritic rock texture. Occasionally, nosean has also been recorded in volcanic bombs.

TESTS This mineral gelatinizes when placed in contact with acid.

well-formed nosean crystals

sanidine, an associated mineral

vitreous luster

Cubic

SG: 2.30–2.40	Cleavage: Indistinct	Fracture: Uneven to conchoidal

Group: SILICATES	Composition: $(Na,Ca)_8(Al_6Si_6)O_{24}(CO_3,SO_4)_2.2H_2O$	Hardness: 5–6

Cancrinite

Prismatic crystals are formed by cancrinite, but they are rare. The usual habit is massive. It is white, yellow, orange, pink, reddish, or bluish and has a colorless streak. It is transparent to translucent, and there is a vitreous, pearly, or greasy luster.

FORMATION Forms in a number of igneous rocks. These include alkali-rich rocks, where it can occur as a primary mineral or as an alteration produce of nepheline. It is often associated with sodalite in syenites. Cancrinite has also been found in high-grade, regionally metamorphosed rocks, including gneisses.

TESTS Cancrinite dissolves in hydrochloric acid, with effervescence, leaving behind a siliceous gel.

nepheline syenite groundmass

vitreous luster

Trigonal/ Hexagonal

SG: 2.42–2.51	Cleavage: Perfect	Fracture: Uneven

Group: SILICATES	Composition: $Na_4Al_3Si_9O_{24}Cl$ to $Ca_4Al_6Si_6O_{24}CO_3$	Hardness: 5–6

Scapolite group

Calcium-rich meionite and sodium-rich marialite form a series of minerals with the group name scapolite. The group occurs as prismatic crystals and also in granular and massive habits. Scapolite varies and may be colorless, white, gray, bluish, greenish, yellowish, brownish, pink, or violet. There is a colorless streak. It is transparent to translucent, with a vitreous to pearly or resinous luster.

FORMATION This group forms in igneous rocks that have been altered from their original mafic composition and in metamorphic rocks, such as high-grade schists and gneisses.
TESTS Soluble in hydrochloric acid.

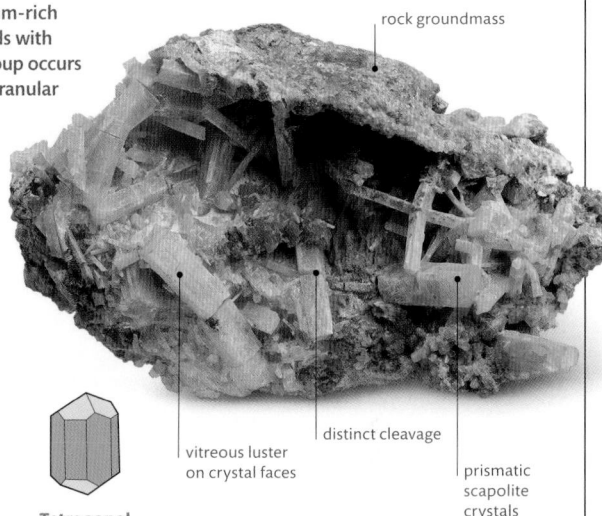

rock groundmass

distinct cleavage

vitreous luster on crystal faces

prismatic scapolite crystals

Tetragonal

SG: 2.50–2.78	Cleavage: Distinct	Fracture: Uneven to conchoidal

---

Group: SILICATES	Composition: $LiAlSi_4O_{10}$	Hardness: $6\frac{1}{2}$

Petalite

This mineral forms rarely as small crystals, which are commonly twinned. More often, petalite forms as large, cleavable masses. It may be white, gray, pinkish, yellow, or colorless, and there is a white streak. Petalite is transparent to translucent, with a vitreous to pearly luster.

FORMATION Forms in very coarse-grained, felsic igneous rocks. It is associated with a number of other minerals, including quartz and lepidolite, spodumene, and other lithium-rich minerals.
TESTS Petalite colors a flame crimson red and is insoluble.

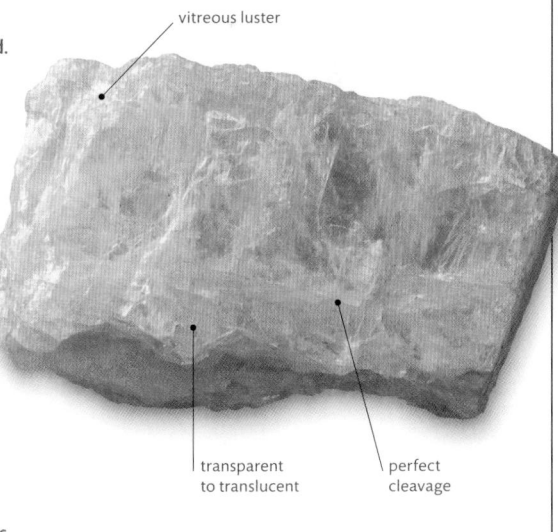

vitreous luster

transparent to translucent

perfect cleavage

Monoclinic

SG: 2.41–2.42	Cleavage: Perfect	Fracture: Subconchoidal

Group: SILICATES	Composition: $NaAlSi_2O_6.H_2O$	Hardness: $5–5\frac{1}{2}$

Analcime

A zeolite mineral that occurs as well-formed trapezohedra, icositetrahedra, and modified cubes, analcime also forms in massive, granular, and compact habits. It may be white, colorless, gray, pink, yellowish, or greenish, with a white streak. Analcime is a transparent to translucent mineral, with a vitreous luster.

FORMATION Occurs in basaltic igneous rocks and may be formed by the alteration of sodalite and nepheline. Analcime is also found in some detrital sediments with other zeolites and calcite.
TESTS When heated, it fuses and colors the flame yellow. This mineral is soluble in acids. It will yield water when heated in a closed test tube.

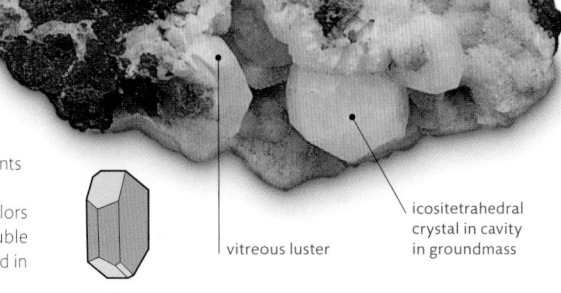

Triclinic

icositetrahedral crystal in cavity in groundmass

vitreous luster

SG: 2.24–2.29	Cleavage: Very poor	Fracture: Subconchoidal

Group: SILICATES	Composition: $CaAl_2Si_4O_{12}.6H_2O$	Hardness: 4–5

Chabazite

A member of the zeolite group of minerals, chabazite occurs as pseudocubic, rhombohedral crystals, which are often twinned. It may be white, yellowish, pinkish, reddish, greenish, or colorless, with a colorless streak. It is a transparent to translucent mineral, and the luster is vitreous.

FORMATION Forms in cavities in basaltic lavas and in some limestones. It is associated with many other zeolites—such as harmotome, phillipsite-K, heulandite-Na, and scolecite—and with quartz and calcite. It can occur in certain metamorphic rocks, such as schists, and forms around hot springs in the crust of minerals deposited from the hot fluids.
TESTS Chabazite gives off water when heated in a closed test tube.

basalt groundmass

vitreous luster

uneven fracture

rhombohedral chabazite crystal

Trigonal/ Hexagonal

SG: 2.05–2.20	Cleavage: Indistinct	Fracture: Uneven

Group: SILICATES	Composition: $Ba_2(Si_{12}Al_4)O_{32}.12H_2O$	Hardness: 4–5

Harmotome

This mineral is a zeolite, which occurs as twinned pseudotetragonal or pseudo-orthorhombic crystals and as radiating aggregates. The color may be white, gray, pink, yellow, brown, or colorless. It has a white streak. It is transparent to translucent, with a vitreous luster.

FORMATION Forms in vesicles in basalts.
TESTS It is fusible and is soluble in hydrochloric acid.

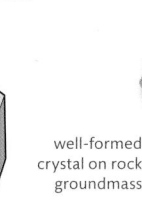

Monoclinic

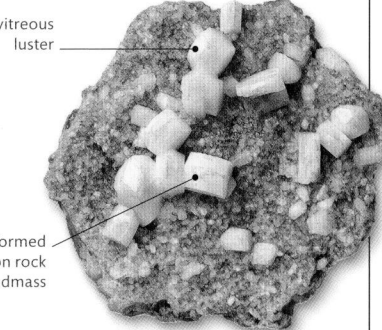

vitreous luster

well-formed crystal on rock groundmass

SG: 2.41–2.47	Cleavage: Distinct	Fracture: Uneven to subconchoidal

Group: SILICATES	Composition: $(Na,Ca,K)_6(Si,Al)_{36}O_{72}.22H_2O$	Hardness: 3–3½

Heulandite-Na

A zeolite which occurs as tabular, trapezoidal crystals, heulandite-Na also forms in massive and granular habits. It can be white, gray, yellow, pink, red, orange, colorless, and brown, and the streak is colorless. It is transparent to translucent, with a vitreous to pearly luster.

FORMATION In vesicles in basalts.
TESTS Heulandite-Na is fusible and is soluble in hydrochloric acid.

Monoclinic

foliated heulandite-Na crystals

rock groundmass

SG: 2.20	Cleavage: Perfect	Fracture: Uneven

Group: SILICATES	Composition: $CaAl_2Si_4O_{12}.4H_2O$	Hardness: 3½–4

Laumontite

This zeolite mineral forms as prismatic crystals and also occurs in massive, fibrous, columnar, and radiating habits. It is white, gray, brownish, pink, or yellowish. The streak is colorless. It has a vitreous to pearly luster and is transparent to opaque.

FORMATION Forms in igneous basaltic cavities.
TESTS Soluble in hydrochloric acid, with gelatinization.

Monoclinic

vitreous to pearly luster

opaque

prismatic crystal

SG: 2.23–2.41	Cleavage: Perfect	Fracture: Uneven

Group: SILICATES	Composition: $Na_2Al_2Si_3O_{10}.2H_2O$	Hardness: 5–5½

Natrolite

This zeolite mineral forms as slender or acicular, prismatic crystals, which are vertically striated. It may also be fibrous, radiating, massive, compact, or granular in habit. The color is white, gray, yellowish, reddish, or colorless, and there is a white streak. It is transparent to translucent, with a vitreous to pearly luster.

FORMATION Forms in vesicles in basalts.
TESTS Natrolite gelatinizes with acid.

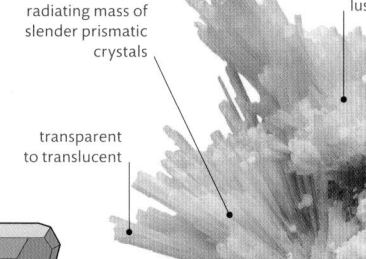

vitreous luster

radiating mass of slender prismatic crystals

transparent to translucent

Orthorhombic

SG: 2.20–2.26	Cleavage: Perfect	Fracture: Uneven

Group: SILICATES	Composition: $Na_2Ca_2Al_6Si_9O_{30}.8H_2O$	Hardness: 5

Mesolite

This zeolite mineral occurs as fibrous or acicular crystals, which form tufts or compact masses. It is always twinned. The mineral is white or colorless. It is transparent and has a vitreous or silky luster.

FORMATION Forms in vesicles in basaltic lavas.
TESTS It gelatinizes with acid. This mineral gives off water when heated in a closed test tube.

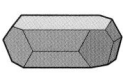

tufts of acicular crystals

silky luster

Orthorhombic

SG: 2.26	Cleavage: Perfect	Fracture: Uneven

Group: SILICATES	Composition: $K_6(Si_{10}Al_6)O_{32}.12H_2O$	Hardness: 4–5

Phillipsite-K

A zeolite which occurs as twinned crystals, phillipsite-K is white, colorless, reddish, or yellowish in color. It is a transparent to translucent mineral, with a vitreous luster.

FORMATION This mineral occurs in vesicular cavities in basalts, in some deep marine deposits and around hot springs.
TESTS Phillipsite-K is soluble in acids. It has two distinct cleavages.

twinned crystals

vitreous luster

Monoclinic

SG: 2.20	Cleavage: Distinct	Fracture: Uneven

Group: SILICATES	Composition: CaAl$_2$Si$_3$O$_{10}$.3H$_2$O	Hardness: 5–5½

Scolecite

This zeolite mineral forms as vertically striated, thin, prismatic crystals. Scolecite may also occur as radiating fibrous masses. The color may be white, yellowish, or colorless. It is a transparent to translucent mineral, and it has a vitreous to silky luster.

FORMATION Forms in vesicles in basalts.
TESTS When heated, scolecite curls into wormlike shapes and fuses.

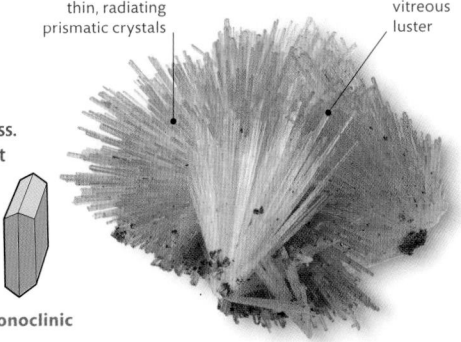

thin, radiating prismatic crystals

vitreous luster

Monoclinic

SG: 2.25–2.29	Cleavage: Perfect	Fracture: Uneven

Group: SILICATES	Composition: NaCa$_4$(Si$_{27}$Al$_9$)O$_{71}$.28H$_2$O	Hardness: 3½–4

Stilbite-Ca

A zeolite occurring as rhombic crystals, stilbite-Ca exhibits cruciform penetration twinning. Other habits are bladed, globular, and radiating masses. The color is white, gray, yellowish, pink, reddish, orange, or brown, and the streak is colorless. Stilbite-Ca is a transparent to translucent mineral, and it has a vitreous or pearly luster.

FORMATION In cavities in basalts and other lavas.
TESTS It is soluble in hydrochloric acid.

sheaflike aggregates of stilbite-Ca crystals on quartz

vitreous luster

Monoclinic

SG: 2.19	Cleavage: Perfect	Fracture: Uneven

Group: SILICATES	Composition: NaCa$_2$Al$_5$Si$_5$O$_{20}$.6H$_2$O	Hardness: 5–5½

Thomsonite-Ca

This zeolite mineral forms as acicular, prismatic crystals, but more often as lamellar or radiating aggregates. The color is white, colorless, yellowish, pink, or greenish. It has a colorless streak. This mineral is transparent to translucent and has a vitreous to pearly luster.

FORMATION Thomsonite-Ca forms in cavities in lavas.
TESTS It is soluble in hydrochloric acid, with gelatinization.

radiating prisms

vitreous luster

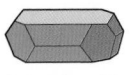

basalt groundmass

Orthorhombic

SG: 2.23–2.29	Cleavage: Perfect	Fracture: Uneven to subconchoidal

ROCKS

IGNEOUS ROCKS

IGNEOUS ROCKS form by the crystallization of once molten material. This molten rock is called magma when underground and lava once on the surface. It is essentially a silicate melt and may contain, as well as silicon and oxygen, other elements—particularly aluminum, iron, calcium, sodium, potassium, and magnesium. These combine, as the magma or lava crystallizes, to form silicate minerals, which make up igneous rocks.

Group: IGNEOUS	Origin: Intrusive	Grain size: Coarse	Crystal shape: Anhedral, Euhedral

Pink granite

One of the most common intrusive rocks, granite has a total silica content above 65 percent and a minimum quartz content of 20 percent. K-feldspars (orthoclase and microcline) are normally dominant over plagioclase (Na-rich) feldspar and often pink. Mica occurs as dark biotite or as silvery muscovite. Hornblende may be present.

TEXTURE Granite is a coarse-grained rock with crystals larger than $\frac{3}{16}$ in (5 mm) in diameter.
ORIGIN Forms at considerable depth in the Earth's crust.

biotite mica

gray quartz crystals

pink orthoclase feldspar

Classification: Felsic	Occurrence: Pluton	Color: Light

Group: IGNEOUS	Origin: Intrusive	Grain size: Coarse	Crystal shape: Anhedral, Euhedral

White granite

A high silica content—over 65 percent total silica and no less than 20 percent quartz—classifies white granite as a felsic rock. K-feldspars (orthoclase and microcline) are dominant and are white in color. Usually, there is some albitic plagioclase. Dark biotite mica and hornblende give the rock a mottled appearance. Light, glittery muscovite is also common.

TEXTURE A coarse-grained rock with euhedral crystals of feldspar and mica and, usually, anhedral quartz.
ORIGIN In plutonic environments.

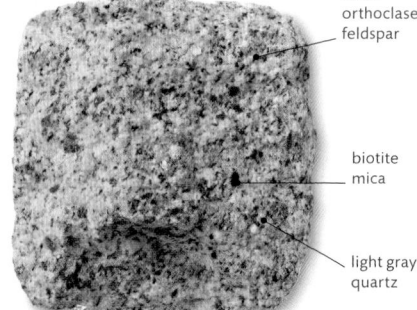

white orthoclase feldspar

biotite mica

light gray quartz

Classification: Felsic	Occurrence: Pluton	Color: Light

| Group: IGNEOUS | Origin: Intrusive | Grain size: Coarse | Crystal shape: Anhedral, Euhedral |

Porphyritic granite

A granitic rock with more than 65 percent silica and a minimum of 20 percent quartz. Pink orthoclase feldspar and white microcline or albitic feldspar are present. Biotite mica crystals and quartz are visible. Hornblende may add to the speckled appearance.

TEXTURE Granite can be equigranular or porphyritic. The phenocrysts are usually of feldspar and may be up to 2½ in (6 cm) long.
ORIGIN Forms by magma cooling in two stages at some depth in the Earth's crust.

biotite mica crystals

quartz crystals

pale phenocrysts of orthoclase feldspar

| Classification: Felsic | Occurrence: Pluton | Color: Light |

| Group: IGNEOUS | Origin: Intrusive | Grain size: Coarse | Crystal shape: Anhedral, Euhedral |

Graphic granite

A felsic igneous rock, this granite contains 20 percent quartz and over 65 percent total silica. It is made up of K-feldspars (orthoclase and microcline), albitic plagioclase, gray quartz, and some dark biotite mica.

TEXTURE Coarse-grained, with a graphic texture.
ORIGIN Forms due to the simultaneous crystallization of quartz and K-feldspars.

pink coloring of orthoclase feldspar

gray quartz

| Classification: Felsic | Occurrence: Pluton | Color: Light |

| Group: IGNEOUS | Origin: Intrusive | Grain size: Coarse | Crystal shape: Anhedral, Euhedral |

Hornblende granite

This granitic rock is made up of more than 20 percent quartz and over 65 percent silica. K-feldspars (orthoclase and microcline) are more abundant than plagioclase feldspar. Hornblende occurs as small masses and as prismatic crystals. Mica is also present in the rock.

TEXTURE Coarse-grained, with equal-sized crystals.
ORIGIN Forms at various depths in the Earth's crust.

dark hornblende crystals

pale orthoclase feldspar

| Classification: Felsic | Occurrence: Pluton | Color: Medium |

| Group: IGNEOUS | Origin: Intrusive | Grain size: Coarse | Crystal shape: Anhedral, Euhedral |

Adamellite

A felsic rock, adamellite has more than 65 percent total silica and less than 20 percent quartz. It contains a large quantity of feldspar—equally divided between K-feldspars (orthoclase and microcline) and plagioclase. Biotite mica gives adamellite a speckled appearance. Small gray grains of quartz occur in the matrix.

TEXTURE This is a coarse-grained, usually equigranular rock, though it can be porphyritic. The crystals are large enough to be seen with the naked eye. Most crystals in adamellite are euhedral, though some of the quartz is anhedral.
ORIGIN Crystallizes in magmas associated with large plutons.

feldspar crystals over ³⁄₁₆ in (5 mm) in diameter

dark biotite mica

light feldspar

| Classification: Felsic | Occurrence: Pluton | Color: Light |

| Group: IGNEOUS | Origin: Intrusive | Grain size: Medium | Crystal shape: Anhedral, Euhedral |

White microgranite

A felsic rock with more than 65 percent total silica and over 20 percent quartz. It contains more K-feldspars (orthoclase and microcline) than plagioclase feldspar. There may be dark biotite and/or light muscovite mica. Patches of biotite can give microgranite a darker color.

TEXTURE Medium-grained, with crystals ³⁄₁₆–¹⁄₆₄ in (5–0.5 mm) in diameter. This makes mineral identification difficult. The texture is generally equigranular but sometimes porphyritic. Many of the crystals are anhedral.
ORIGIN In the outer margins of pegmatites. Also forms as minor intrusions, such as sills and dykes, from the crystallization of magma at moderate depth.

light orthoclase feldspar

gray quartz

biotite mica gives speckled appearance

| Classification: Felsic | Occurrence: Dyke, Sill | Color: Light, Medium |

| Group: IGNEOUS | Origin: Intrusive | Grain size: Medium | Crystal shape: Anhedral, Euhedral |

Pink microgranite

A felsic rock with more than 65 percent total silica and over 20 percent quartz. If the predominant feldspar is pink orthoclase, this will influence the color of the rock. When biotite mica is present in microgranite, it will appear as dark specks. The gray grains of quartz in the groundmass are often anhedral.

TEXTURE Medium-grained, with crystals ³⁄₁₆–¹⁄₆₄ in (5–0.5 mm) in diameter. The crystals are generally of similar size.
ORIGIN Usually forms in dykes and sills, from the solidifying of magma.

pink orthoclase

dark biotite mica crystals

| Classification: Felsic | Occurrence: Dyke, Sill | Color: Light, Medium |

| Group: IGNEOUS | Origin: Intrusive | Grain size: Medium | Crystal shape: Anhedral, Euhedral |

Porphyritic microgranite

This felsic rock contains over 65 percent total silica and more than 20 percent quartz. As with other granites, there is more K-feldspar (orthoclase and microcline) than plagioclase feldspar in porphyritic microgranite. This specimen has light-colored feldspar phenocrysts set into a matrix that also contains dark biotite mica.

TEXTURE This is a medium-grained rock, with crystals ³⁄₁₆–¹⁄₆₄ in (5–0.5 mm) in diameter. The phenocrysts that give the rock its porphyritic texture usually have good crystal shape and may be aligned due to flow. These phenocrysts are generally of feldspar and are often euhedral.
ORIGIN Porphyritic microgranite forms in minor intrusions, such as sills and dykes.

phenocrysts of feldspar

medium-grained matrix

| Classification: Felsic | Occurrence: Dyke, Sill | Color: Medium |

| Group: IGNEOUS/MET. | Origin: Various | Grain size: Medium to fine | Crystal shape: Anhedral, Euhedral |

Xenolith

Xenolith is a term applied to rock fragments that are foreign to the body of igneous rock in which they occur. They are usually engulfed by magma and partly altered. This specimen is a dark mass of mafic lava within pink granite. The granite's feldspar, mica, and quartz contrast noticeably with the dark xenolith.

TEXTURE Xenolith is a medium- to fine-grained rock. The granite is coarse-grained.
ORIGIN Xenoliths occur in many igneous rocks.

granite around margins

xenolith

coarse grains

| Classification: Felsic to mafic | Occurrence: Pluton, Volcano | Color: Dark |

| Group: IGNEOUS | Origin: Intrusive | Grain size: Medium | Crystal shape: Anhedral, Euhedral |

Quartz porphyry

A felsic rock with more than 65 percent total silica and over 10 percent quartz, it contains phenocrysts of quartz and alkali feldspar (usually orthoclase) in a microcrystalline matrix. In quartz porphyry, orthoclase feldspar exceeds plagioclase feldspar. Some crystals of hornblende are also visible in this specimen.

TEXTURE This is a medium-grained rock, but with some larger crystals (phenocrysts) of various essential minerals, surrounded by smaller mineral grains. These smaller grains in the matrix are of similar size. A porphyritic rock, quartz porphyry may have formed in two stages during the cooling of magma.
ORIGIN Quartz porphyry forms in minor intrusive structures, such as sills and dykes, from the intrusion and cooling of magma. It does not usually form at great depth.

phenocrysts in matrix

| Classification: Felsic | Occurrence: Dyke, Sill | Color: Light, Medium |

Group: IGNEOUS	Origin: Intrusive	Grain size: Very coarse	Crystal shape: Euhedral

Feldspar pegmatite

This felsic rock has the same mineral composition as granite. It contains a high proportion of feldspar (which is usually pink or white), grayish quartz, and biotite, amphibole, and/or tourmaline. The total silica content is well over 65 percent.

TEXTURE Due to rapid cooling of water-rich magmas, pegmatites are very coarse-grained; some have crystals many feet long. In this specimen, the mass of white feldspar is over 4 in (10 cm) long. The minerals can be easily identified without a magnifying glass.

ORIGIN Forms in plutonic environments and often in dykes and veins. Pegmatites tend to be concentrated at the margins of granite intrusions.

amphibole crystals

white feldspar crystals

large crystals

Classification: Felsic	Occurrence: Pluton, Dyke, Sill	Color: Light

Group: IGNEOUS	Origin: Intrusive	Grain size: Very coarse	Crystal shape: Euhedral

Mica pegmatite

This is a felsic rock of granitic composition, with more than 65 percent total silica and over 20 percent quartz. White muscovite mica may form as large sheets, over 2½ in (6 cm) long, within the rock mass. There is also some feldspar and biotite. The name pegmatite generally refers to rocks of felsic composition, but the term applies to any igneous rock of very coarse grain size.

TEXTURE Pegmatites owe their very coarse grain size to slow cooling. Large crystals, some several feet long, may be found.

ORIGIN Forms deep below the Earth's surface in plutonic environments. Cooling of magma is rapid and often associated with late-stage fluids, which may carry some rarer elements (e.g., Li, Be, B) into the rock mass.

gray quartz

large, glittering, muscovite mica crystals

Classification: Felsic	Occurrence: Pluton, Dyke, Sill	Color: Light

Group: IGNEOUS	Origin: Intrusive	Grain size: Very coarse	Crystal shape: Euhedral

Tourmaline pegmatite

dark, prismatic tourmaline crystals

This rock has a felsic composition similar to that of granite, with well over 20 percent quartz and more than 65 percent total silica. A high proportion of gray quartz, pink K-feldspars, and dark biotite mica may be present. The dark, prismatic crystals are the borosilicate mineral, tourmaline.

TEXTURE Consists of very coarse-grained crystals. Some of the larger crystals in this specimen are 2–2½ in (5–6 cm) long. Most are euhedral (well-shaped). The tourmaline forms coarse, striated prismatic crystals.

ORIGIN Tourmaline pegmatite forms in large intrusions and also in dykes or sills. The rock is created by the rapid cooling of water-rich magma at depth in the Earth's crust.

pink orthoclase feldspar

Classification: Felsic	Occurrence: Pluton, Dyke, Sill	Color: Light

Group: IGNEOUS	Origin: Intrusive	Grain size: Medium	Crystal shape: Anhedral, Euhedral

Granophyre

ferromagnesian minerals give dark color

This rock has a felsic composition, with more than 20 percent quartz and a total silica content of over 65 percent. It contains both K-feldspars and plagioclase feldspars, mica, and amphibole. When ferromagnesian minerals are present in granophyre, they give the rock a darker color.

TEXTURE This is a medium-grained rock but can be porphyritic, characterized by a texture formed by an intergrowth of feldspars and quartz—called granophyric—and a finer version of graphic texture found in some granites. The texture is best seen with a magnifying glass or viewed under a microscope.

ORIGIN The rock occurs on the margins of large plutonic, intrusive masses and also in hypabyssal intrusions.

similar-sized grains

Classification: Felsic	Occurrence: Pluton, Dyke	Color: Light, Medium

| Group: IGNEOUS | Origin: Intrusive | Grain size: Coarse | Crystal shape: Anhedral, Euhedral |

Pink granodiorite

This is a plutonic rock generally consisting of quartz, plagioclase, and lesser amounts of alkali feldspar. Minor constituents of pink granodiorite may be hornblende, biotite, or pyroxene.

TEXTURE A medium- to coarse-grained rock, usually with well-formed crystals.
ORIGIN Forms in many types of igneous intrusions. This is probably the commonest rock of the granite family.

hornblende crystal

| Classification: Intermediate | Occurrence: Pluton, Dyke | Color: Light, Medium |

| Group: IGNEOUS | Origin: Intrusive | Grain size: Coarse | Crystal shape: Anhedral, Euhedral |

White granodiorite

The total silica content of this rock is lower than that of granite, being between 55 and 65 percent. This light form of granodiorite contains a high proportion of gray quartz and plagioclase feldspar. Dark mica and hornblende give the rock a speckled appearance.

TEXTURE A coarse-grained rock, white granodiorite has well-formed crystals. Some of the interstitial quartz may be anhedral.
ORIGIN Forms in many types of igneous intrusions.

light feldspar

dark ferromagnesian minerals

| Classification: Intermediate | Occurrence: Pluton | Color: Light |

| Group: IGNEOUS | Origin: Intrusive | Grain size: Medium to coarse | Crystal shape: Anhedral, Euhedral |

Diorite

A rock of intermediate composition, diorite has 55 to 65 percent total silica content. Essentially composed of plagioclase feldspar (oligoclase or andesine) and hornblende. Biotite mica and pyroxene may also occur in diorite.

TEXTURE The grain size of diorite is medium to coarse (sometimes pegmatitic). It may be equigranular or porphyritic with phenocrysts of feldspar or hornblende.
ORIGIN Sometimes forms as independent intrusions, such as dykes, but usually comprises parts of major granitic masses.

light plagioclase feldspar

| Classification: Intermediate | Occurrence: Pluton, Dyke | Color: Medium, Dark |

| Group: IGNEOUS | Origin: Intrusive | Grain size: Coarse | Crystal shape: Anhedral, Euhedral |

Syenite

A coarse-grained plutonic rock generally devoid of quartz (up to 10 percent quartz in quartz syenites), syenite is a light-colored rock often confused with granite. This intermediate rock, with total silica between 55 and 65 percent, is principally formed of alkali feldspar and/or sodic plagioclase and is usually associated with biotite, amphibole, or pyroxene.

TEXTURE A coarse-grained rock with all minerals visible to the naked eye and with grains generally the same size. It is sometimes porphyritic—where larger crystals are enclosed by a finer-grained matrix. Crystals are mainly anhedral to euhedral.

ORIGIN Usually forms in minor intrusions, dykes, and sills, often associated with granites.

amphibole

pale pink feldspar

| Classification: Intermediate | Occurrence: Pluton, Dyke, Sill | Color: Light, Dark |

| Group: IGNEOUS | Origin: Intrusive | Grain size: Coarse | Crystal shape: Euhedral |

Nepheline syenite

This rock has the typical intermediate igneous rock composition of 55 to 65 percent total silica content. It contains a high proportion of feldspar, amphibole, and mica. Pyroxene can sometimes be present. Nepheline syenite contains the feldspathoid mineral, nepheline, from which its name is derived. There is no quartz present in this rock.

TEXTURE Nepheline syenite is coarse-grained; the minerals can be seen clearly without a magnifying glass. The crystals generally have the same grain size (equigranular). This rock can sometimes be pegmatitic.

ORIGIN Nepheline syenite forms from the crystallization of magmas that are often associated with highly alkaline rocks. These are rocks that contain minerals rich in sodium and potassium.

dark patches of ferromagnesian minerals

coarse-grained texture

| Classification: Intermediate | Occurrence: Pluton, Dyke | Color: Light, Dark |

Group: IGNEOUS	Origin: Intrusive	Grain size: Coarse	Crystal shape: Euhedral

Larvikite

A variety of augite syenite, larvikite is an intermediate rock consisting of feldspar, pyroxene (usually Ti–augite), mica, and amphibole. It contains minor amounts of nepheline and olivine. Dark to light gray in color, the feldspars usually display a distinctive schiller.

TEXTURE Larvikite is a coarse-grained rock. In this specimen, the minerals are seen to form in clots.
ORIGIN Forms in relatively small intrusions, such as sills.

coarse-grained rock

mass of grayish feldspar crystals with ferromagnesian minerals in between

Classification: Intermediate	Occurrence: Sill, Dyke	Color: Light, Dark

Group: IGNEOUS	Origin: Intrusive	Grain size: Coarse	Crystal shape: Euhedral

Gabbro

A mafic rock in which quartz is rare. Gabbro is poorer in silica than granite (about 50 percent by weight) and is composed essentially of calcic plagioclase, pyroxene (usually augite), olivine, and magnetite.

TEXTURE Gabbro is a coarse-grained and equigranular rock.
ORIGIN Forms in major plutonic intrusions, which are commonly layered.

light plagioclase feldspar

coarse grain size

dark pyroxene

Classification: Mafic	Occurrence: Pluton	Color: Medium

Group: IGNEOUS	Origin: Intrusive	Grain size: Coarse	Crystal shape: Euhedral

Layered gabbro

With a mafic composition as in gabbro, the main minerals are calcium-rich plagioclase and pyroxene, with olivine and magnetite also present. Layering, defined by alternate layers of light- and dark-colored minerals, varies from a few feet to a few inches in thickness and is due to gravity settling.

TEXTURE A coarse-grained rock with euhedral crystals.
ORIGIN Forms in mafic plutonic intrusions, sometimes as major structures (lopoliths).

alternating layers

light plagioclase feldspar

dark ferro-magnesian minerals and magnetite

Classification: Mafic	Occurrence: Pluton	Color: Medium

| Group: IGNEOUS | Origin: Intrusive | Grain size: Coarse | Crystal shape: Anhedral, Euhedral |

Olivine Gabbro

This rock has a mafic composition, with a total silica content of less than 55 percent. Quartz occurs only rarely. The high content of ferro-magnesian minerals gives the rock a dark coloring. It is of higher density than the granitic rocks. Olivine gabbro contains plagioclase feldspar (a calcium-rich variety), pyroxene, and olivine. Magnetite is generally present in small amounts.

TEXTURE A coarse-grained rock, the crystals—which are mostly euhedral—are over 3/16 in (5 mm) and easy to see with the naked eye. The grains are all of similar size, though gabbros can be porphyritic—having larger crystals surrounded by a finer matrix.
ORIGIN Forms in plutonic environments, often in stocks, sills, and other sheetlike intrusions.

plagioclase feldspar

abundance of olivine evident as dark greenish patches

| Classification: Mafic | Occurrence: Pluton, Dyke, Sill | Color: Medium, Dark |

| Group: IGNEOUS | Origin: Intrusive | Grain size: Coarse | Crystal shape: Anhedral, Euhedral |

Leucogabbro

Mafic in composition, leucogabbro has a total silica content of less than 55 percent. It is paler than other gabbros because of a high percentage of plagioclase feldspar. This is usually associated with the clinopyroxene, augite. Olivine and magnetite can also sometimes be present.

TEXTURE Leucogabbro is a coarse-grained rock. The crystals are over 3/16 in (5 mm) in diameter and can easily be seen with the naked eye.
ORIGIN This rock forms in plutonic environments, often in major intrusions. During crystallization, crystals and liquid may be separated under the influence of gravity. The separation of the liquid fraction can lead to the formation of a variety of rock types, a process known as fractional crystallization.

dark pyroxene equal in quantity to feldspar

white plagioclase feldspar

| Classification: Mafic | Occurrence: Pluton | Color: Medium, Light |

Group: IGNEOUS	Origin: Intrusive	Grain size: Coarse	Crystal shape: Anhedral, Euhedral

Bojite

A plutonic rock consisting of plagioclase feldspar (labradorite), brown hornblende, minor augite, and biotite. The brown hornblende is thought to be of primary formation. A common accessory mineral is iron oxide (magnetite). Bojite is often visually striking, with patches and streaks and a layering of mafic minerals.

TEXTURE Coarse-grained, with crystals greater than ³⁄₁₆ in (5 mm) in diameter. Grains are of the same size, but dark minerals tend to be in patches and layers.

ORIGIN Forms in plutonic environments at considerable depth in the Earth's crust.

recognizable areas of different-colored minerals

areas of iron-rich alteration

Classification: Mafic	Occurrence: Pluton		Color: Dark

Group: IGNEOUS	Origin: Intrusive	Grain size: Coarse	Crystal shape: Anhedral, Euhedral

Anorthosite

A rock of mafic composition, the total silica content is less than 55 percent, and quartz is virtually absent. Anorthosite comprises at least 90 percent plagioclase feldspar (labradorite-bytownite). Other minerals in the rock include olivine, pyroxene, and iron oxides. Garnet sometimes forms in reaction rims around pyroxene.

TEXTURE Generally coarse-grained, granular, and light in color, these rocks may have a parallel alignment of dark minerals.

ORIGIN Forms in plutonic environments in stocks, dykes, and sheet-shaped intrusions. It is often associated with gabbros in layered sequences and makes up the light-colored regions on the Moon's surface.

coarse grain size

mass of light plagioclase feldspar crystals

ferro-magnesian minerals

Classification: Mafic	Occurrence: Pluton		Color: Light

| Group: IGNEOUS | Origin: Intrusive | Grain size: Medium | Crystal shape: Anhedral, Euhedral |

Dolerite

This rock has a mafic composition, with a total silica content of less than 55 percent; the quartz content is usually lower than 10 percent. Dolerite consists of calcium-rich plagioclase feldspar and pyroxene—often augite—with some quartz and sometimes magnetite and olivine. (If olivine is present, it is known as olivine dolerite; if the rock contains quartz, it is called quartz dolerite.)

TEXTURE A medium-grained rock with crystals between ¼₄–³⁄₁₆ in (0.5–5 mm) in diameter. Euhedral or anhedral crystals of plagioclase are embedded in pyroxene crystals.

ORIGIN This rock usually forms as dykes and sills in basaltic provinces. It may also occur as dyke swarms—hundreds of individual intrusions associated with a single igneous center.

plagioclase feldspar

| Classification: Mafic | Occurrence: Dyke, Sill | Color: Dark |

| Group: IGNEOUS | Origin: Intrusive | Grain size: Medium | Crystal shape: Anhedral, Euhedral |

Norite

Similar to gabbro, this is a rock of mafic composition, with less than 55 percent total silica. Norite is composed of plagioclase feldspar and pyroxene. Importantly, it is a variety of gabbro in which orthopyroxene is dominant over clinopyroxene. Olivine may be present in some varieties of the rock. Biotite mica, hornblende, and cordierite can sometimes also occur.

TEXTURE A coarse-grained rock, which is granular in texture, norite often shows a layered structure.

ORIGIN Forms by the freezing of magma in a plutonic environment. Norite is associated with larger mafic igneous bodies and is often found in layered igneous intrusions; different rock types may form within one intrusion by a separation of their mineral content, often due to the effects of gravity settling.

dark ferromagnesian minerals

light plagioclase feldspar

| Classification: Mafic | Occurrence: Pluton | Color: Dark |

Group: IGNEOUS	Origin: Intrusive	Grain size: Coarse, Medium	Crystal shape: Anhedral, Euhedral

Troctolite

A variety of gabbro, troctolite has a total silica content of less than 55 percent. It is composed essentially of highly calcic plagioclase and olivine, with virtually no pyroxene. The olivine is often altered to serpentine. Troctolite is generally dark gray, often with a mottled appearance.

TEXTURE This is a medium- to coarse-grained rock with many crystals about ³⁄₁₆ in (5 mm) in diameter. The grains are generally of a similar size.

ORIGIN This rock forms in a plutonic environment where the magma cools slowly. Troctolite is usually associated with gabbros or anorthosite, sometimes in layered complexes.

gray-colored plagioclase feldspar

mottled appearance

Classification: Mafic	Occurrence: Pluton	Color: Dark

Group: IGNEOUS	Origin: Intrusive	Grain size: Medium	Crystal shape: Euhedral

Dunite

A rock of ultramafic composition, dunite contains less than 45 percent total silica and no quartz. It is made up almost entirely of olivine, which gives the rock its recognizable greenish or brownish coloring. The alternative name, olivinite, refers to its mineral composition. Chromite occurs in this rock as an accessory mineral.

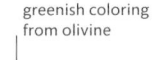

greenish coloring from olivine

TEXTURE A medium-grained rock with crystals ¹⁄₆₄–³⁄₁₆ in (0.5–5 mm) in diameter. The texture of dunite is granular and sugary.

ORIGIN Small volumes of ultramafic rocks are often formed as cumulates during the differentiation of mafic rocks in a plutonic environment. Minerals in some dunites are sometimes crushed, and they may be emplaced in a near-solid state due to Earth movements. This can produce a mass of ultramafic rock from a magma that is otherwise of mafic composition.

typical sugary texture

Classification: Ultramafic	Occurrence: Pluton	Color: Dark, Medium

| Group: METAMORPHIC | Origin: Intrusive | Grain size: Coarse to medium | Crystal shape: Anhedral, Euhedral |

Serpentinite

Serpentinite forms the low-temperature metamorphism of intrusive or extrusive mafic and ultramafic igneous. It is composed almost entirely of serpentine minerals, such as antigorite and chrysotile. Small amounts of olivine are often present. Other ferromagnesian minerals such as garnet, pyroxene, hornblende, and mica are also commonly found, as are chromite or chrome spinels. Serpentinite is dark in color, with areas of black, green, or red. Serpentinite is now classified as a metamorphic rock.

TEXTURE This is a compact, often banded rock commonly veined by fibrous serpentine.
ORIGIN Occurs as dykes, stocks, and lenses. Serpentinite is formed by the serpentinization of other rocks, principally peridotite. It commonly occurs in folded metamorphic rocks, probably from altered olivine-rich intrusions.

easily seen coarse-grained crystals

overall dark coloring

patches of different color

| Classification: Ultramafic | Occurrence: Orogenic belts | Color: Dark |

| Group: IGNEOUS | Origin: Intrusive | Grain size: Coarse to medium | Crystal shape: Anhedral, Euhedral |

Pyroxenite

This is an ultramafic, plutonic rock with less than 45 percent total silica. As the name suggests, it is composed almost entirely of one or more pyroxenes. Some biotite, hornblende, olivine, and iron oxide may also be present. The light-colored crystals in pyroxenite are of feldspar in very small amounts.

TEXTURE Pyroxenite is a coarse- to medium-grained rock. It has a granular texture, with well-formed crystals sometimes forming layers. The grains can easily be seen with the naked eye.
ORIGIN Pyroxenite forms in small, independent intrusions that are usually associated with gabbros or types of ultramafic rock.

dark coloring

pyroxene mineral

granular texture

| Classification: Ultramafic | Occurrence: Pluton | Color: Dark |

| Group: IGNEOUS | Origin: Intrusive | Grain size: Coarse | Crystal shape: Euhedral |

Kimberlite

An ultramafic rock consisting of major amounts of serpentinized olivine. It is associated with phlogopite, ortho- or clino-pyroxene, carbonates, and chromite. Pyrope garnet, rutile, and perovskite may also be present. Kimberlite is dark in color.

TEXTURE This is a coarse-grained rock, often with a porphyritic texture. Kimberlite can have a brecciated appearance.

ORIGIN Forms at the base of the Earth's crust and is brought to the surface by steep-sided pipes. The pipes are usually less than a mile in diameter. Kimberlite pipes are the primary source of diamonds and are mined, especially in South Africa, for their high diamond content.

dark matrix

crystal of a ferromagnesian mineral

| Classification: Ultramafic | Occurrence: Hypabyssal, Pluton | Color: Dark |

| Group: IGNEOUS | Origin: Intrusive | Grain size: Coarse to medium | Crystal shape: Anhedral, Euhedral |

Garnet peridotite

A rock with less than 45 percent total silica content, garnet peridotite is composed only of dark minerals: feldspar is virtually absent, olivine is essential, as is garnet. Pyroxene and/or hornblende are often present.

TEXTURE This is a coarse- or medium-grained rock with garnets set into a granular matrix. The garnets may vary in size from very small grains to larger patches over ³⁄₁₆ in (5 mm) in diameter.

ORIGIN Garnet peridotite forms in intrusive dykes, sills, and stocks and is sometimes associated with large masses of gabbro, pyroxenite, and anorthosite. It is found in basalts and as xenoliths in high-grade metamorphic rocks. Garnet peridotite is often derived from the Earth's mantle.

small patches of red garnet

| Classification: Ultramafic | Occurrence: Pluton, Dyke, Sill | Color: Dark |

Group: IGNEOUS	Origin: Extrusive	Grain size: Fine	Crystal shape: Anhedral

Rhyolite

This is an extrusive rock with the same general composition as granite. Like granite, rhyolite is often rich in quartz and alkali feldspar, but glass is usually one of the major components of rhyolite. Biotite mica is usually present.

TEXTURE A fine-grained felsic volcanic rock which may have phenocrysts, giving a porphyritic texture. The matrix crystals are too small to be seen with the naked eye, and the rapid cooling of the lava causes the magmatic liquid to quench as a glass. Rhyolite may also have vesicles and amygdules.

ORIGIN These rocks erupt from volcanoes with explosive violence and are the result of the cooling of viscous lava. Such lavas may plug the volcano's vent, causing a buildup of gaseous pressure.

phenocrysts include quartz

porphyritic texture

Classification: Felsic	Occurrence: Volcano	Color: Light

Group: IGNEOUS	Origin: Extrusive	Grain size: Fine	Crystal shape: Anhedral

Banded rhyolite

A group of rocks similar in composition to granites. Quartz, feldspar, and mica along with glass are the major components of banded rhyolite, while hornblende may also be present.

TEXTURE A fine- or very fine-grained rock in which the minerals are too small to be seen with the naked eye. Flow-banding is common in rhyolites and is defined by swirling layers of different color and texture. These rocks may also have a spheroidal texture formed by radial aggregates of needles composed of quartz and feldspar.

ORIGIN Produced by the rapid cooling of lava, leading to the formation of minute crystals or glass. The magma is highly viscous.

flinty appearance

bands of different colors

Classification: Felsic	Occurrence: Volcano	Color: Light, Medium

| Group: IGNEOUS | Origin: Extrusive | Grain size: Fine | Crystal shape: Anhedral, Euhedral |

Dacite

A volcanic rock of intermediate composition. Quartz and plagioclase feldspar are the major constituents in dacite, with minor amounts of biotite and/or hornblende or pyroxene.

TEXTURE Dacite is a fine-grained rock, though it can have a porphyritic texture. The crystals are anhedral or euhedral.
ORIGIN Although a volcanic rock, dacite can also occur in small intrusions.

porphyritic texture

| Classification: Intermediate | Occurrence: Volcano | Color: Light, Medium |

| Group: IGNEOUS | Origin: Extrusive | Grain size: Very fine | Crystal shape: Anhedral |

Obsidian

This is a silica-rich volcanic rock. With glass as its main component, obsidian is sometimes defined as being a glassy volcanic rock, with less than 1 percent water content in its structure.

TEXTURE Glassy obsidian may contain rare phenocrysts of quartz and feldspar. It breaks with a very sharp conchoidal fracture that has been exploited since Paleolithic times for making cutting tools.
ORIGIN Volcanic, formed by the very rapid cooling of viscous felsic lava.

conchoidal fracture

glass rather than crystals of minerals

| Classification: Felsic | Occurrence: Volcano | Color: Dark |

| Group: IGNEOUS | Origin: Extrusive | Grain size: Very fine | Crystal shape: Anhedral |

Snowflake obsidian

Like obsidian, this rock is composed of a high percentage of glass rather than crystals. The characteristic pale "snowflakes" are patches where the glass has become devitrified around distinct centers.

TEXTURE This is an extremely fine-grained rock. It also displays microcrystalline patches of white color.
ORIGIN A volcanic rock, snowflake obsidian is formed from lava that has cooled rapidly.

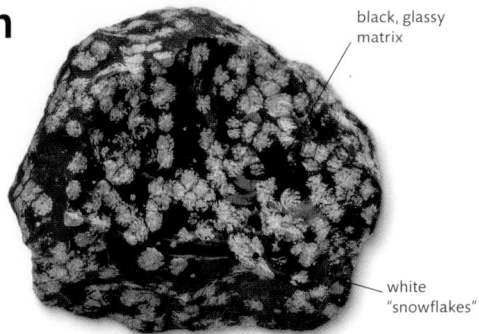

black, glassy matrix

white "snowflakes"

| Classification: Felsic | Occurrence: Volcano | Color: Dark |

| Group: IGNEOUS | Origin: Extrusive | Grain size: Very fine | Crystal shape: Anhedral |

Pitchstone

This rock has a composition equivalent to a wide range of other volcanic rocks. It is essentially a volcanic glass containing a few phenocrysts. Pitchstone is usually very dark in color and has a luster similar to that of tar or pitch.

TEXTURE Although the proportion of glass in pitchstone is very high, this rock contains more water than obsidian. It may also be spotted or flow-banded. Even under microscopic examination, the crystals appear to be poorly formed.

ORIGIN The rock is produced by the very rapid solidification of lava, especially in dykes and flows. The large quantity of glass contained in pitchstone is a result of this rapid cooling.

tarlike surface | fine-grained crystals

| Classification: Felsic to mafic | Occurrence: Volcano, Dyke, Sill | Color: Dark |

| Group: IGNEOUS | Origin: Extrusive | Grain size: Very fine | Crystal shape: Anhedral |

Porphyritic pitchstone

A very dark and glassy rock in appearance, porphyritic pitchstone is usually of felsic composition, although, as in the case of pitchstone, the chemistry is variable. This pitchstone is rich in phenocrysts, generally of quartz, feldspar, and pyroxene. Some authorities distinguish between pitchstone and obsidian by the water content of the rocks—pitchstone has as much as 10 percent, while obsidian usually contains less than 1 percent.

TEXTURE Because of the two stages in its rapid cooling history, porphyritic pitchstone contains phenocrysts of feldspar, which are set into the fine-grained matrix.

ORIGIN Forms in lava flows and small sills and dykes, often near to granitic masses. In both of these situations, the lava solidifies rapidly, giving the crystals no time to grow—hence the glassy appearance.

porphyritic texture

pale phenocrysts

| Classification: Felsic to mafic | Occurrence: Volcano, Dyke, Sill | Color: Dark |

| Group: IGNEOUS | Origin: Extrusive | Grain size: Medium | Crystal shape: Anhedral, Euhedral |

Lamprophyre

A group of rocks of variable composition, characterized by being potassium-rich and strongly porphyritic in mafic minerals, typically biotite, amphibole, and pyroxene—any feldspar (whether alkali or plagioclase feldspar) is confined to the matrix. Accessory minerals include hornblende, calcite, titanite, and magnetite.

TEXTURE Medium-grained, this group of rocks is typically porphyritic. Both biotite and hornblende phenocrysts give the rocks a distinctive appearance.
ORIGIN Forms in minor intrusions and in dykes and sills. The rocks often show signs of hydrothermal alteration. They can be associated with a variety of other igneous rocks, such as granites, syenites, and diorites.

porphyritic texture

| Classification: Felsic to mafic | Occurrence: Dyke, Sill | Color: Medium |

| Group: IGNEOUS | Origin: Extrusive | Grain size: Fine | Crystal shape: Anhedral, Euhedral |

Andesite

An intermediate volcanic rock, andesite usually has 55 to 65 percent total silica content. Plagioclase feldspar (andesine or oligoclase) is the most significant constituent, along with pyroxene, amphibole, and biotite mica.

TEXTURE A fine-grained, often porphyritic rock. The phenocrysts set into the matrix are usually white tabular feldspar crystals or biotite, hornblende, or augite.
ORIGIN This rock forms as lava flows from andesitic volcanoes, which are second in abundance only to basaltic volcanoes. Andesitic volcanoes are often associated with subduction zones, as in the Andean mountains of South America.

phenocrysts of light plagioclase feldspar

fine-grained groundmass

| Classification: Intermediate | Occurrence: Volcano | Color: Medium |

| Group: IGNEOUS | Origin: Extrusive | Grain size: Fine | Crystal shape: Anhedral, Euhedral |

Amygdaloidal andesite

This is an intermediate volcanic rock that is usually porphyritic. Amygdaloidal andesite consists of plagioclase feldspar (frequently zoned labradorite-oligoclase), pyroxene, and/or biotite. The rock matrix tends to be a medium-colored gray rather than the black of basalt.

TEXTURE This rock has a fine-grained matrix, although it may often be porphyritic. Many small, rounded vesicles are visible on the rock surface. These vesicles are left after gas bubbles have escaped from the lava. Infilled vesicles are known as amygdales and are commonly infilled by minerals of the zeolite group. The cavities can be widened by the growth of minerals.

ORIGIN Amygdaloidal andesite forms by the rapid cooling of lava from a gas-rich volcanic eruption.

gas bubble cavities, infilled with minerals

fine-grained matrix

| Classification: Intermediate | Occurrence: Volcano | Color: Medium |

| Group: IGNEOUS | Origin: Extrusive | Grain size: Fine | Crystal shape: Anhedral, Euhedral |

Porphyritic andesite

euhedral phenocrysts set into the matrix

This rock has the same composition as andesite. It is an intermediate rock with 55 to 65 percent total silica. Plagioclase feldspar is an important constituent, as are pyroxene, amphibole, and biotite mica. Andesite is usually a darker-colored volcanic rock than rhyolite, though it is lighter than basalt.

TEXTURE The matrix is fine-grained, and the crystals can be studied in detail only under a microscope. Larger phenocrysts of feldspar and pyroxene are set into the matrix. This texture indicates that some crystals grew in the magma below the Earth's surface and that, on eruption, the lava solidified rapidly.

ORIGIN Porphyritic andesite forms as lava flows usually associated with andesitic volcanoes.

fine-grained matrix

| Classification: Intermediate | Occurrence: Volcano | Color: Medium |

| Group: IGNEOUS | Origin: Extrusive | Grain size: Fine | Crystal shape: Anhedral, Euhedral |

Trachyte

This is a volcanic rock with a total silica content of between 55 and 60 percent. Trachyte is rich in alkali feldspar and also contain either nepheline or small amounts of quartz (less than 10 percent). Dark minerals, such as the pyroxene, aegerine, are present in small amounts, though trachyte is generally light in color.

TEXTURE A fine-grained rock, usually porphyritic. Feldspar microcrystals exhibit flow structure.
ORIGIN Trachyte forms as lava flows and narrow dykes and sills.

small phenocrysts

| Classification: Intermediate | Occurrence: Volcano | Color: Medium |

| Group: IGNEOUS | Origin: Extrusive | Grain size: Fine | Crystal shape: Anhedral, Euhedral |

Porphyritic trachyte

This rock has a similar composition to trachyte and has 55 to 65 percent total silica. Dominantly composed of alkali feldspar, some quartz and oligoclase feldspar may be present, as well as pyroxene, hornblende, and biotite mica.

TEXTURE This rock has a fine-grained matrix, and euhedral phenocrysts are common, giving the porphyritic texture.
ORIGIN Formed by the cooling of lava.

fine-grained matrix

| Classification: Intermediate | Occurrence: Volcano | Color: Medium |

| Group: IGNEOUS | Origin: Extrusive | Grain size: Medium | Crystal shape: Euhedral |

Rhomb porphyry

A rock of intermediate chemistry, rhomb porphyry is often called microsyenite. It has 55 to 65 percent total silica content and up to 10 percent quartz. The main minerals are alkali feldspar with hornblende, pyroxene, and biotite mica.

TEXTURE This rock derives its name from the distinctive rhombic shape of the cross-section of its feldspar phenocrysts.
ORIGIN Occurs as lava flows and dykes.

plagioclase feldspar phenocrysts / medium-grained matrix

| Classification: Intermediate | Occurrence: Dyke, Sill | Color: Medium |

| Group: IGNEOUS | Origin: Extrusive | Grain size: Fine | Crystal shape: Anhedral, Euhedral |

Basalt

A mafic volcanic rock consisting of calcic-plagioclase feldspar and pyroxene, basalt is the most abundant of all lava types. Apatite and magnetite are nearly always present in small quantities, while olivine may also occur.

TEXTURE A fine-grained rock, basalt has crystals that are both euhedral and anhedral. The crystals, however, are not easy to see, even with a magnifying glass.
ORIGIN Produced by the cooling of highly mobile basaltic lavas. Because of their fluidity, they may form very thick lava sheets. Basalt occurs widely in continental areas and is the principal rock of the ocean floor. One of the best-studied active basaltic volcanoes, Mauna Loa, forms much of the island of Hawaii.

dark-colored, fine-grained crystals

| Classification: Mafic | Occurrence: Volcano | Color: Dark |

| Group: IGNEOUS | Origin: Extrusive | Grain size: Fine | Crystal shape: Anhedral, Euhedral |

Porphyritic basalt

fine-grained matrix

This rock is of a similar mafic composition to basalt. It contains between 45 and 55 percent total silica and less than 10 percent quartz. Plagioclase—usually calcium-rich—and pyroxene make up the bulk of the rock. Olivine and magnetite may also be present.

TEXTURE This is a fine-grained rock, with phenocrysts set into the matrix. These phenocrysts are usually of olivine (green), pyroxene (black), or plagioclase (white-gray). The resulting porphyritic texture indicates two stages in the cooling of the lava.
ORIGIN Erupted from volcanoes in oceanic areas. Basalt is a nonviscous lava and flows for great distances. The lava flows may form lava plateaus extending over thousands of square miles.

relatively large phenocrysts of pyroxene

| Classification: Mafic | Occurrence: Volcano | Color: Dark |

| Group: IGNEOUS | Origin: Extrusive | Grain size: Fine | Crystal shape: Anhedral |

Amygdaloidal basalt

A mafic volcanic rock with a total silica content of 45 to 55 percent. Calcium-rich plagioclase feldspar and pyroxene are the main minerals. Olivine and magnetite are other minerals that are frequently associated with amygdaloidal basalt.

TEXTURE Numerous amygdales (small, rounded gas-bubble cavities infilled with minerals) are characteristic of some basalts. Zeolites and quartz—often in the form of agate—are common minerals.
ORIGIN This rock is produced by the cooling of lava.

numerous rounded amygdales

rusty weathering of iron minerals

| Classification: Mafic | Occurrence: Volcano | Color: Dark |

| Group: IGNEOUS | Origin: Extrusive | Grain size: Fine | Crystal shape: Anhedral, Euhedral |

Vesicular basalt

This rock has a very similar composition to that of basalt, with calcic-plagioclase feldspar and pyroxene being the essential minerals. Olivine and magnetite are also usually present in vesicular basalt.

TEXTURE The rock is riddled with empty gas-bubble cavities called vesicles. The matrix is fine-grained, often porphyritic. If the cavities are infilled with minerals, vesicular basalt becomes an amygdaloidal basalt.
ORIGIN Forms from the cooling of basaltic lava.

rounded cavities

| Classification: Mafic | Occurrence: Volcano | Color: Dark |

| Group: IGNEOUS | Origin: Extrusive | Grain size: Fine | Crystal shape: Anhedral, Euhedral |

Spilite

pale green amygdales set in fine-grained matrix

A mafic rock with a silica content averaging 40 percent, spilite occurs as pillow lavas. A distinctive feature of this rock is that the plagioclase feldspar is albite (Na-rich). The pyroxene content in spilite is often altered to chlorite, although augite sometimes remains.

TEXTURE A fine-grained rock with infilled gas-bubble cavities. These amygdales are often visible, set in the rock matrix.
ORIGIN Found in underwater lava flows and in pillow lava formed on the ocean floor.

| Classification: Mafic | Occurrence: Volcano | Color: Dark |

Group: IGNEOUS	Origin: Pyroclastic	Grain size: Coarse	Crystal shape: Fragments

Agglomerate

A consolidated or unconsolidated, coarse, pyroclastic rock material, agglomerate may be composed of both volcanic and country rock fragments that are completely unsorted.

TEXTURE The size of the particles varies considerably; the rock texture often consists of angular to subrounded fragments set into a finer-grained matrix. The lava particles are vesicular, sometimes spindle-shaped.

ORIGIN This rock generally accumulates in volcanic craters or on the flanks of a volcano. Agglomerate consists of lava fragments and blocks of country rock that have been caught up in the volcanic activity and have erupted with the lava through a volcanic vent. Usually associated with other extrusive deposits, such as tuff.

many rock fragments held together in fine matrix

Classification: Felsic to mafic	Occurrence: Volcano	Color: Medium

Group: IGNEOUS	Origin: Pyroclastic	Grain size: Fine	Crystal shape: Fragments

Lithic tuff

small fragments of lava and ash cemented together

This is a pyroclastic rock (tuff) in which lithic fragments are more abundant than either crystal or vitric (glassy) fragments.

TEXTURE A fine-grained rock, tuff consists of consolidated volcanic fragments that are usually less than $\frac{1}{12}$ in (2 mm) in diameter. Lithic tuff contains a variety of crystalline rock fragments that may be of rhyolitic, trachytic, or andesitic composition.

ORIGIN This rock forms as a deposit from volcanic ash blown into the atmosphere. Lithic tuff sometimes accumulates underwater, when strata may develop. Grading of these layers may take place, and the tuff can have a variety of structures associated with sedimentation, including layering and banding. From very explosive eruptions, ash is often carried many miles into the atmosphere. Wind systems then carry the ash to settle a long way from the original volcano. When this happens, the dust particles, blown high into the atmosphere, may cause beautiful sunsets.

fine-grained matrix

Classification:Felsic to mafic	Occurrence: Volcano	Color: Medium

| Group: IGNEOUS | Origin: Pyroclastic | Grain size: Fine | Crystal shape: Anhedral, Euhedral |

Crystal tuff

This is a variety of tuff in which crystal fragments are more abundant than either lithic or vitric fragments. Most tuffs are mixtures of lithic, vitric, or crystal fractions. The minerals present in crystal tuff usually include feldspars and pyroxenes, as well as amphiboles.

TEXTURE This is a fine- to medium-grained rock, with masses of crystals set into an ash matrix. The crystals are often euhedral.
ORIGIN Forms when ashes are blown out from volcanoes during eruption. Previously formed crystals are separated from lava and may accumulate on land or underwater. When underwater deposition occurs, tuff becomes stratified and takes on the features of a sedimentary rock.

dark color due to ferro-magnesian mineral content

| Classification: Felsic to mafic | Occurrence: Volcano | Color: Medium, Dark |

| Group: IGNEOUS | Origin: Extrusive | Grain size: Fine | Crystal shape: Anhedral |

Pumice

This is a porous rock with the composition of rhyolite. It contains minute crystals of various silicate minerals, such as feldspar and ferro-magnesians, and also has a considerable amount of glass.

TEXTURE Pumice usually tends to be used as a textural term—applied to vesiculated lavas that may resemble froth or foam. This rock has a highly scoriaceous texture, with many hollows and cavities. The vesicles sometimes join to form elongated passages and tubes throughout the rock. Zeolites may fill these cavities. The density of pumice is so low that it can easily float in water.
ORIGIN Forms as frothy lavas associated with rhyolitic volcanic eruptions. When erupted into the ocean, patches may drift for great distances. Pumice can also be produced by land-bound volcanic eruptions.

hollow, gas-bubble cavities (vesicles)

typically elongated vesicles

| Classification: Felsic to mafic | Occurrence: Volcano | Color: Medium |

Group: IGNEOUS	Origin: Extrusive	Grain size: Fine	Crystal shape: Anhedral

Ignimbrite

This is a hard, volcanic tuff consisting of crystal and rock fragments in a matrix of glass shards that are usually welded together, leading in some cases to the original texture being lost. Ignimbrite has a similar composition to rhyolite.

TEXTURE It is often a fine-grained rock with a banded structure. In the field, wavy flow-banding may be seen through an exposure. The glass shards in the rock are often curved where they have formed around gas bubbles in the original frothy flow of ash, tuff, and lava droplets.

ORIGIN Produced as a deposit from a rapidly moving, turbulent, ignited pyroclastic density current. Associated with especially violent eruptions, producing clouds of incandescent gas and lava drops. These flow from volcanic eruptions at great speed, close to the ground.

shard glass

pale-colored felsic rock with darker patches

Classification: Felsic	Occurrence: Volcano	Color: Light, Medium

Group: IGNEOUS	Origin: Extrusive	Grain size: Fine	Crystal shape: Anhedral

Breadcrust volcanic bomb

Volcanic bombs usually have the composition of the lava erupted by a particular volcano. The lava clots have a high silica content, with a high proportion of quartz. Clots from intermediate composition lavas have a silica content of 55 to 65 percent. Mafic volcanoes are mainly nonexplosive, and bombs are less likely to form.

TEXTURE Breadcrust volcanic bombs have a fine-grained crust and may show coarser crystals within. The crust is marked and cracked because of the force of impact with the ground. They may contain small fragments of country rock torn from around the volcanic pipe.

ORIGIN Volcanic bombs are small to large molten lava clots that have been ejected from a volcano by violent eruption and have landed on the Earth. The lava clots are usually made of viscous lava, which cools on the outside during flight, forming a skin that cracks on impact of landing to produce the "breadcrust" surface. The bombs may sometimes measure over 3 ft (1 m) in diameter. When they land in volcanic ash, these bombs will often form a crater.

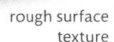

rough surface texture

Classification: Felsic to mafic	Occurrence: Volcano	Color: Dark

Group: IGNEOUS	Origin: Extrusive	Grain size: Fine	Crystal shape: Anhedral

Rounded spindle bomb

Spindle bombs usually have the composition of the lava erupted by a particular volcano, whether it be andesitic or basaltic. However, they also tend to be associated with felsic and other intermediate lava volcanoes.

TEXTURE These rocks are composed of fine-grained crystals, which need microscopic examination. The shape results from the molten lava clot twisting during flight.

ORIGIN Rounded spindle bombs form as molten lava clots thrown from violently erupting volcanoes.

rough, vesicular surface

twisted shape

dark color

Classification: Felsic to mafic	Occurrence: Volcano	Color: Medium, Dark

Group: IGNEOUS	Origin: Extrusive	Grain size: Fine	Crystal shape: Anhedral

Ropy lava

This rock tends to be formed from mafic volcanic eruptions and is usually of a basaltic composition. It contains a high proportion of plagioclase feldspar and augite and small amounts of iron oxide. Such a composition gives ropy lava a dark color and a high specific gravity.

TEXTURE These lavas are often highly vesicular, containing many gas-bubble cavities. The cavities can be filled at a subsequent time by a variety of minerals, including quartz, calcite, and zeolites. The rock is described as amygdaloidal when the cavities are filled.

ORIGIN Ropy lava forms when mobile lava flows from mafic volcanoes and continues to move beneath a relatively solid but plastic crust. Basaltic lavas with a low silica content and a high gas content are usually very mobile. The flowing lava causes the crust to stretch, making folds and rope-shaped patterns. In Hawaii, where ropy lava is common, it is called *pahoehoe*, an accepted geological term.

dark color, but weathered surface is paler and brownish

folded, ropelike surface

Classification: Mafic	Occurrence: Volcano	Color: Dark

METAMORPHIC ROCKS

METAMORPHIC ROCKS form from the alteration of a preexisting rocks. Contact metamorphism is caused by direct heat, and the resulting rock is usually crystalline. Regional metamorphism is due to heat and pressure and produces foliation, or cleavage, in rocks where the minerals have been aligned by pressure and recrystallization. Dynamic metamorphism is associated with the alteration of rocks along major thrust zones (fault planes).

Group: METAMORPHIC	Origin: Mountain ranges	Grain size: Fine	Classification: Regional

Green slate

A low-grade metamorphic rock, slate is derived from pelitic rocks. Green slate is formed from quartz, some feldspar, and mica. The presence of chlorite gives this slate its green color.

TEXTURE Fine-grained, with grains of a similar size. The grain size is too fine to be seen without a microscope.
ORIGIN Forms when fine-grained sediments, such as clay or volcanic ash, undergo regional metamorphism. Minerals like mica and chlorite become aligned, giving a perfect, slaty cleavage.

greenish color across cleavage surface

many small dark patches of carbon and pyrite

Pressure: Low	Temperature: Low	Structure: Foliated

Group: METAMORPHIC	Origin: Mountain ranges	Grain size: Fine	Classification: Regional

Black slate

This rock is formed from pelitic sediments—clays, mudstones, shales, and fine-grained tuff. It contains clay minerals, quartz, mica, and feldspar. Organic matter, such as graphite, give black slate its dark color.

TEXTURE This is a fine-grained rock. It has the characteristic perfect, slaty cleavage produced by the alignment of flaky minerals, such as mica, making it easily split into thin sheets.
ORIGIN Forms when fine-grained, pelitic sediments, such as mudstones or shales, undergo regional metamorphism at low temperatures and low pressures.

small, raised pyrite porphyroblasts

dark color

fine grain size

Pressure: Low	Temperature: Low	Structure: Foliated

| Group: METAMORPHIC | Origin: Mountain ranges | Grain size: Fine | Classification: Regional |

Slate with pyrite

Formed from pelitic sediments, as with other slates, this rock is composed of quartz, clay minerals, chlorite, mica, and feldspar. As its name suggests, there is also pyrite present. This can be either finely disseminated small crystals or larger porphyroblasts (distinct crystals) set in a fine-grained matrix. The pyrite is often in the form of cubic crystals.

TEXTURE This slate is fine-grained, with only the pyrite porphyroblasts visible to the naked eye. The fine-grained matrix can be studied in detail only under a microscope. Like other slates, this rock is characterized by its perfect, slaty cleavage, which has resulted from the alignment of flaky minerals due to pressure conditions.

ORIGIN Slate forms under low temperatures and low pressure conditions. The distinct pyrite crystals grow in response to this regional metamorphism.

small pyrite crystal

fine-grained matrix

| Pressure: Low | Temperature: Low | Structure: Foliated |

| Group: METAMORPHIC | Origin: Mountain ranges | Grain size: Fine | Classification: Regional |

Fossiliferous slate

This rock contains minerals associated with the original pelitic sediments from which it was formed. Quartz, clay minerals, and mica, with feldspar and chlorite, are the main minerals in this slate. There may also be minute crystals of pyrite. Fossils can be preserved in the slates formed from fossiliferous shales, because the metamorphic grade is low.

TEXTURE Fine-grained rock, sometimes with a few porphyroblasts of pyrite.

ORIGIN Fossiliferous slate forms by the low-grade regional metamorphism of fossiliferous shale. Fossils, such as this brachiopod, can survive in identifiable form but may be distorted due to metamorphism, which produces rock cleavage.

fine-grained matrix

distorted fossil

| Pressure: Low | Temperature: Low | Structure: Foliated |

| Group: METAMORPHIC | Origin: Mountain ranges | Grain size: Medium, Fine | Classification: Regional |

Phyllite

Derived from low-grade metamorphosed sediments, phyllites are comparable with slates but are not restricted to very fine clays. Quartz and feldspars are more abundant than in shales. The essential constituents mica and chlorite impart a characteristic sheen and a gray or green color to the rock.

TEXTURE This is a foliated rock of fine to medium grain size. Phyllite may have small, distinct crystals (porphyroblasts) of garnet set into the wavy foliation. This foliation results from the alignment of mica and chlorite under low to moderate pressure. Phyllites often show small-scale folding.

ORIGINS Forms from pelitic sediments during low to moderate pressure and low-temperature regional metamorphism.

pale grayish-green coloring

"sheen" on surfaces due to high mica and chlorite content

| Pressure: Low, Moderate | Temperature: Low | Structure: Foliated |

| Group: METAMORPHIC | Origin: Mountain ranges | Grain size: Medium | Classification: Regional |

Garnet schist

The group of rocks known as schists is characterized by the alignment of visible flaky or tabular minerals. Garnet schist is rich in the micas biotite and muscovite, with quartz and feldspar also present. The usually well-shaped crystals of garnet are about 3⁄16 in (5 mm) in diameter and have grown in the rock during pressure and temperature changes. The garnet is usually a reddish variety.

TEXTURE A medium- to coarse-grained rock. A schistosity is always well-developed due to the parallel alignment of micas. The rock may show small-scale folding.

ORIGIN Forms in conditions of medium-grade, regional metamorphism at deeper levels than phyllite. The pressure is moderately high, and temperature has been influential in changing the rock's original character.

wavy foliation

dark-colored rock

mica gives glittery, silvery sheen

red garnet porphyroblasts

| Pressure: Moderate | Temperature: Low to moderate | Structure: Foliated |

Group: METAMORPHIC	Origin: Mountain ranges	Grain size: Medium	Classification: Regional

Folded schist

This rock contains quartz, feldspar, and biotite and muscovite micas. Folded schist is characterized by small-scale folds accentuated by glittering, mica crystals.

TEXTURE A medium-grained rock, the constituent minerals are often segregated into distinct bands. Schistosity, a wavy foliation caused by the rock splitting along planes of weakness, is emphasized by the mica crystals.

ORIGIN Formed by moderate pressures and low to moderate temperatures very deep in the crust within fold mountain belts.

pale muscovite

dark biotite

wavy folds picked out by mineral bands

Pressure: Moderate	Temperature: Low to moderate	Structure: Foliated

Group: METAMORPHIC	Origin: Mountain ranges	Grain size: Medium	Classification: Regional

Muscovite schist

This is a rock rich in silvery muscovite mica, which is aligned on the planes of wavy foliation within the rock. Muscovite schist also contains quartz and feldspar and some biotite mica. Garnet and chlorite minerals can be present in the rock.

TEXTURE A medium-grained rock with mica crystals $\frac{1}{12}$–$\frac{1}{8}$ in (2–3 mm) in size. The schistosity, or wavy foliation, may be emphasized by bands rich and poor in muscovite.

ORIGIN Muscovite schists form from pelitic rocks under conditions of medium-grade regional metamorphism, where pressures are moderate and temperature influences low to moderate. Such conditions typically lead to the alteration of mud- and clay-based rocks. Other rocks are also affected by this metamorphism, but these tend to show less foliation.

silvery mica on foliation

Pressure: Moderate	Temperature: Low to moderate	Structure: Foliated

Group: METAMORPHIC	Origin: Mountain ranges	Grain size: Medium	Classification: Regional

Biotite schist

This rock contains a high proportion of mica, together with quartz and feldspar. It is especially rich in biotite mica, which gives it a darkish coloring. Compositionally, biotite schist is very similar to the pelitic sediments from which it developed during metamorphism.

TEXTURE A medium-grained rock with crystals that are visible to the naked eye. Biotite schist is, however, best studied with a hand lens. This specimen shows the dark flakes of mica aligned with the foliation.

ORIGIN Forms during medium-grade regional metamorphism of pelitic sediments and other rocks, but these may not become foliated.

quartz

wavy foliation from alignment of flaky minerals

Pressure: Moderate	Temperature: Low to moderate	Structure: Foliated

Group: METAMORPHIC	Origin: Mountain ranges	Grain size: Medium, Coarse	Classification: Regional

Kyanite schist

The bulk of this rock is composed of quartz, feldspar, and mica, though it is characterized by the presence of mineral kyanite. This forms blue porphyroblasts of bladed habit which lie parallel to the foliation, or as clusters of crystals. Other minerals can be garnet and staurolite. The overall color is grayish but may be darker. Kyanite schist is often folded.

TEXTURE A medium- to coarse-grained rock; the crystals are easy to see with the naked eye.

ORIGIN Found in the central high-grade part of metamorphic belts under moderate to high pressure and temperate regimes. This rock is associated with sillimanite and staurolite schists. Kyanite is one of the minerals used by geologists to map metamorphic zones. Each zone is defined according to a mineral formed under certain pressure-temperature conditions.

gray rock with foliated structure

dark mica

gray quartz

blue, bladed kyanite

medium- to coarse-grained

Pressure: Moderate	Temperature: Moderate to high	Structure: Foliated

| Group: METAMORPHIC | Origin: Mountain ranges | Grain size: Coarse | Classification: Regional |

Gneiss

Gneiss is characterized by compositional banding of metamorphic origin. Feldspar and quartz are abundant, while muscovite, biotite, and hornblende are commonly present. Other minerals typical of high-grade regional metamorphism, such as pyroxene and garnet, may also occur.

alternating bands of dark and light minerals

TEXTURE A medium- to coarse-grained rock characterized by discontinuous, alternating light and dark bands. The presence of quartz and feldspar helps form the lighter bands, which usually have a granular texture. The darker bands of ferro-magnesian minerals tend to be foliated.

ORIGIN This rock forms from the high-grade regional metamorphism of any preexisting rock. The minerals are segregated into bands as a result of high temperatures and pressures. Gneisses may be either meta-sediments or meta-igneous rocks and occur in association with migmatites and granites. Gneiss is thought to comprise much of the lower continental crust.

| Pressure: High | Temperature: High | Structure: Foliated, Crystalline |

| Group: METAMORPHIC | Origin: Mountain ranges | Grain size: Coarse | Classification: Regional |

Folded gneiss

As with other gneisses, this rock is composed of segregated bands: the lighter bands are rich in quartz and feldspar, and the dark bands are made up of ferro-magnesian minerals, such as hornblende and biotite mica. In folded gneiss, these bands are often very obvious. The composition may be similar to that of granite.

folded, separate bands of pale and dark minerals

TEXTURE A coarse-grained rock with all the minerals easy to see with the naked eye. The folded structure is emphasized by the segregation of the minerals and indicates that parts of the rock were plastic when formed.

ORIGIN Folded gneiss is formed under conditions of high-grade regional metamorphism. All rock types may become gneiss under these conditions.

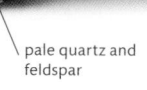

pale quartz and feldspar

dark hornblende and biotite mica

| Pressure: High | Temperature: High | Structure: Foliated, Crystalline |

| Group: METAMORPHIC | Origin: Mountain ranges | Grain size: Coarse | Classification: Regional |

Augen gneiss

This is a metamorphic rock of granitic composition that contain large lens-shaped crystals ("eyes") of feldspar in a banded matrix of quartz, feldspar, and mica. ("Augen" is the German word for "eyes.")

TEXTURE A coarse-grained rock, the gneissose banding is somewhat displaced by the augen structure.
ORIGIN Augen gneiss forms in the highest temperature and pressure zones of regional metamorphism.

large patch of feldspar

dark and light banding

| Pressure: High | Temperature: High | Structure: Foliated, Crystalline |

| Group: METAMORPHIC | Origin: Mountain ranges | Grain size: Coarse | Classification: Regional |

Granular gneiss

High proportions of light gray quartz, white and pink feldspar, and light and dark mica make up this rock. Amphibole and pyroxene may be present. The composition is often granitic.

TEXTURE The crystals are streaked out into typical gneissose banding, with dark and light bands. The texture is granular, with interlocking crystals.
ORIGIN Forms in very high-grade metamorphic environments deep in the Earth's crust.

dark- and light-colored foliated bands

pale feldspar

dark mica

| Pressure: High | Temperature: High | Structure: Foliated, Crystalline |

| Group: METAMORPHIC | Origin: Mountain ranges | Grain size: Coarse | Classification: Regional |

Migmatite

This is a mixed metamorphic rock consisting of a schistose or gneissose component together with a granitic component that forms as layers or pods. Migmatite may approach granite in composition.

TEXTURE A coarse-grained rock with a granular texture, it often shows gneissose banding. The various components may display schistosity.
ORIGIN Forms on a regional scale in areas of high-grade metamorphism.

small-scale folds

light mineral band

dark mafic material

| Pressure: High | Temperature: High | Structure: Foliated, Crystalline |

Group: METAMORPHIC	Origin: Base of crust	Grain size: Coarse	Classification: Regional

Eclogite

A rock predominantly composed of green pyroxene and red garnet. Kyanite crystals may sometimes occur in eclogite.

TEXTURE A medium- to coarse-grained rock that may be banded.
ORIGIN Formed under the highest temperature and pressure conditions at considerable depth in the Earth's crust. Found in association with peridotites and serpentinites.

greenish pyroxene

red garnet

Pressure: High	Temperature: High	Structure: Foliated, Crystalline

Group: METAMORPHIC	Origin: Base of crust	Grain size: Coarse	Classification: Regional

Granulite

This rock has a characteristically high content of pyroxene and either diopside or hypersthene. Garnet, kyanite, biotite, quartz, and feldspar are sometimes present.

TEXTURE These are tough, massive, coarse-grained rocks that may be banded but are not usually schistose.
ORIGIN Believed to be formed at very high temperatures and pressures. Found in ancient continental shield areas.

pale, distinct crystals set in finer matrix

Pressure: High	Temperature: High	Structure: Crystalline

Group: METAMORPHIC	Origin: Mountain ranges	Grain size: Coarse	Classification: Regional

Amphibolite

amphibole crystals

This rock is predominantly formed of amphibole, commonly hornblende, but sometimes actinolite or tremolite. Feldspar, pyroxene, chlorite, epidote, and garnet are also often present.

TEXTURE This is a coarse-grained rock. A well-developed foliation or schistosity can occur, and there may be porphyroblasts, particularly of garnet.
ORIGIN Medium- to high-grade rocks, amphibolites are formed mostly from the metamorphism of igneous rocks such as dolerites.

Pressure: High	Temperature: High	Structure: Foliated, Crystalline

Group: METAMORPHIC	Origin: Contact aureoles	Grain size: Fine, Coarse	Classification: Contact

Green marble

This rock is composed essentially of calcite, derived from the original limestone, but may contain lesser amounts of dolomite. Other minerals formed from impurities in the limestone can include brucite, olivine, tremolite, and serpentine—all of which give the otherwise whitish rock a greenish coloring.

greenish veins of calc-silicate minerals

TEXTURE This is a crystalline rock which, when looked at through a hand lens, but especially under a microscope, is seen to have a mosaic of interlocking and fused crystals of calcite. The original limestone would probably have contained fossils, but these will have been lost during the metamorphic recrystallization.

ORIGIN This rock results from the thermal metamorphism of limestone around igneous intrusions.

Pressure: Low	Temperature: High	Structure: Crystalline

Group: METAMORPHIC	Origin: Contact aureoles	Grain size: Fine, Coarse	Classification: Contact

Blue marble

Composed essentially of calcite, which forms the original limestone, but may contain smaller amounts of dolomite. If the limestone is impure, new minerals develop when the rock is recrystallized due to thermal metamorphism. The new minerals can include forsterite, wollastonite, serpentine, brucite, diopside, and tremolite. The blue coloring, which makes this marble attractive, is due mainly to the diopside in its composition.

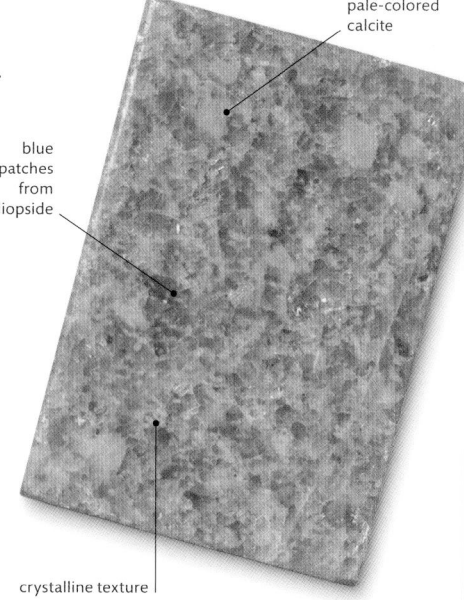

pale-colored calcite

blue patches from diopside

TEXTURE A crystalline rock with a mosaic of fused calcite crystals, just visible with a magnifying glass. Other minerals are set into the matrix.

ORIGIN Forms when limestone is intruded by igneous rock. The heat from such events causes recrystallization of the calcite, destroying original structures in the limestone, and leads to the formation of new minerals.

crystalline texture

Pressure: Low	Temperature: High	Structure: Crystalline

Group: METAMORPHIC	Origin: Contact aureoles	Grain size: Fine, Coarse	Classification: Contact

Gray marble

Unlike other marbles, this rock forms from relatively pure limestones, and therefore few calc-silicate minerals develop. Gray marble is a calcite-rich rock which, when studied under a microscope, is seen to contain a small amount of wollastonite, brucite, tremolite, serpentine, or diopside. Marbles will effervesce in a weak hydrochloric acid solution—this is a very useful test.

TEXTURE This is a crystalline rock with interlocking calcite crystals, forming a pale rock. The sugary surface can be scratched easily with a knife blade.

ORIGIN Forms in the metamorphic aureoles of igneous rocks, where limestone has been heated and recrystallized, especially near granite intrusions.

crystalline texture

Pressure: Low	Temperature: High	Structure: Crystalline

Group: METAMORPHIC	Origin: Contact aureoles	Grain size: Fine, Coarse	Classification: Contact

Olivine marble

This rock contains a very high percentage of calcite, which is recrystallized from the original premetamorphic limestone. Other minerals are produced as a result of metamorphic conditions, the most important of which is olivine. This mineral occurs in the marble as greenish-brown granular crystals.

TEXTURE A rock with a crystalline texture, olivine marble is formed from an interlocking mass of calcite crystals. It differs from the original limestone, in which the calcite grains may have pore spaces between them. Fossils occur only rarely in marble, because the calcite is recrystallized. The olivine crystals are granular in texture.

ORIGIN This rock is formed when limestone is thermally metamorphosed by the intrusion of igneous rock.

individual crystals of olivine

calcite matrix

Pressure: Low	Temperature: High	Structure: Crystalline

| Group: METAMORPHIC | Origin: Contact aureoles | Grain size: Fine | Classification: Contact |

Cordierite hornfels

A rock that contains a variety of minerals, the final assemblage depends on the composition of the original rock and on the temperature conditions of metamorphism. Cordierite hornfels is usually a dark-colored rock containing cordierite—which develops during metamorphism.

TEXTURE A fine- to medium-grained crystalline rock, it contains porphyroblasts of cordierite, which are often several inches in size. The original sedimentary structures are usually destroyed by metamorphic recrystallization. The equigranular composition of the rock causes it to be tough and splintery in texture.

ORIGIN Forms in contact metamorphic aureoles, which occur in rocks close to large igneous (often granite) intrusions. These aureoles grade outward into lower-grade rocks, such as spotted slate.

dark-gray, fine-grained rock

| Pressure: Low | Temperature: High | Structure: Crystalline |

| Group: METAMORPHIC | Origin: Contact aureoles | Grain size: Fine | Classification: Contact |

Pyroxene hornfels

Tough, fine-grained, dark-colored rock essentially composed of quartz, mica, and pyroxene. Pyroxene in the hornfels often occurs as porphyroblasts. Some of the other minerals may not be visible to the naked eye, and all primary sedimentary structures are destroyed by recrystallization. Hornfels lacks planar structures, and its coloration can be grayish, greenish, or black.

TEXTURE This is a fine- to medium-grained rock with an even grain size. Porphyroblasts of pyroxene, cordierite, or andalusite are often developed. The high degree of recrystallization that has occurred removes any original sedimentary structures.

ORIGIN Pyroxene hornfels forms in the innermost part of contact metamorphic aureoles, where the temperature is highest following granite intrusion.

overall dark coloring

| Pressure: Low | Temperature: High | Structure: Crystalline |

| Group: METAMORPHIC | Origin: Contact aureoles | Grain size: Fine | Classification: Contact |

Garnet hornfels

This is generally a dark-colored rock. Garnet hornfels has reddish patches and crystals of garnet set into the matrix. It also contains quartz, mica, and feldspar and metamorphic minerals such as cordierite and andalusite.

reddish garnet porphyroblasts

TEXTURE This is a fine- to medium-grained rock with a tough, splintery texture. The distinct garnet crystals give garnet hornfels a porphyroblastic texture.
ORIGIN Develops in the contact aureoles of large igneous intrusions. These can be formed of granite, syenite, and gabbro.

| Pressure: Low | Temperature: High | Structure: Crystalline |

| Group: METAMORPHIC | Origin: Contact aureoles | Grain size: Fine | Classification: Contact |

Spotted slate

This is a black, greenish, or gray rock with dark spots, which are metamorphic minerals, such as cordierite or andalusite. Spotted slate also has in its composition many of the original nonmetamorphic minerals, such as quartz and mica.

TEXTURE This rock has the same good cleavage as slate and is characterized by the presence of spots, which are often indistinct.
ORIGIN Forms in the perimeter zones of contact aureoles, often grading into hornfels.

| Pressure: Low | Temperature: Moderate to high | Structure: Crystalline |

| Group: METAMORPHIC | Origin: Contact aureoles | Grain size: Fine | Classification: Contact |

Chiastolite hornfels

A gray or brownish rock, this hornfels contains minerals such as quartz and mica, with andalusite and cordierite. The thin-bladed crystals that are clearly seen in the matrix are of chiastolite, a variety of andalusite.

chiastolite crystal

TEXTURE This rock consists of fine-grained crystals of even size. Porphyroblasts of andalusite occur as inclusions of chiastolite, which are cross-shaped in section.
ORIGIN Forms close to the igneous intrusion that provides the heat for metamorphism.

bladed chiastolite

| Pressure: High | Temperature: Moderate to high | Structure: Crystalline |

| Group: METAMORPHIC | Origin: Contact aureoles | Grain size: Medium | Classification: Contact |

Metaquartzite

crystalline
texture

This rock contains well over 90 percent quartz, giving it a pale, almost sugary appearance. It is formed from quartz-rich sandstones. At high magnification, minerals such as mica and feldspar, along with iron oxides, may be seen.

TEXTURE A medium-grained rock, its texture is very even, with the quartz crystals fused to form a tough crystalline rock. The texture is very different from that of the original arenaceous (sandy) sediment, in which there would have been pore spaces between the grains.

ORIGIN Metaquartzite forms by contact metamorphism of sandstone near a large igneous intrusion.

| Pressure: Low | Temperature: High | Structure: Crystalline |

| Group: METAMORPHIC | Origin: Contact aureoles | Grain size: Fine to coarse | Classification: Contact |

Skarn

typical veined
and banded
structure

While containing a variety of minerals, skarn is essentially calcite-rich. It may contain olivine, periclase, wollastonite, diopside, garnet, tremolite, and other minerals that are typical of metamorphosed limestones. Ore minerals—such as pyrite, sphalerite, galena, and chalcopyrite—may also be present.

TEXTURE With a grain size that is fine to medium to coarse, skarn has euhedral crystals of a number of minerals, which often concentrate into patches and nodules in the rock.

ORIGIN The complex mineral assemblages found in skarns are the result of its formation from the contact metamorphism of limestone, usually by granite or syenite intrusions. Impurities in the limestone, as well as fluids from intrusions, cause the formation of various minerals. Ore deposits, including copper, manganese, and molybdenum, which are of sufficient size to be of economic use, are often found in skarns.

dark mineral
patch

pale calcite

| Pressure: Low | Temperature: High | Structure: Crystalline |

| Group: METAMORPHIC | Origin: Contact aureoles | Grain size: Fine | Classification: Contact |

Halleflinta

This is a rock containing a variety of minerals related to its original premetamorphosed composition as a volcanic tuff. Halleflinta, therefore, contains quartz and has been enriched with silica during metamorphism. It is frequently pale-colored and can vary from brown to pink, green, gray, or yellowish brown.

TEXTURE Halleflinta is a fine-grained rock— a microscope is needed to study its mineral composition. Texture is even, with a flinty, crystalline appearance. This rock breaks with a sharp, splintery fracture. It may show a layered structure related to the original stratification of the volcanic tuff. Porphyroblastic textures with large, isolated crystals are sometimes found.

ORIGIN Forms by the contact metamorphism of tuffs, which have usually been impregnated by secondary silica. It is often associated with hornfels.

brownish, flinty rock

splintery fracture

| Pressure: Low | Temperature: High | Structure: Crystalline |

| Group: METAMORPHIC | Origin: Thrust zones | Grain size: Fine | Classification: Dynamic |

Mylonite

The minerals contained in mylonite vary depending on the rocks being subjected to metamorphic alteration. Mylonite contains two main groups of material: one is derived from fragments of rock, called "rock flour," and the other consists of minerals that have crystallized at or soon after metamorphism. The rock can be dark- or light-colored.

TEXTURE This is a rock that has been destroyed by deformation and the particles streaked out into small lenses and patches. It tends to be fine-grained. However, in some coarser specimens, the streaked-out structure may be visible, and the surfaces can exhibit foliation.

ORIGIN Forms when large-scale thrust faults develop. The rocks near the thrust plane suffer great shearing stress and are fragmented and drawn out in the direction of thrust movement. This occurs during Earth movements associated with mountain formation.

foliation

| Pressure: Shearing stress | Temperature: Low | Structure: Streaked out |

SEDIMENTARY ROCKS

SEDIMENTARY ROCKS are deposited at the Earth's surface, many on the sea bed, and are often layered. The rocks have layers that are often visible to the naked eye. Detrital sediments result from weathering, erosion, and accumulation of particles from rocks already formed. Organic sediments are composed of fossils and material derived from once-living organisms. Chemical sediments are formed from chemical precipitation of material such as rock salt and calcite.

Group: SEDIMENTARY	Origin: Marine, Freshwater	Grain size: Very coarse

Quartz conglomerate

This rock contains many light-colored quartz fragments set in a much finer matrix, which usually comprises sand or silt, small rock fragments, and iron oxides, often cemented by silica or calcite.

TEXTURE The large grains are rounded; the matrix may be angular or rounded. Quartz conglomerates rarely contain fossils because of their coarse nature and the often turbulent conditions associated with their formation. Bedding structures are seldom seen in small specimens.
ORIGIN Forms in environments such as beaches and river systems, where there is sufficient energy to move large fragments of material.

large fragments of quartz

fine sandstone matrix

Classification: Detrital	Fossils: Very rare	Grain shape: Rounded

Group: SEDIMENTARY	Origin: Marine, Freshwater	Grain size: Very coarse

Polygenetic conglomerate

Containing a variety of different materials, polygenetic conglomerates can have fragments derived from igneous, metamorphic, and sedimentary rocks, as well as particles of individual minerals. The fragments can be cemented by various minerals, including quartz, iron oxides, and calcite.

TEXTURE The grains in a polygenetic conglomerate are rounded or subrounded by the action of water. There may be some smaller angular fragments in the matrix between the large grains.
ORIGIN Forms in high-energy environments, such as powerful water currents, which are able to move the large fragments of rock.

large subrounded fragment

Classification: Detrital	Fossils: Very rare	Grain shape: Rounded

| Group: SEDIMENTARY | Origin: Transitional, Water | Grain size: Very coarse |

Breccia

Fragments in breccia are angular and may be of any type of igneous, metamorphic, and sedimentary rock. These fragments are bound together in a fine- to medium-grained matrix.

TEXTURE Bedding structures are usually visible only on a large scale in the field. Fossils are uncommon in such rocks. The large fragments of rocks and minerals in breccia are angular, and the surrounding matrix material is also angular.

ORIGIN Often forms as scree at the base of cliffs. Breccia has a similar origin to limestone breccia, but the fragments in it are not calcareous. The accumulation of the large, angular fragments can cake place in a number of environments, especially where mechanical weathering is active.

angular fragment showing no preferred orientation

yellowish matrix

gray siliceous fragment

| Classification: Detrital | Fossils: Uncommon | Grain shape: Angular |

| Group: SEDIMENTARY | Origin: Transitional, Water | Grain size: Very coarse |

Limestone breccia

This is a rock that contains fragments of limestone, usually set in a fine-grained matrix cemented with calcite. Other minerals such as quartz may be present in limestone breccia, as may particles of other rocks.

TEXTURE The grains are large and angular in contrast to the rounded fragments in conglomerate. The individual fragments in limestone breccia may contain fossils.

ORIGIN Found in transitional environments near continental margins. Limestone breccia may form as deposits at the base of cliffs. As water seeps through the cliff and the accumulated scree, it deposits calcite that will cement together the fragments.

finer matrix

dark, angular fragment of limestone

| Classification: Detrital | Fossils: Invertebrates | Grain shape: Angular |

Group: SEDIMENTARY	Origin: Glacier, Ice sheet	Grain size: Fine

Boulder clay

This rock consists of angular and rounded pebbles, varying in size and set in a fine, unconsolidated matrix of clay or sand. The glacial fragments included in the boulder clay are called glacial erratics. These are fragments carried away from their place of origin by the ice. They can be of assistance to geologists in helping them work out the general direction of ice movement.

TEXTURE The fragments in boulder clay are mainly angular. The rock is made up of various unsorted materials, ranging from clay size to boulder size.
ORIGIN Boulder clay usually forms as a deposit from melting glaciers and ice sheets.

rock fragment

brown, fine-grained clay

Classification: Detrital	Fossils: Rare	Grain shape: Angular, Rounded

Group: SEDIMENTARY	Origin: Continental	Grain size: Fine

Loess

This is a yellowish or brownish clay made up of very small particles of quartz, feldspar, calcite, and other minerals and rock fragments.

TEXTURE Loess is a fine-grained aeolian clay, which is porous and earthy. It is poorly cemented, which makes it crumbly. The grains may be rounded because of wind action, and bedding can be difficult to determine.
ORIGIN Forms by the winds blowing out from glaciated regions. Loess is found in thick layers, especially in China, but also in areas of western Europe.

yellowish coloring due to the presence of limonite

Classification: Detrital	Fossils: Rare	Grain shape: Rounded, Angular

Group: SEDIMENTARY	Origin: Marine, Freshwater, Continental	Grain size: Medium

Sandstone

This rock is predominantly made up of quartz grains but is often accompanied by feldspar, mica, or other minerals. Grains may be cemented by silica, calcite, or iron oxides.

TEXTURE Sandstone is a medium-grained rock. The grains are usually well-sorted (grains all of a similar size) and can either be angular (gritstone) or rounded (sandstone).
ORIGIN Sandstones are extremely common rocks that form in a great variety of geological situations. The majority of sandstones, however, are accumulated in either water, usually marine, or as wind-blown deposits in arid continental areas.

numerous grains of quartz make up the matrix

fine stratification

Classification: Detrital	Fossils: Invertebrates, Vertebrates, Plants	Grain shape: Angular, Rounded

Group: SEDIMENTARY	Origin: Marine	Grain size: Medium

Greensand

This is a quartz sandstone that contains a few percent of glauconite (a green-colored mineral that forms only under marine conditions). Small quantities of detrital mica, feldspar, and rock fragments are usually cemented by calcite. The glauconite may have formed in place (authigenic) and occurs as flaky grains.

TEXTURE Greensand is a medium-grained rock, with the majority of the grains being angular. The sediment is well-sorted.
ORIGIN Greensand forms in a marine environment. The constituent mineral glauconite, a potassium iron silicate, may be used to help in radiometric age-dating.

glauconite gives green coloring

Classification: Detrital	Fossils: Invertebrates, Vertebrates, Plants	Grain shape: Angular

| Group: SEDIMENTARY | Origin: Continental, Marine | Grain size: Medium |

Red sandstone

This rock is predominantly formed by quartz grains but also accompanied by some mica and feldspar. The red coloration is due to coatings of hematite over the sand grains. Hematite is an iron oxide derived by the oxidation of iron-rich minerals swept in from a source area.

TEXTURE This is a well-sorted sediment, and the grains may be angular or rounded. Red sandstone often displays sedimentary structures, including cross-bedding, ripple marks, and desiccation cracks.

ORIGIN Forms as continental deposits, where iron may be oxidized. Red sandstone also commonly forms in shallow marine environments.

iron oxide gives reddish color

rounded grains

well-sorted sediment

| Classification: Detrital | Fossils: Invertebrates, Vertebrates, Plants | Grain shape: Angular, Rounded |

| Group: SEDIMENTARY | Origin: Continental | Grain size: Medium |

Millet-seed sandstone

A quartz sandstone with conspicuous rounding of the grains, producing what is known as a millet-seed texture, the rock may also contain some feldspar and rock fragments, but mica is usually absent. There is often a thin coating of iron oxides on the grains.

TEXTURE This is a very well-sorted sediment, with the quartz grains all the same size. The grains are rounded and are of medium size. Fossils are very rare.

ORIGIN Millet-seed sandstone forms in arid environments. The quartz sand grains are rounded by the action of the wind. In the field, large-scale dune bedding may be a feature of this rock, indicating continental deposition.

medium-sized grain of rounded quartz

iron oxide gives brown coloring

| Classification: Detrital | Fossils: Rare | Grain shape: Rounded |

Group: SEDIMENTARY	Origin: Marine, Freshwater	Grain size: Medium

Micaceous sandstone

A rock containing abundant quartz but also considerable amounts of mica. It may contain detrital feldspar and rock fragments. On the bedding planes, the surfaces where the sand is deposited, there are many small, glittering flakes of mica. These can be muscovite, biotite mica, or both.

TEXTURE This rock is well-sorted and medium-grained. The majority of the grains are angular, the mica occurring typically as flakes.

ORIGIN Mica is a rare mineral in continental, wind-deposited sandstones, because its flaky habit causes it to be blown away. Its presence in micaceous sandstone suggests water deposition, in either lakes and rivers, or the sea.

patch of iron oxide on surface

small mica flake

Classification: Detrital	Fossils: Invertebrates, Vertebrates, Plants	Grain shape: Angular, Flattened

Group: SEDIMENTARY	Origin: Marine, Freshwater	Grain size: Medium

Limonitic sandstone

Rich in quartz grains, limonitic sandstone may contain small rock fragments and minerals such as feldspar and mica. The presence of the iron mineral "limonite"–from which the rock gets its name—may give it a yellowish or dark-brownish coloring.

TEXTURE This is a well-sorted sediment, with most of the grains the same size. The fragments are angular and coated with limonite, which acts as a cement. As with other sandstones, bedding surfaces may be discernible, although this may not be particularly obvious in a hand specimen.

ORIGIN Limonitic sandstone can form in a number of different environments, including marine and freshwater.

dark brown coloring due to limonite

angular grains cemented with limonite

well-sorted sediment

Classification: Detrital	Fossils: Invertebrates, Vertebrates, Plants	Grain shape: Angular

| Group: SEDIMENTARY | Origin: Marine, Freshwater | Grain size: Medium |

Pink orthoquartzite

As with all orthoquartzites, this rock is a sandstone with a quartz content greater than 95 percent. The pinkish, iron-stained quartz grains are bound together with a silica cement. With a magnifying glass, other materials may occasionally be visible, including some feldspar or rock fragments. Fossils in orthoquartzite are very rare.

TEXTURE This is a medium-grained, well-sorted rock with a crystalline appearance.
ORIGIN As orthoquartzites contain very little feldspar, they are said to be mature rocks. This is because the long-term processes of weathering, erosion, and deposition have removed virtually all the less-resistant materials from the source rocks, and quartz becomes the dominant mineral.

high quartz content

crystalline appearance

| Classification: Detrital | Fossils: Rare, Invertebrates | Grain shape: Angular |

| Group: SEDIMENTARY | Origin: Marine, Freshwater | Grain size: Medium |

Gray orthoquartzite

Compositionally the same as pink orthoquartzite, the gray coloring of this rock comes from the constituent quartz grains. The cement is also quartz, and this binds the grains very firmly. Orthoquartzite may be difficult to distinguish from metaquartzite (metamorphosed quartz sandstones), though the occasional presence of fossils can help in identification. There are often stratification and other sedimentary structures, such as cross or graded bedding, in orthoquartzite. These are not usually evident in metaquartzite.

TEXTURE This is a rock of medium grain size, and it is usually well-sorted.
ORIGIN Gray orthoquartzite forms in marine and freshwater environments. With so much quartz present, this, as with other orthoquartzites, is known as a mature sediment.

medium-grained quartz

| Classification: Detrital | Fossils: Rare, Invertebrates | Grain shape: Angular |

| Group: SEDIMENTARY | Origin: Marine | Grain size: Medium, Fine |

Greywacke

This rock contains abundant quartz, feldspar, and rock fragments. The matrix is of clay, chlorite, quartz, and pyrite, but the minerals are too small to be seen with the naked eye.

TEXTURE Greywacke has a poorly sorted nature, with a great variety of different grain sizes apparent.
ORIGIN This rock is composed of marine sediments. It may form from a slurry of sediment deposited in deep ocean environments from fast-moving currents. When this is the case, the rock may exhibit a variety of sedimentary features.

poorly sorted

fine-grained matrix

| Classification: Detrital | Fossils: Rare | Grain shape: Angular |

| Group: SEDIMENTARY | Origin: Marine, Freshwater, Continental | Grain size: Medium |

Arkose

A medium- to coarse-grained rock that is pinkish to gray in color. Although predominantly made up of quartz, feldspar can contribute as much as a third of the rock. Constituents are usually well-sorted. Together with mica flakes, they are cemented in a calcitic or ferruginous cement.

TEXTURE The grains in this rock are angular and usually well-sorted.
ORIGIN Forms in marine and freshwater environments and continental deposits. Arkose is said to be an immature rock because of its high feldspar content. The sediment that forms this rock is deposited rapidly or in an arid environment preventing the feldspar from decomposing. The effect of a long process of chemical weathering, erosion, and deposition would be to alter and decompose the feldspar. Most arkoses are derived from granite disintegration.

pinkish feldspar

quartz grains

| Classification: Detrital | Fossils: Rare | Grain shape: Angular |

| Group: SEDIMENTARY | Origin: Marine, Freshwater, Continental | Grain size: Coarse, Medium |

Quartz gritstone

This rock contains over 75 percent quartz and some feldspar and mica. There can also be small rock fragments of varying types, depending on the rocks in the source area from which the sediment is derived. The cementing mineral may be quartz, and a yellowish coating of limonite on the grains is often evident.

well-sorted sediment

TEXTURE This is a coarse- to medium-grained rock. The grains are fairly well-sorted and angular in shape. Gritstones are sometimes poorly cemented, and the individual grains can often be rubbed off with the fingers.
ORIGIN Forms in a number of different environments, ranging from marine and freshwater to continental. Most gritstones are formed in water, often in river systems and deltas. In all these environments, a reasonable amount of energy is needed to carry the coarse particles.

| Classification: Detrital | Fossils: Invertebrates, Vertebrates, Plants | Grain shape: Angular |

| Group: SEDIMENTARY | Origin: Marine, Continental | Grain size: Coarse, Medium |

Feldspathic gritstone

This rock contains a high percentage of quartz but also has as much as 25 percent feldspar. Mica is present, and there are often small rock fragments derived from the source area. Feldspathic gritstone has a similar composition to arkose, which is its fine-grained equivalent. It is a brownish-colored rock and may take on a pinkish tinge when pink orthoclase feldspar is present. A cement of quartz or iron oxide binds the grains together.

medium grain size

TEXTURE This is a coarse- to medium-grained rock. The grains are angular, although the feldspar may have flattened faces where it has broken along cleavage planes. It is well-sorted (most of the grains are of the same size).
ORIGIN Forms by rapid deposition in transitional environments. Feldspar decomposes during protracted weathering.

feldspar grain

| Classification: Detrital | Fossils: Invertebrates, Vertebrates, Plants | Grain shape: Angular |

Group: SEDIMENTARY	Origin: Marine	Grain size: Fine

Black shale

This, like other shales, consists of a mixture of clay minerals together with detrital quartz, feldspar, and mica. Black shales are rich in carbonaceous matter, and pyrite and gypsum commonly occur. The pyrite content may result from the rock forming under reducing conditions in deep, still water. This mineral can occur as cubic crystals on bedding planes, and fossils in black shale are often replaced by pyrite.

TEXTURE This is a very fine-grained rock, with mineral grains invisible except under a microscope. It is finely laminated and splits easily along the bedding planes, sometimes revealing flattened fossils.
ORIGIN Forms as a clay deposit in deep marine environments. The fossils in black shale are often marine creatures, such as mollusks.

fine-grained rock

Classification: Detrital	Fossils: Invertebrates, Vertebrates, Plants	Grain shape: Angular

Group: SEDIMENTARY	Origin: Marine, Freshwater	Grain size: Fine

Fossiliferous shale

Compositionally similar to other shales, fossiliferous shale may also have a high calcite content derived from the fossils it contains. As well as complete fossils, it usually has detrital fossil fragments.

TEXTURE Because of its fine grain size, shale can preserve a variety of fossils with very fine detail. Fossils commonly found in shales include brachiopods and mollusks, such as ammonoids, bivalves, and gastropods. There are often arthropods, such as trilobites, and graptolites—delicate structures which are not found in coarser rocks. Plants and vertebrates may also be present.
ORIGIN Usually forms under relatively shallow marine conditions. Fossiliferous shale can also be found under freshwater conditions. The nature of the fossils found in the rock is usually a good indicator of the environment in which the rock was formed.

fossil brachiopod

shale matrix

Classification: Detrital	Fossils: Invertebrates, Vertebrates, Plants	Grain shape: Angular

Group: SEDIMENTARY	Origin: Marine, Freshwater	Grain size: Fine

Siltstone

This rock contains more quartz than either mudstone or shale. Siltstone is commonly laminated due to variations in grain size, organic content, or amounts of calcium carbonate.

TEXTURE This is a fine-grained sediment. The individual rock fragments and mineral grains in siltstone are too small to be visible to the naked eye.
ORIGIN Siltstone forms by the compaction of sediment of silt grade, which may have accumulated in a variety of environments, both marine and freshwater. The fossil content can be a guide to the precise environment of deposition. Because of the presence of feldspar, siltstone is said to be immature. A long-term weathering process would decompose feldspar.

fine-grained sediment

Classification: Detrital	Fossils: Invertebrates, Vertebrates, Plants	Grain shape: Angular

Group: SEDIMENTARY	Origin: Marine, Freshwater	Grain size: Fine

Mudstone

This rock consists of a mixture of clay minerals together with detrital quartz, feldspar, and mica. Iron oxides are also often present.

TEXTURE Mudstone is a very fine-grained rock; the grains cannot be seen with the naked eye. It shares many characteristics with shale and may contain fossils, though it has less well-defined lamination compared to shale.
ORIGIN Mudstone forms in a variety of environments resulting from the deposition of mud in, for example, oceans and freshwater lakes. Studying the fossils contained in a specimen of mudstone and comparing them with the lifestyles of related modern organisms can help identify the type of environment in which the rock was formed.

fine-grained rock

Classification: Detrital	Fossils: Invertebrates, Vertebrates, Plants	Grain shape: Angular

| Group: SEDIMENTARY | Origin: Marine, Freshwater | Grain size: Fine |

Calcareous mudstone

As its name suggests, this rock is similar to mudstone but has a high calcite content. Detrital quartz and feldspar may also be present. Fossils are not uncommon. The rock is often light-colored.

TEXTURE A very fine-grained rock in which the particles cannot be seen with the naked eye. The grains are much the same size, but recrystallization may change their original shape. The rock may break in a distinctive way, with a subconchoidal fracture. Because of the high calcite content, it will effervesce when tested with cold hydrochloric acid.

ORIGIN Forms in marine and freshwater conditions. Being very fine-grained, calcareous mud is easily transported by water into the sea and lakes where it may accumulate with sand, silt, and calcareous organisms.

curved fracture

calcite vein

| Classification: Detrital | Fossils: Invertebrates, Vertebrates, Plants | Grain shape: Angular |

| Group: SEDIMENTARY | Origin: Marine, Freshwater, Continental | Grain size: Fine |

Clay

This rock is very rich in clay minerals, together with detrital quartz, mica, and feldspar.

TEXTURE The grain size is so fine that the individual minerals cannot be seen except with a microscope. Clays often have a characteristic smell, and the grains absorb water to become plastic.

ORIGIN Clay forms in many different environments. It can occur in deep and shallow marine conditions, in lakes, and as a continental sediment. Glacial clays develop from the powdering of rock by ice action. Clay minerals are formed by the decay and alteration of certain silicate minerals, such as feldspars, under chemical weathering. Fossils are often well preserved in clay because of its very fine grain size.

very fine grains

this fossil shell suggests a marine environment

| Classification: Detrital | Fossils: Invertebrates, Vertebrates, Plants | Grain shape: Angular |

| Group: SEDIMENTARY | Origin: Marine, Freshwater | Grain size: Fine |

Red marl

This rock is a sediment intermediate between clays and limestones and includes gradations between calcareous clays and muddy limestones. The amount of calcareous material varies between 40 and 60 percent, with detrital quartz, clay, and silt particles. The red coloring is due to the presence of iron oxide.

TEXTURE Because marl is such a fine-grained rock, it can be examined in detail only under a microscope. The grains are well-formed and cemented by calcite.
ORIGIN Marls are often found in shallow lakes with a lot of vegetation. They are also associated with evaporite deposits formed in saline basins. In this case, they may be interbedded with gypsum and rock salt.

fine-grained rock

reddish-brown color

| Classification: Detrital | Fossils: Invertebrates, Vertebrates, Plants | Grain shape: Angular |

| Group: SEDIMENTARY | Origin: Marine, Freshwater | Grain size: Fine |

Green marl

As with its red counterpart, green marl is an intermediate sediment between the clays and the limestones. It differs only in color, with the greenish coloring due to the presence of minerals such as glauconite and chlorite. Green marl also has a high calcite content. The calcite present causes the rock to effervesce when it is tested with cold, dilute hydrochloric acid.

TEXTURE Green marl is a fine-grained rock. The individual particles can be seen only under a microscope.
ORIGIN This rock forms in marine and freshwater conditions. When glauconite is present in green marl, it indicates that the rock formed in a marine environment.

fine-grained sediment

| Classification: Detrital | Fossils: Invertebrates, Plants | Grain shape: Angular |

Group: SEDIMENTARY	Origin: Marine, Salt lakes	Grain size: Coarse

Rock salt

This rock is essentially composed of halite, often with impurities of clay minerals and iron oxides. The rock is colored reddish brown when iron oxides are present.

TEXTURE Rock salt is usually massive and coarsely crystalline, sometimes occurring as distinct cubic crystals. Under pressure, the rock may flow, forming salt plugs that intrude other strata.
ORIGIN Forms from saline waters, such as salt lakes, in a sequence that includes other evaporite minerals, such as dolomite and gypsum.

orange-brown crystal

Classification: Chemical	Fossils: None	Grain shape: –

Group: SEDIMENTARY	Origin: Marine, Salt lakes	Grain size: Coarse to fine

Rock gypsum

This rock normally occurs as massive gypsum (hydrated calcium sulfate).

TEXTURE This coarse- to fine-grained rock has a fibrous habit. It may also show bedding, which is often strongly distorted. Rock gypsum is usually interbedded with sandstones, marls, and limestones. A soft rock, it can be scratched easily with a fingernail.
ORIGIN Forms in evaporite rock sequences in association with dolomite rock and marl and the minerals anhydrite, halite, and calcite.

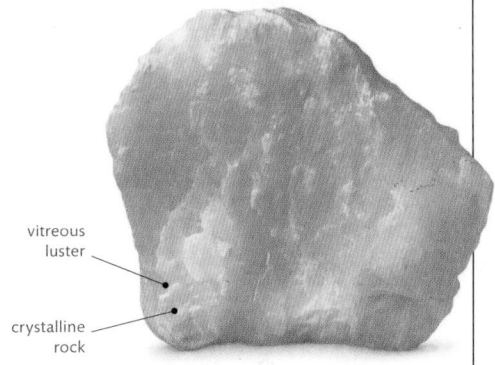

vitreous luster

crystalline rock

Classification: Chemical	Fossils: None	Grain shape: –

Group: SEDIMENTARY	Origin: Marine, Salt lakes	Grain size: –

Potash rock

This rock is essentially a mixture of sylvite and halite. The crystalline sylvite is a pale gray color when it is pure, while orange-red sylvite gets its color from iron oxide staining.

TEXTURE This is a crystalline rock.
ORIGIN Deposited from saline waters, potash rock forms in a sequence that includes evaporites and rocks such as dolomite, marl, and mudstone.

rough, partly dissolved surface

iron impurities give reddish coloring

Classification: Chemical	Fossils: None	Grain shape: –

Group: SEDIMENTARY	Origin: Marine	Grain size: Coarse

Pisolitic limestone

This rock is similar to oolitic limestones but contains larger and more irregular structures up to pea size, known as pisoliths. These are formed of calcite precipitated around a nucleus, such as a sand grain or a fragment of shell. The cementing material is calcite.

TEXTURE This limestone is a coarse-grained rock with pisoliths all of much the same size. These can often be flattened, unlike the spherical ooliths. Fossils are common and include many invertebrates.

ORIGIN Pisolitic limestone forms in moderately shallow marine conditions, similar to those where oolite forms. Such environments favor the precipitation of calcite. These conditions were common during the past, especially during the Mesozoic era.

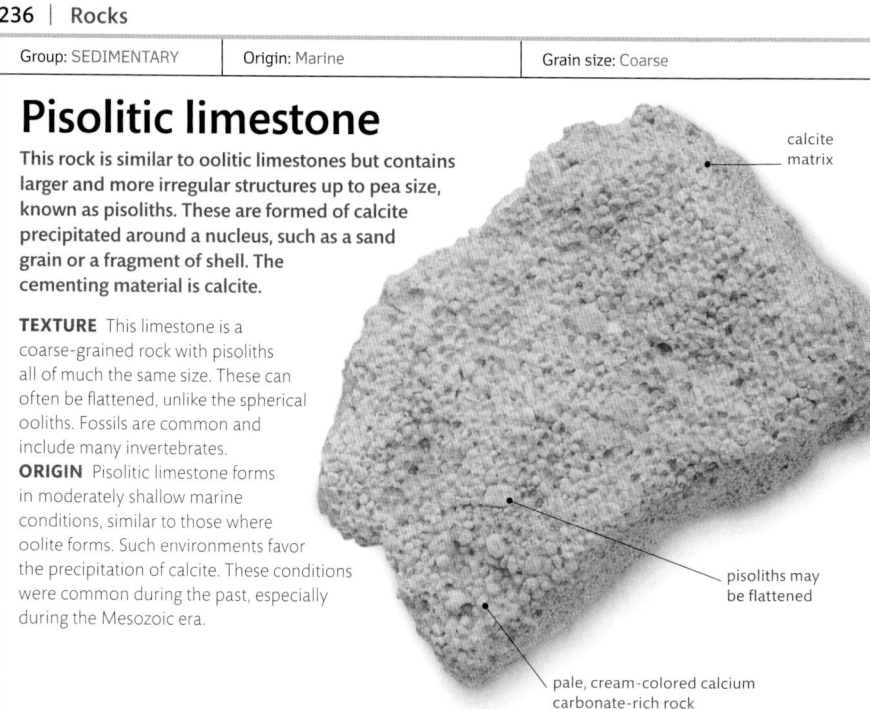

calcite matrix

pisoliths may be flattened

pale, cream-colored calcium carbonate-rich rock

Classification: Chemical	Fossils: Invertebrates	Grain shape: Rounded

Group: SEDIMENTARY	Origin: Marine	Grain size: Medium

Oolitic limestone

Containing a high degree of calcium carbonate, oolitic limestone may also contain small amounts of quartz and other detrital minerals. Fossil fragments are common.

TEXTURE Rock essentially composed of closely packed ooliths is called oolite. Oooliths are spheroidal or ellipsoidal structures built of concentric layers—usually composed of calcite. The rounded ooliths are easy to see with the naked eye in the typically light-colored rock matrix.

ORIGIN Forms in warm, shallow, and strongly agitated marine conditions. The constant action of tides, currents, and waves encourages the precipitation of calcium carbonate around quartz grains and fossil fragments.

medium-grained, rounded ooliths set in calcite cement

pale-colored matrix

Classification: Chemical	Fossils: Invertebrates	Grain shape: Rounded

Group: SEDIMENTARY	Origin: Marine	Grain size: Fine

Chalk

This is a very pure limestone formed of calcite and containing only small amounts of silt or mud. It consists mainly of the tests of microorganisms, such as coccoliths and foraminiferans, which cannot be seen without the aid of a microscope. Macrofossils, which can be seen with the naked eye, are often present, and these include ammonites and bivalves, brachiopods, and echinoderms. Chalk may contain detrital material, mainly quartz, as well as other mineral fragments.

TEXTURE A very fine-grained, powdery, soft rock. It effervesces strongly when in contact with cold, dilute hydrochloric acid.

ORIGIN Formed in marine conditions during the Cretaceous period. During this period, the continental shelves, where the chalk was deposited, were below a much greater depth of seawater than today. The small amount of detrital material suggests that nearby continental areas were low-lying and arid.

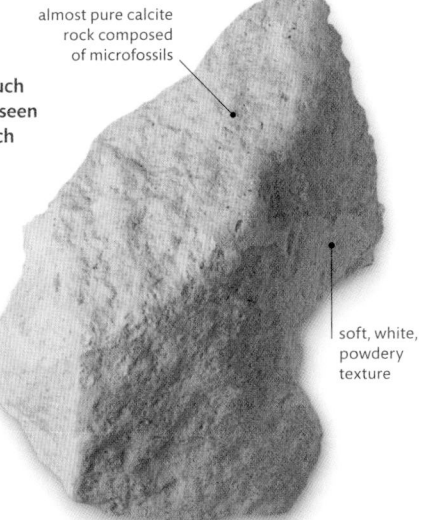

almost pure calcite rock composed of microfossils

soft, white, powdery texture

Classification: Organic	Fossils: Invertebrates, Vertebrates	Grain shape: Rounded, Angular

Group: SEDIMENTARY	Origin: Marine	Grain size: Fine

Red chalk

A fine-grained calcareous rock, red chalk gets its color from a detrital component of iron oxide (hematite). It may also contain scattered quartz pebbles. Many of the minute grains in red chalk are microfossils, such as coccoliths. Macrofossils, including belemnites, ammonites, bivalves, and echinoderms, are frequently present in red chalk.

TEXTURE The grain size is small and the individual particles are too minute to be detected except with a microscope.

ORIGIN Thought to be formed under slow marine deposition. The red coloring agent hematite may be derived from a nearby land surface. A study of the fossils in red chalk will give a much more detailed indication of the environment of deposition.

reddish coloring due to iron oxide

fine grain size

Classification: Organic	Fossils: Invertebrates	Grain shape: Rounded

| Group: SEDIMENTARY | Origin: Marine | Grain size: Fine to coarse |

Crinoidal limestone

This rock is essentially formed of calcite as fine or larger crystals. These may have been derived from animal skeletons such as crinoid plates. Ossicles of crinoid stems are conspicuous ingredients of this rock.

TEXTURE The large fragments in the rock are the broken stems of crinoids. These may be long, cylindrical pieces, as well as single, rounded ossicles. They are bound in a matrix of massive calcite, with a calcite cement.

ORIGIN This limestone is formed in marine conditions and takes its name from crinoids—a group of sea-dwelling creatures related to starfish and sea urchins. Crinoids' presence in coral limestone suggests that they inhabited shallow marine environments. Crinoids are not the only fossils that are commonly found in crinoidal limestone—it can be rich in brachiopods, mollusks, and corals.

pale grayish-pink rock with a lot of fragmented calcite

broken crinoid stem

| Classification: Organic | Fossils: Invertebrates | Grain shape: Angular, Rounded |

| Group: SEDIMENTARY | Origin: Marine | Grain size: Fine |

Coral limestone

This limestone is almost entirely formed from the calcareous remains of fossil coral. The individual structures are called corallites, and they are held in a matrix of lime-rich mud. As well as a high proportion of calcite, this mud, now limestone, contains small amounts of detrital material such as clay and quartz.

TEXTURE The texture is determined by the type of coral preserved in the rock. The matrix of this limestone is fine-grained.

ORIGIN These rocks form in marine conditions, and by studying the individual corals, it may be possible to give more precise details of the environment. Most coral limestone forms on the continental shelf. Though these rocks are rich in coral, they can also contain other shallow-water marine invertebrates, including brachiopods, cephalopods, gastropods, and bryozoans.

unusual coloring

mass of coral held in lime mud matrix

| Classification: Organic | Fossils: Invertebrates | Grain shape: Angular |

| Group: SEDIMENTARY | Origin: Marine, Freshwater | Grain size: Medium, Fine |

Shelly limestone

A general name for calcareous rocks containing a high proportion of fossil shells. This limestone can contain a great variety of brachiopod and bivalve shells. The rock matrix is usually cemented by calcite. Any brownish coloring the rock exhibits is due to detrital minerals and iron oxides.

TEXTURE The matrix of this rock is medium- or fine-grained and has angular fragments.
ORIGIN These limestones are essentially of marine origin, although a rare few of them may form in freshwater environments. As with many of the rocks that contain fossils, it is often possible to discover the actual environment in which a specimen formed by a careful study of the fossils found within the shelly limestone.

gray calcite
brachiopod shell

brownish coloring
from iron oxides

| Classification: Organic | Fossils: Invertebrates | Grain shape: Angular |

| Group: SEDIMENTARY | Origin: Marine | Grain size: Fine |

Bryozoan limestone

The percentage of calcite in bryozoan limestone is very high. This rock also contains a small amount of detrital material, such as quartz and clay. These detrital materials may give the rock a coloring that is darker than the pale gray of purer limestone. Essentially, bryozoan limestone is lime mud characterized by the netlike structures of fossil bryozoans.

TEXTURE The lime mud that forms the matrix is fine-grained and even-textured.
ORIGIN This rock forms in marine conditions. It commonly originates in calcareous reef deposits, where the bryozoans, such as *Fenestella*, help bind the mounds of reef sediment. Besides bryozoans, the reef environment also supports a wealth of other organisms, and these limestones are rich in mollusks, brachiopods, and other marine invertebrates.

small bryozoans within
a lime mud

| Classification: Organic | Fossils: Invertebrates | Grain shape: Angular |

Group: SEDIMENTARY	Origin: Freshwater	Grain size: Medium, Fine

Freshwater limestone

Less common than marine limestone, the freshwater variety is distinguished by the nature of the fossils contained in it, associated with freshwater environments. As with other limestones, this rock has a high proportion of calcium carbonate and can also contain detrital quartz and clay. The high calcite content causes the rock to effervesce when it comes into contact with cold, dilute hydrochloric acid.

TEXTURE The calcareous matrix is crystalline and binds the rock together. This rock consists essentially of a calcareous mud, with a number of coiled gastropod shells. The chief way to determine if a limestone is marine or freshwater is by identifying the fossils.

ORIGIN This limestone forms in freshwater lakes with a high lime content and is unusual in the stratigraphic record.

nonmarine gastropod shell

lime mud matrix

Classification: Organic	Fossils: Invertebrates, Plants	Grain shape: Angular

Group: SEDIMENTARY	Origin: Marine	Grain size: Fine

Nummulitic limestone

This rock contains a very high percentage of calcium carbonate, mainly in the form of whole and fragmented, circular-shaped shells of a foraminiferid fossil called *Nummulites*. These are cemented together with calcite. In common with other biogenic limestones, which are composed largely of one type of fossil, nummulitic limestone can contain other fossils. Some detrital material, usually quartz, may also be present.

TEXTURE The matrix of this limestone is fine-grained, whereas the whole fossil can measure up to about ¾ in (2 cm) in diameter.

ORIGIN This rock is formed under marine conditions and is commonly found in localized areas. The Egyptian pyramids are made of this particular limestone.

fossil *Nummulites*

fine matrix

Classification: Organic	Fossils: Invertebrates	Grain shape: Angular

Group: SEDIMENTARY	Origin: Marine	Grain size: Medium, Fine

Dolomite

This rock, also known as dolostone, contains a high proportion of the mineral dolomite (calcium magnesium carbonate), from which it gets its name. Detrital minerals and secondary silica (chert) are also present. Dolomite rocks are usually darker than other limestones (often creamy brown). Dolomites also tend to be less fossiliferous than other limestones, possibly because of the recrystallization that has often taken place during their formation.

TEXTURE Dolomite usually has an equigranular crystalline texture but sometimes occurs as compact and earthy masses.
ORIGIN This rock forms in marine environments. Most dolomites are believed to be of secondary origin, replacing original limestones.

equigranular texture

fine-grained matrix

Classification: Chemical	Fossils: Invertebrates	Grain shape: Angular

Group: SEDIMENTARY	Origin: Continental	Grain size: Fine

Tufa

This rock is principally composed of calcite (calcium carbonate). Impurities of iron oxides are responsible for tufa's yellowish or reddish coloration. Calcrete is a name given to the pebbly form of tufa. This is a porous and usually nonbedded deposit. Travertine is a more dense and banded form of tufa.

TEXTURE This is a crystalline material and may have pebbles and grains of sediment caught up in it.
ORIGIN The rock forms when calcium carbonate is precipitated from lime-rich waters. This may occur on cliffs, in caves, and on quarry faces, especially in limestone regions. Plants and mosses are often covered with tufa, and thus preserved as crusty, lime-rich fossils. Such preservation is very rapid, and modern organisms can become encrusted in a matter of months in favorable conditions.

noticeable lack of any bedding

crusty, porous structure

Classification: Chemical	Fossils: Plants, Invertebrates	Grain shape: Angular

Group: SEDIMENTARY	Origin: Continental	Grain size: Fine

Travertine

Consisting of almost pure calcium carbonate, travertine may also contain some detrital quartz and clay. Fossil material is virtually absent. Travertine is a very light-colored rock unless it contains iron compounds or other impurities, which can give it a darker coloring. Travertine deposits are often rounded and may be banded.

TEXTURE This rock is formed of small crystals of calcite that bind together other sediment particles. In many situations, travertine occurs in strata.

ORIGIN Many hot springs, especially in volcanic regions, give rise to travertine by the deposition of calcium carbonate.

iron minerals give slight staining

porous, spongy texture

Classification: Chemical	Fossils: Rare	Grain shape: Angular

Group: SEDIMENTARY	Origin: Continental	Grain size: Fine to medium

Stalactite

Sedimentary structures formed of calcium carbonate, stalactites are sometimes colored by impurities, such as iron oxide.

TEXTURE These crystalline structures occur in the shape of pendants grown from the roofs of caves, especially in limestone regions. While stalactites are long, slender forms, the corresponding structures—stalagmites—that grow up from the cave floor are stumpy and shorter. The two sometimes join together to form calcite columns.

ORIGIN These structures form by inorganic precipitation of calcium carbonate from waters seeping through fractures in the roofs of caves. When lime-rich waters meet the air and carbon dioxide is released, calcium carbonate is deposited, while evaporation of the water speeds up the process. Lime-rich water, dropping from the end of a stalactite, results in the formation of a stalagmite.

pale calcite

pendant-shaped

Classification: Chemical	Fossils: None	Grain shape: Angular

Group: SEDIMENTARY	Origin: Continental	Grain size: Medium, Fine

Banded ironstone

This rock is ferruginous chert, showing a marked banded structure mainly consisting of alternating layers of chert and magnetite or hematite in which considerable recrystallization has taken place. Magnetite and pyrite may also occur in the iron-rich bands of the rock.

prominent banding

TEXTURE Banded ironstones are fine- to medium-grained rocks.

ORIGIN Mostly formed in the Precambrian, between 2,000 and 3,000 million years ago. It is open to interpretation whether or not banded ironstones were deposited by precipitation in enclosed lakes or basins. They do, however, occur in rocks from many sedimentary environments, from shallow and intertidal to deep water situations. The disappearance of banded ironstone from the rock record around 2000 million years ago is evidence of increasing oxygen in the Earth's atmosphere, likely due to the emergence of life on Earth.

alternating gray and red bands of iron oxides and iron-rich chert

Classification: Chemical	Fossils: None	Grain shape: Crystalline

Group: SEDIMENTARY	Origin: Marine	Grain size: Medium

Oolitic ironstone

dark-red, iron-rich rock

This rock consists of closely packed ooliths rich in siderite and other iron minerals. Quartz, feldspar, and other detrital minerals can be present. The rock may have originally been calcium carbonate-rich, and replacement has converted the calcium carbonate to iron minerals. The ooliths, which give the rock its name, are small and rounded like they are in oolitic limestone.

TEXTURE Detrital grains in the rock may be angular. Calcite is a common cement between the ooliths.

ORIGIN Forms in marine environments; the rock may undergo change shortly after deposition, or it may be deposited already rich in iron.

rounded ooliths form body of rock

Classification: Chemical	Fossils: Invertebrates	Grain shape: Rounded

| Group: SEDIMENTARY | Origin: Continental | Grain size: Medium, Fine |

Lignite

crumbly surface

This is a brown-colored coal, having a carbon content between that of peat and bituminous coal. Lignite still has a large amount of visible plant material in its structure and is friable.

TEXTURE Less compact than other coals, lignite has a high moisture content and is crumbly. It also contains more volatiles and impurities.
ORIGIN A type of low-rank coal most commonly found in Tertiary and Mesozoic strata where changes have not occurred to the vegetable matter. Lignite also occasionally results from shallow burial of peat.

| Classification: Organic | Fossils: Plants | Grain shape: None |

| Group: SEDIMENTARY | Origin: Continental | Grain size: Medium, Fine |

Bituminous coal

dull patches

shiny patches

The action of pressure and temperature on the rock lignite leads to the formation of bituminous or "household" coal. It is hard, brittle, and has a high carbon content. This rock has alternating shiny and dull layers and may contain some recognizable plant material. It is dirty to handle.

TEXTURE This coal is even-textured, with the appearance of being fused material. Bituminous coal breaks into cubelike fragments due to its structure with two sets of joints at right angles.
ORIGIN It forms by the accumulation of peat and subsequent changes due to burial causing pressure and heat that drives off volatiles.

| Classification: Organic | Fossils: Plants | Grain shape: None |

| Group: SEDIMENTARY | Origin: Continental | Grain size: Medium, Fine |

Anthracite

dark, shiny matrix

This differs from other coals because of its extremely high content of carbon with a correspondingly low proportion of volatile matter. It is normally an unbanded type of coal.

TEXTURE More glassy and cleaner to handle than bituminous coal, anthracite ignites at much higher temperatures compared to other coals.
ORIGIN Forms by accumulation of peat. It is suggested that the increase of pressure and especially heat has caused volatiles to be driven off, forming a higher grade of coal.

uneven surfaces

| Classification: Organic | Fossils: Plants | Grain shape: None |

| Group: SEDIMENTARY | Origin: Continental | Grain size: Medium, Fine |

Peat

This rock represents the initial stage in the modification of plant material to lignite and bituminous coal. Peat is dark brown to black in color and contains about 50 percent carbon, as well as a great deal of volatile material. It is crumbly and easily broken in the hand.

TEXTURE There are many plant fragments visible in peat, often including large roots. It is frequently high in water and breaks unevenly when dry. Peat is a soft rock.

ORIGIN Forms from the deposition of plant debris on forest floors, in fens, or on moorland. Much of the vegetable matter in the peat that accumulates today is mosses, rushes, and sedges. The deposits may be many feet thick. By decay and reconstruction, the bottom layers of peat banks become compacted, darkened, and hardened, while the carbon content increases.

plant fragments

crumbly surface

| Classification: Organic | Fossils: Plants, Invertebrates | Grain shape: None |

| Group: SEDIMENTARY | Origin: Continental, Marine | Grain size: Medium, Fine |

Jet

Due to its high carbon content, jet is classified as a type of coal. It is a compact substance found in bituminous shales, and it produces a brown streak. Jet has a conchoidal fracture, and it is hard enough to take a good polish, a characteristic that has been exploited for making jewelry and ornaments. It rarely forms in geographically extensive seams.

TEXTURE When examined in close detail, jet shows woody tissue structures.

ORIGIN The formation of jet has been open to debate. It is generally believed that this black, coal-like rock developed in marine strata from logs and other drifting plant material, which then became waterlogged and sank into the mud on the seabed. It is found in rocks of marine origin, unlike other forms of coal, which form from plant matter accumulated on the land surface.

bedded structure

| Classification: Organic | Fossils: Plants | Grain shape: None |

Group: SEDIMENTARY	Origin: Marine	Grain size: Fine

Chert

This occurs as siliceous nodules or sheets, especially in sedimentary rocks such as limestone and among lavas. Chert is usually grayish in coloring.

TEXTURE It is composed of crypto-crystalline silica, and its components can be seen only under a microscope. Chert breaks with an uneven to subconchoidal fracture. It is a hard rock that cannot be scratched with a knife.
ORIGIN Chert is produced from the accumulation of silica, possibly in a gelatinous form on seabeds. This silica may come from organic sources.

fine grain size

subconchoidal fracture

Classification: Chemical	Fossils: Invertebrates, Plants	Grain shape: Crypto-crystalline

---

Group: SEDIMENTARY	Origin: Marine	Grain size: Fine

Flint

The term flint is used principally for siliceous nodules in the chalk of western Europe. It is a hard, compact substance with a homogenous appearance and breaks with a conchoidal fracture. Its sharp-edged flakes were used as tools by primitive peoples.

TEXTURE Consists entirely of crypto-crystalline silica, which appears to be derived from organic opal held in sponge spicules.
ORIGIN Occurs as bands and nodular masses in fine-grained limestones, especially chalk. Flint frequently contains fossils.

sharp edges

conchoidal fracture

Classification: Chemical	Fossils: Invertebrates	Grain shape: Crypto-crystalline

---

Group: SEDIMENTARY	Origin: Continental	Grain size: None

Amber

This material is the fossil resin of coniferous trees. Amber is soft, with a resinous or subvitreous luster. It is transparent to translucent. Insects and small vertebrates trapped in the original sticky resin may be found fossilized in amber. Amber is often used in jewelry. It is now regarded as an organic mineral.

TEXTURE When broken, amber has a conchoidal fracture.
ORIGIN Forms from the resin of coniferous trees and is found in sedimentary deposits.

resinous luster

conchoidal fracture

Classification: Biogenic	Fossils: Vertebrates, Invertebrates	Grain shape: None

Group: SEDIMENTARY	Origin: Post depositional	Grain size: None

Septarian concretion

Concretions are often formed of the same material as the host sediment but are cemented (concreted) together by silica, carbonate minerals, or iron oxides. Septarian concretions have radiating and polygonal internal patterns of veins—usually of calcite.

TEXTURE The structure is one of radiating and concentric cracks in a tough outer shell. When opened, this internal veined structure is apparent.
ORIGIN It may form by the segregation of minerals during diagenesis (the processes that turn soft, muddy material into rock) and their concentration around a nucleus, which may be a grain of sediment or even a fossil. After formation of the concretion, the cracks known as septa may develop during shrinkage.

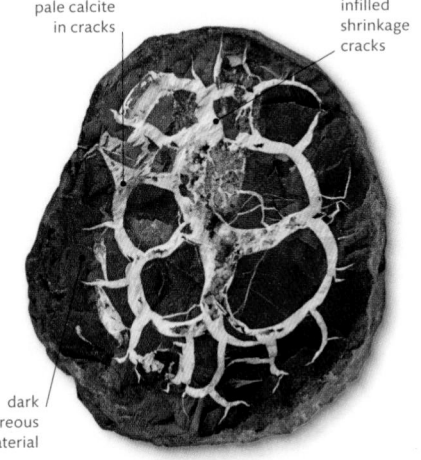

pale calcite in cracks

infilled shrinkage cracks

dark calcareous material

Classification: Chemical	Fossils: Invertebrates	Grain shape: Crystalline

Group: SEDIMENTARY	Origin: Post depositional	Grain size: None

Pyrite nodule

These rocks occur as spherical, botryoidal, or cylindrical nodules formed by the bronzy yellow mineral pyrite. On weathered surfaces, the nodules usually have a yellow-black coloring. Pyrite nodules are commonly found in shales and mudstones.

TEXTURE The internal structure of these rounded nodules reveals acicular crystals radiating from a central nucleus. Nodules can be a great variety of shapes, such as tubular or ovoid.
ORIGIN Pyrite nodules commonly form in shales, clays, and other pelitic rocks, which are themselves rich in pyrite. Also often found in chalk. Pyrite nodule formation is not fully understood, but precipitation of pyrite around a central nucleus is a possible explanation.

bronzy yellow acicular pyrite crystals

internal radiating structure

brownish coating

outer surface dull and weathered

Classification: Chemical	Fossils: Rare	Grain shape: Crystalline

Group: TEKTITE	Origin: Terrestrial	Grain size: Glass

Tektite

These are silica-rich glass objects that were once believed to be meteorites. However, their distribution on the Earth and their chemistry have now led scientists to suggest that they do not in fact have an extraterrestrial origin. Tektites actually have a composition not unlike that of some volcanic rocks. In addition to having a high silica content, they are also rich in oxides of potassium, calcium, and aluminum.

TEXTURE These rocks are small in size, usually about 7–10 oz (200–300 g) in weight, and have a disk or ovoid shape. Their surface may be smooth or rough.
ORIGIN Tektites result from the melting of terrestrial rocks on the impact of a meteorite. It seems unlikely that they were fired toward the Earth from a large volcano on the Moon, as has been suggested in the past.

typical rounded shape

smooth surface

indentation

Classification: Tektite	Shape: Rounded	Composition: Silicate

Group: METEORITE	Origin: Extraterrestrial	Grain size: Fine

Stony iron

Stony iron meteorites are composed of about 50 percent metal and 50 percent silicate material. The metallic content is nickel-iron alloy. The silicate components are minerals recognized in many rocks on Earth and include olivine, pyroxene, and plagioclase feldspar.

TEXTURE These are rocklike objects and have a surface showing various components, including crystals. The silicate minerals, such as olivine, may be removed by weathering, giving the surface a pitted appearance.
ORIGIN These are rare meteorites, and only about 4 percent of known meteorites are in this group. Stony iron meteorites help geologists understand how certain elements combine with iron or silica during the process of melting and vein formation. They give an insight into planets with an iron-rich core and a silicate outer shell.

rough surface

cavities on surface

Classification: Stony Iron	Shape: Angular, Rounded	Composition: Silicate, Metal

Group: METEORITE	Origin: Extraterrestrial	Grain size: Fine

Chondrite

These rocks form the largest group of meteorites classified as stones. Chondrites contain silicate minerals—mostly pyroxene, olivine, and small amounts of plagioclase feldspar. There is also a small proportion of nickel-iron.

TEXTURE These meteorites have a structure consisting of chondrules, which are small, spherical grains. The overall shape of chondrites varies, but many are rounded or even dome-shaped. Angular specimens are those that have fragmented on impact.

ORIGIN How chondrites form is not certain, but their chemistry seems to represent the mantle material of planet-forming bodies, planetesimals. This type of meteorite gives the oldest radiometric date yet obtained from rocky material—4,600 million years— a figure generally accepted as the date of the formation of the solar system.

angular fragmented specimen

crust around edges showing features of melting on entry into the Earth's atmosphere

Classification: Chondrite	Shape: Rounded, Angular	Composition: Silicate, Metal

Group: METEORITE	Origin: Extraterrestrial	Grain size: Medium, Coarse

Achondrite

These rocks differ from chondrites in both structure and composition. Achondrites contain a high proportion of silicate material, similar to that found in rocks on the Earth. This includes pyroxene and olivine, as well as plagioclase feldspar. However, the composition of achondrites is more variable than that of chondrites, and they generally contain very little iron.

TEXTURE Achondrites are coarser-grained than chondrites, and they lack chondrules.

ORIGIN As achondrites resemble the rocks found in the mantle and basaltic crust of the Earth, their origin may possibly be volcanic.

medium to coarse grains

rough surface

Classification: Achondrite	Shape: Angular, Rounded	Composition: Silicate

GLOSSARY

TECHNICAL EXPRESSIONS have been avoided wherever possible, but a limited use of them is essential in a book of this nature. The terms listed below, many of which are particular to minerals and rocks, are defined in a concise manner. Some definitions have been simplified and generalized in order to avoid obscure terminology. Words that appear in bold type in the definitions are explained elsewhere in the glossary. Many keywords are also explained with color photographs in the introductory section of the book.

■ **Accessory minerals**
The mineral constituents of an igneous rock that occur in such small amounts that they are not considered in its definition.

■ **Acicular habit**
Needle-shaped mineral habit.

■ **Adamantine luster**
Very bright mineral **luster** similar to that of diamond.

■ **Aeolian sediments**
Sediments deposited by the wind.

■ **Amphibole group**
Group of common rock-forming minerals, often with complex composition but mostly **ferromagnesian** silicates.

■ **Amygdale**
In-filled **vesicle** in an igneous rock.

■ **Anhedral crystal**
Poorly formed crystal.

■ **Arenaceous rocks**
Sedimentary rocks composed of sand grains.

■ **Batholith**
Very large, irregularly shaped mass of igneous rock formed from the **intrusion** of magma at great depth.

■ **Bedding**
Layering of sedimentary rocks.

■ **Bladed habit**
Blade-shaped habit in minerals.

■ **Clay minerals**
Alumino-silicate group of minerals common in sedimentary rocks.

■ **Cleavage**
The way certain minerals break along planes related to their internal atomic structure.

■ **Conchoidal fracture**
Curved or shell-like fracture in many minerals and some rocks.

■ **Concordant**
Following existing rock structures.

■ **Concretion**
Commonly discrete, rounded, nodular rock masses formed in beds of shale or clay.

■ **Country rock**
Any rock intruded by magma or lying beneath a lava flow.

■ **Cryptocrystalline**
With minute crystals, which can only be seen with a microscope.

■ **Dendritic habit**
Treelike mineral habit.

■ **Detrital rocks**
Group of sedimentary rocks formed essentially of fragments and grains derived from preexisting rocks.

■ **Discordant**
Cutting across existing rock structures.

■ **Dull luster**
Luster with little reflectiveness.

■ **Dike**
Sheet-shaped **discordant** igneous **intrusion**. Cuts across existing rock structures.

■ **Earthy luster**
Nonreflective, mineral **luster**.

■ **Essential minerals**
The mineral constituents of a rock that are necessary to its classification.

■ **Euhedral crystal**
Well-formed crystal that shows good faces.

■ **Evaporite**
Mineral or rock formed by the evaporation of saline water.

■ **Fault**
A break in the rocks of the Earth's crust where one side has moved relative to the other.

■ **Feldspathoid minerals**
Group of minerals similar in chemistry and structure to the feldspars, but with less silica.

■ **Felsic rock**
Igneous rock with over 65 percent total silica and over 20 percent quartz.

■ **Ferromagnesian minerals**
Minerals rich in iron and magnesium. These are dense, dark-colored silicates, such as the olivines, pyroxenes, and amphiboles.

■ **Fossil**
Any record of past life preserved in the crustal rocks. As well as bones and shells, fossils can be of footprints, excrement, and borings.

■ **Glassy texture**
A noncrystalline texture caused by the very rapid cooling of lava.

■ **Graded bedding**
Sedimentary structure where coarser grains gradually give way to finer grains upward through a bed.

■ **Granular**
Composed of grains.

■ **Graphic texture**
Rock texture resembling writing resulting from the regular intergrowth of quartz and feldspar.

■ **Groundmass**
Also called matrix. Mass of rock in which larger crystals may be set.

■ **Hackly fracture**
Jagged mineral fracture.

■ **Hemimorphic crystal**
Crystal with a different termination at each end.

■ **Hopper crystal**
Crystal with faces that are hollowed, as in the "stepped" faces of some halite crystals.

■ **Hydrothermal vein**
Fracture in rocks in which minerals have been deposited from hot magmatic fluids rich in water.

■ **Hypabyssal**
Occurring at relatively shallow depths in the Earth's crust.

■ **Inclusion**
A fragment or crystal of another material enclosed in a crystal or rock.

■ **Intermediate rock**
Igneous rock with between 65 percent and 55 percent total silica.

Intrusion
A body of igneous rock that invades older rock.

Laccolith
Mass of intrusive igneous rock with a dome-shaped top and usually a flat base.

Lamellar
In thin layers or scales; composed of plates or flakes.

Luster
The way in which a mineral reflects light.

Mafic rock
Igneous rock that contains between 45% and 55% total silica. These have less than 10% quartz and are rich in **ferro-magnesian** minerals.

Magma
Molten rock that may consolidate at depth or be erupted as lava.

Massive habit
Mineral habit of no definite shape.

Matrix *see* **Groundmass**

Metallic luster
A luster like that of fresh metal.

Metamorphic aureole
Area around an igneous **intrusion** where contact metamorphism of the original **country rock** has occurred.

Metasomatic alteration
Process that changes composition of a rock or mineral by the addition or replacement of chemicals.

Meteoric water
Water originating as rain or snow.

Microcrystalline
With very small crystals only visible with a microscope.

Oolith
Individual, spheroidal sedimentary grains from which oolite rocks are chemically formed. Usually calcareous, with a concentric or radial structure.

Orogenic belt
Region of the Earth's crust that is or has been active, and in which fold mountains are or have been formed.

Ossicle
Fragment of the stem of a crinoid, belonging to a group of creatures within the phylum *Echinodermata*.

Pelitic sediment
Sediment made of mud or clay.

Phenocryst
Relatively large crystal set into the **groundmass** of an igneous rock to give a **porphyritic** texture.

Pillow lava
Masses of lava formed on the sea bed, shaped like rounded pillows.

Pisolith
Pea-sized sediment grain with concentric internal structure.

Placer deposit
Deposit of minerals often in alluvial conditions, or on a beach, formed because of their high specific gravity and/or resistance to weathering.

Platy habit
Mineral habit with flat, thin crystals.

Pluton
Large mass of igneous rock that has formed deep beneath the surface of the Earth by consolidation of magma.

Porphyritic texture
Igneous rock **texture** with relatively large crystals set in the **matrix**.

Porphyroblastic texture
Metamorphic rock **texture** with relatively large crystals set into rock **matrix**.

Pseudomorph
A crystal with the outward form of a different mineral.

Pyroclast
Detrital volcanic material that has been ejected from a volcanic vent.

Radiometric dating
A variety of methods by which absolute ages for minerals and rocks can be obtained by studying the ratio between daughter products and their parent elements.

Recrystallization
Formation of new mineral grains in a rock while in the solid state.

Resinous luster
A luster with the reflectivity of resin.

Reticulated
Having a netlike structure.

Rock flour
Very fine-grained rock dust, often the product of glacial action.

Salt dome
Large intrusive mass of salt.

Schillerization
Brilliant play of bright colors, often produced by minute rodlike **inclusions** in certain minerals.

Schistosity
Wavy structure that occurs in medium- and coarse-grained rocks. Generally resulting from the alignment of **platy** mineral grains.

Scoriaceous rock
Lava or other volcanic material that is heavily pitted with hollows and empty cavities.

Scree
Mass of unconsolidated rock waste found on a mountain slope or below a cliff face, caused by weathering.

Secondary mineral
Any mineral forming in a rock after the rock has cooled.

Sill
Concordant, sheet-shaped igneous **intrusion**.

Slaty cleavage
Structure in some regionally metamorphosed rocks, allowing them to be split into thin sheets.

Texture
Size and shape of rock grains or crystals and their relationship.

Thrust fault line 1
Type of **fault** that has a low angle plane of movement, where older rock is pushed over younger rock.

Twinned crystals
Crystals that grow together, with a common crystallographic surface.

Ultramafic rock
Igneous rock having less than 45 percent total silica.

Vein
Sheet-shaped mass of mineral material, usually cutting through rock.

Vesicle
An unfilled gas-bubble cavity in lava.

Vitreous luster
A glasslike luster.

Volcanic pipe
Fissure through which lava flows.

Well-sorted texture
A sedimentary rock texture where all the grains are very similar in size.

Zeolite minerals
Group of hydrated alumino-silicates characterized by their easy and reversible loss of water.

INDEX

ACKNOWLEDGMENTS

The authors would like to thank the following people for their help with the original edition of the book: Stella Vayne, Gillian Roberts, Mary-Clare Jerram, and James Harrison for editorial work at Dorling Kindersley. Expert geological advice was given by Dr. George Rowbotham of Keele University and Dr. Robert Symes of the Natural History Museum. For the revised edition, thanks go to Angeles Gavira at Dorling Kindersley in London and Devangana Ojha at Dorling Kindersley in Noida, India, for their valued editorial help and guidance throughout the project.

Dorling Kindersley would like to thank: Janashree Singha, Tanya Singhal, Nandini D. Tripathy, David Preston, Marcus Hardy, Susie Behar, Irene Lyford, Gillian Roberts, and Sophy Roberts for their invaluable editorial work; Arthur Brown, Peter Howlett of Lemon Graphics, and Alastair Wardle for additional design; Michael Allaby for compiling the index; Picture Research Manager Taiyaba Khatoon, and Senior Picture Researcher Surya Sarangi.

The authors and publisher are greatly indebted to the Natural History Museum for making available for photography most of the rocks and minerals illustrated, and Alan Hart of the Mineralogy department for selecting the specimens.

PICTURE CREDITS

All photographs are by Harry Taylor except for: 8 Dorling Kindersley: Stephen Oliver (cb). Dreamstime.com: Cosmin Constantin Sava/ iPhone® is a trademark of Apple Inc., registered in the US and other countries. (clb); Anton Starikov (cr). 9 Dorling Kindersley: Richard Leeney/Holts Gems (cra). Dreamstime.com: Justin Skinner (tc). 10 Dreamstime.com: May1985 (cb). 11 Dorling Kindersley: Richard Leeney/Holts Gems (crb). 12 Dreamstime.com: Re06179e (cr); Chris Pellant (tr), 16 (bl), 17 (b), 18 (bl and br), 19 (tr and bl), 30 (bl and br), 31 (bl), 32 (bl), 33 (tr (3) and c), 34 (l and tr), 35 (tr and bl), 37 (cl), 38 (bl), 39 (c); Colin Keates (Natural History Museum) 17 (t, r, and c), 24 (br), 25 (cl, bl, and br); C.M. Dixon/ Phorosources 26 (b). Line illustrations by Chris Lyon; airbrushing by Janos Maffry; color illustrations, 7, 30, and 31 by Andy Farmer; and endpaper illustrations by Caroline Church.

All other images © Dorling Kindersley

For further information see: www.dkimages.com

Endpaper images: Front and Back: **Alamy Stock Photo:** Universal Images Group North America LLC / DeAgostini / A. Rizzi cb; **Dreamstime.com:** Nicolae Gherasim c; **Getty Images** / **iStock:** GeorgePeters b.
For further information see: **www.dkimages.com**